Fast Takes:

Slices of Life Through a Journalist's Eye

Fast Takes:

Slices of Life Through a Journalist's Eye

by Mike D'Orso

HAMPTON ROADS
PUBLISHING COMPANY, INC.

"Saturday's Hero: A Beat" appears by permission of *Sports Illustrated* magazine.

"From Petersburg to The Promised Land," "150 MPH for God, Country and STP," and "Bustin' Loose" appear by permission of *Commonwealth* magazine.

All other stories permission of *The Virginian-Pilot and The Ledger-Star*, Norfolk, Virginia.

Hampton Roads Publishing Co., Inc.
5661 Virginia Beach Blvd.
Norfolk, VA 23502

Cover design by Jeryl Barnett
Printed in the United States of America

Acknowledgements

The list of people who, in so many ways, have been by my side from my beginning in this business is a long one. It includes:

Bill O'Donovan, editor and publisher of the *Virginia Gazette* (who helped me get my feet wet),

Susan Harb and Deborah Marquardt, former editors of *Commonwealth Magazine* (who guided me through a three-year baptism),

Carol Wood, former features editor of *The Virginian-Pilot and The Ledger-Star* (who brought me into the VP/LS family),

Marian Anderfuren, former features editor of the VP/LS (whose door and heart have always been open),

Sandy Rowe, VP/LS executive editor, and Jim Raper, VP/LS managing editor, (who continue to share their faith and support),

Frank DeMarco, vice president of Hampton Roads Publishing (who believed in this book and made it come to be), and

Fred Kirsch (who will always inspire me, as a writer and as my friend).

To all these people — and many more not named — I give my thanks.

PREFACE

This is a book of stories. True stories. The people are real, the places exist. Moses Malone is still playing basketball in the NBA, Philip Berrigan and his family are still battling nuclear annihilation from their Baltimore ghetto home, Elisabeth Kubler-Ross continues to usher the dying toward death from her headquarters in the Appalachian foothills. These people were in these places before I visited them, and they remained when I left.

That is what a journalist is — a visitor. He drops into people's lives, probing, prodding, collecting, then returning to his desk to sort, sift through and make sense of what he has seen. He is an explorer. As a reporter in the field, his tools are his eyes and his ears. And his heart. As a writer at his pad or his keyboard, his tools become his vision and his voice. And everywhere, his terrain is the truth.

That is, of course, the truth as he sees it. Journalism is, in the end, a matter of trust: trust from the subject that the reporter hears, sees, and understands what the subject shares and shows (perhaps more clearly than the subject hears, sees, and understands himself); trust from the reader that the story, filtered through the writer's point of view and his own feelings, is focused on facts (the reader then is free to decide whether he shares the same point of view); and trust from the journalist himself in his own effort and instincts.

Trust does not come easily. Reporters themselves often wonder about the nature of their relationship with the people they interview. They wonder at what point sincerity stops and manipulation begins. A writer named Janet Malcolm began a 1989 New Yorker magazine story with this assessment of the reporter-subject relationship:

> *Every journalist who is not too stupid or too full of himself to notice what is going on knows that what he does is morally indefensible. He is a kind of confidence man, preying on people's vanity, ignorance, or loneliness, gaining their trust and betraying them without remorse.*

Harsh words, but any writer who wants to get beyond pat predictability in his stories struggles with this issue. It is in their murkier depths that people and places reveal themselves, but it's not easy getting down there. Rarely will someone simply invite a stranger in. It's safer to stay on the surface. But a journalist's — a **storyteller's** — job is to dig deeper, to get at what makes a person or a place tick, to dive into the soul of the subject and capture it alive. It can get complex and confusing down there, close to the bone. Often there are wounds. Often they are raw. But any story worth telling demands that this dive be made.

Rarely can the reporter make it alone. At some point the subject — wittingly or not — must take him in. It is then that the interview becomes a delicate dance. But it does not require deceit. There is a difference between being exposed and being betrayed. A subject may not be comfortable or even happy with the way he is finally laid bare in print, but if the truth has been told, then the trust was not betrayed. And the subject, like the writer, knows if the truth has been told — whether he likes it or not.

As for ultimate objectivity, there is no such thing. A story is by definition subjective. It depends totally on the teller. It is seen through his eyes, told in his voice. He interprets. He concludes. The best he can be is fair. The worst he can do is pretend he is not there. To hide behind a distanced voice of dispassionate authority is to cheat the reader and rob the story.

The 29 stories in this book were written between 1983 and 1990. Most appeared in the newspaper I work for — *The Virginian-Pilot and The Ledger-Star*. Several appeared in magazines. I spent days with some of these subjects, hours with most, mere minutes with many. But they each have their place in these stories. And the stories each have a place in the landscape we call our culture.

It has become well-established that non-fiction can resonate with the same timeless power as any short story or novel. Writer James Agee had this to say in the beginning of his classic portrait of rural poverty, *Let Us Now Praise Famous Men*:

In a novel, a house or person has his meaning, his existence, entirely through the writer. Here, a house or a person has only the most limited of his meaning through me: his true meaning is much huger. It is that he exists, in actual being, as you do and as I do, and as no character of the imagination can possibly exist. His great weight, mystery and dignity are in this fact. As for me, I can tell you of him only what I saw, only so accurately as in my terms I know how: and this in turn has its chief stature not in any ability of mine but in the fact that I too exist, not as a work of fiction, but as a human being. Because of his immeasurable weight in actual existence, and because of mine, every word I tell of him has inevitably a kind of immediacy, a kind of meaning, not at all necessarily "superior" to that of imagination, but of a kind so different that a work of the imagination (however intensely it may draw on "life") can at best only faintly imitate the least of it.

Mystery. Meaning. Immediacy.
Agee wrote these words more than 50 years ago.
They will always be true.

Contents

I. THE PROMISED LAND

From Petersburg
to the Promised Land

Game night in Philadelphia, and the Spectrum is hopping. Ticket windows are jammed, the pretzel man can't pocket his bills fast enough, it's an hour before tipoff and 10,000 people already have pushed their way in from the night's bitter chill to catch the hottest act in town, the 76ers.

The Utah jazz, still sore from a pounding in Boston the night before, are out on the floor loosening up, but the Sixers are only now trickling into their dressing room after catching an early flight home from their win in Cleveland.

One by one, down a drafty concrete corridor, they arrive. Marc Iavaroni, late of the University of Virginia and professional ball in Europe, ducks into the locker room after showing his father and sister to their seats. Maurice Cheeks, normally a starting guard but sidelined with an injury, strolls down the hallway alone. He won't dress tonight. Then, surrounded by a gaggle of well-wishers, comes Doctor J., Julius Erving, as smooth as the cashmere coat and thin leather gloves he wears, shaking hands, making small talk, glowing. And, finally, Moses Malone, nondescript in casual slacks and black leather jacket, walking alone, his dark, massive frame moving slowly, almost awkwardly, head slightly bowed, eyes fixed on the floor ahead of him.

In the locker room, Iavaroni ribs the ball boys and trades barbs with another rookie, Mitchell Anderson from Bradley. Erving jokes and jives with the small cluster of reporters gathered around his cubicle. And Malone sits in his corner alone, silently pulling socks over his taped ankles. No flash, no flair, but to the 13,000 fans who are now rocking to the pregame music upstairs, Malone is the show, the answer, the Second Coming. It doesn't make him comfortable, but it is a role he has come to know well.

Moses Malone was no more than a babe in the bulrushes, a skinny teenager still buying milk in his high school cafeteria, when he gazed up past the foothills of a collegiate career to the distant peaks of play-for-pay basketball and heard a voice whispering, "Go pro, Moses, go pro."

Almost nine years have passed since Malone heeded that call, becoming the first basketball player ever to jump from the schoolyards to the big time, breaking the heart of the NCAA by leapfrogging directly from Petersburg High School to the Utah Stars of the now-defunct American Basketball Association. In Salt Lake City, then in Houston and, this season, in Philadelphia, he has shouldered the burden of a man who knows the way to the promised land of a world championship. Twice he has been named the most valuable player in the National Basketball Association. The workingman's ballplayer, they call him. A blue-collar laborer, he earns his money in the sweaty, bloody, body-mashing frenzy of the inside game.

King of the rack. Chairman of the boards. If Malone quit tomorrow, he already would have marked his place in the annals of basketball history: Jerry West had the jumper, Bob Cousy handled the ball, Elgin Baylor had the moves, Bill Russell blocked the shots, but there has never been a rebounder as awesome as Moses Malone.

Yet Malone has never worn an NBA championship ring. It was worth $13.2 million to Harold Katz, owner of the Philadelphia 76ers, to lure the big man to a city starving for the crown, to pair him with the league's living legend, Erving, and to start collecting those rings. Malone will get $2.2 million a year for the next six years, the highest salary in the game. If Philadelphia makes it to the finals this season, if they play 100 games on their way to the crown, if Malone averages 44 minutes of playing time per 48-minute game, he will collect $500 *a minute*.

He will be worth every cent, says Katz, if Philadelphia wins the title. But for some people, even a championship will not be enough. Malone can score 50 points, pull down 30 rebounds, fold up the chairs and turn out the lights, but these people want something more. They want Moses to *talk* to them.

It is Malone's other side, the sullen face he wears when he's off the court, that lingers in the public eye. He has never been friendly with pens, pads, microphones and cameras. When he was with Utah, he would slap on a pair of stereo headphones and stare at the floor as reporters flocked around him, firing questions. When he did talk, his voice swelled from somewhere deep in his Nikes and the words came slowly, painfully. "Mumbles Malone," a Salt Lake City disc jockey called him, and Malone pulled the shades down even farther.

Mean, shy, mysterious, dumb. Before he had his hand on a high school diploma, the words were ringing in the young boy's ears, the chorus of frustrated reporters. When he turned pro, the questions came faster, heavier, as Malone was pressured to answer for his audacious affront to the colleges of America. Bucking the system has its price, and Malone paid by wearing the stigma of ignorance. He still wears it today.

There is more to Moses Malone than unanswered phone calls, two-word interviews and silent stares, but it can't be found in the glare of a press conference or the steam of a locker room. It can't even be found in the plush comfort of Malone's Philadelphia condominium. To know Moses Malone, look back to where he grew up, to Petersburg.

The Crater and Central State Hospital. These are the two things Petersburg was known for before Malone. One is the most celebrated hole in the ground produced by the Civil War; the other is the state's largest mental institution. For most people, Petersburg is nothing more than a stop on Interstate 95, a place to grab a bite to eat and then move on. But for the people who live in The Heights, there is very little moving on.

Every city has its backwater, its haven for have-nots, its ghetto. In Petersburg, that place is The Heights. On a bleak knoll in the center of the city stand rows of loose-shingled houses leaning together behind rotting porches, sagging chain link fences and broken sidewalks. Perched in the midst of it all, looking down on the surrounding neighborhood, is the Virginia Avenue Elementary School. Day or night, winter or summer, the school's playground is filled with the shouts of children playing tackle football in the dirt, the thuds of baseballs bouncing off the bricks of the school building, the chants of girls jumping rope. But the most revealing sound, the key to this playground and others like it, is the hollow echo of a bouncing basketball.

It is the city game, they say. The ticket out. If a boy is gifted enough, if he can turn away from the call of the streets, he can ride his jump shot to college, to a job, even to the pros. The dream is always there, hovering above the rusting backboards like a mirage.

Moses Malone was born a block away from the Virginia Avenue playground in 1955. Before he was 2, his father was gone, and it was up to Mary Malone to raise her only child with her will and the salary she made working as a nurse's aide and later wrapping and pricing meat at a local supermarket. She made sure her son went to Sunday School and that he knew where his grandfather's old Bible was. Years later, Malone would make that Bible famous.

Fame on the courts was slow to come. Malone's first love was the football field, where he starred as a gangly end in elementary and junior high school. Basketball was just another game, and Malone, who was called "Tiny" by his friends, was just another kid.

"We used to hustle bottles together," remembers Eugene "Ickey" Hollins, a childhood friend of Malone's and his teammate at Petersburg High. "That's how we got money on Saturdays. You know, you get all the bottles you can, two cents a bottle, take them to the store, and you buy your candy. To most people, Malone seems quiet, very reserved, but to me and the fellow ballplayers he dealt with and the guys in the neighborhood that hung out on the corner, you could not get him to stop talking."

Nine of the 15 players on his high school basketball team came from Virginia Avenue Elementary School, and Malone was well over six-feet tall before he was out of the sixth grade, but then he was an also-ran under the backboards. "He was not an avid player like the rest of us at first," says Hollins, who is an assistant sales manager at a Petersburg automobile dealership. "We always played at night, and he'd go out and play with us sometimes, get a couple of blocked shots here and there just because his arms were tall. We thought of him as simply a human being, just somebody, just a tall guy."

But the more Malone came out, the more he liked the game, until, by the time he was 13, it was in his blood. "Just crazy about basketball," remembers his mother. Soon, even the afternoon and evening games were not enough. To Johnny Byrd, who runs the neighborhood confectionary one house away from the two-story flat in which Malone was raised, the tall boy was like any other kid in the neighborhood. Almost.

"I never really noticed him much," Byrd says, a .38-caliber pistol gleaming on his hip as he bags some penny candy for a group of children, "except when I'd close up some nights, 2, 2:30 in the morning, and I'd hear him bouncing a ball alone over on the courts."

It wasn't long before Malone caught the eye of Robertnette "Pro" Hayes. Hayes was the assistant basketball coach at Petersburg High, and the Virginia Avenue playground was where he found most of his athletes. Amid the mad, feverish whirl of street ball, among the un-polished gems with their flashy "in your face" dunks and drives, Hayes saw the Hope Diamond in Malone.

"Moses was fast all the time, and quick. He had real quick hands," says Hayes, who is now an administrative assistant at Petersburg High School. "He was a lean boy, but he was strong for his size." Hayes lured Malone to the school's junior varsity practices, but after two weeks the boy left and went back to the playground. "He couldn't make the adjustment," explains Hayes. "In street ball, Moses was everything, but now he had to make some concessions. He had to learn to set a pick, for example. He had to learn to do things from a team concept."

Hayes got Malone to return and slowly introduced him to a different game, one played in uniforms, with referees, scoreboards, and rims with nets. But there was more for Malone to adjust to than the X's and O's of organized ball. One was his initial discomfort with whites. "Living in a ghetto area, where you don't see members of the opposite race, It's natural to be leery," says Hayes, who had his captain at the time, a white ballplayer named Tim Antozzi, help bring Moses out of his shell.

It was one thing to open new horizons of basketball to Malone and quite another to show him the world that stretched beyond the tattered blocks of The Heights. Vacations in the mountains, weekends at the beach, an evening at the theater — these experiences are not on the itinerary of a boy in the inner city. "Moses was isolated in a ghetto, played basketball in the ghetto, everything he did was in that area," explains Hayes. "That was the main thing, to get him out of that area."

Bus rides to away games, trips to other schools gave Malone a glimpse of people and places he had not seen before. Hayes filled the shoes of the boy's absent father, giving him advice when he asked for it, offering help when he needed it. When the team made its first trip to the University of Virginia to play in the state basketball tournament, Hayes bought Malone a pair of new shoes and a suit of clothes to wear in the spotlight.

But home, in The Heights, was where Malone was comfortable. He would stay home and play the organ his mother bought him, or go out and shoot pool with the basketball team's trainer, Nathan "Panther" Dickerson. When his teammates got together, Malone would join them, but on his own terms. "After high school games, all the guys used to get together and just drink beer, you know, and hang out with the ladies," recalls Hollins. "Everybody would put in money to buy the beer, and Moses would always put in money to help, but he didn't drink. He would go and buy a little box of cereal, some milk, get a bowl and eat his cornflakes. I will never forget that."

Malone's closest friend was David Pair, who was several years older than Malone and a big brother to many of the neighborhood kids. Pair still lives in the same crowded house where Malone would retreat after high school games, hiding from college scouts and eating the pineapple upside-down cakes Pair would bake for him. "I wasn't the partying type," says Pair, whose walls are lined with medals and trophies won in judo competition. "I didn't drink, didn't smoke, so I guess I was kind of down Mo's line."

Even in The Heights, though, the only place Malone was really at home was on the court. "Moses would always be out there, at the playground, shooting bank shots, shooting bank shots, shooting bank shots," says Hollins. "We had put our time in during the day, but he was out there at night, dribbling the basketball, taking it through his legs, trying to dunk the ball, layups, all the fundamentals."

His sophomore year, Malone had his first showdown in a Petersburg uniform against a name player, Michael James, a seven- foot senior from Hopewell High School. James, who went on to play for Nebraska and ended his promising career when he was convicted of shooting a cab driver, ran roughshod over the 6-foot-8-inch Malone. After the game, Malone vowed no one would beat him like that again, and he spent even more time on the playground, searching out older, tougher ballplayers to test his game. Street stars with nicknames like Babyhead and Snake gave Malone the competition he couldn't find at school. Ballplayers from other towns would come to match their reputations against Malone's. Ed Gholson was a senior at Hopewell when Malone was a junior, and they both made the All-State team that season. But they had met long before that, on the playground.

"When me and Mo used to go to Lee Park and play, there would be 100 people watching us go at it," says Gholson, who played at Cleveland State and still talks hopefully of playing professionally in Europe. When the Houston Rockets were beaten in the 1981 NBA finals by the Boston Celtics, a disgusted Malone commented that he could take "four guys from back in Petersburg" and beat Boston. "Yeah, he was talking about me and some of the others that play over at Lee Park," says Gholson.

Occasionally, in the summer, the Petersburg players would drive to the Federal Prison Camp on the edge of the town or to the Virginia State Penitentiary in Richmond to play against some of the convicts. They called the prison "the serious joint," and the games were top quality. Mike James played for the federal prison team, as did Skip Wise, who had starred for Clemson and been derailed on his way to the NBA by a drug problem. Other prison stars were known only by their nicknames. Helicopter, Two-Booty. And the Milkman. Malone mentioned the Milkman once in an interview. When asked where the nickname had come from, he just smiled and said, "'Cause he killed one, man."

By the time Malone went head-to-head with another celebrated center in a high school game, this time against a player for Thomas Dale High School named Melvin Friend, his skills had moved beyond the level of schoolboy basketball. He blew Friend out of the gym and never looked back. Before his sophomore year was over, Moses Malone was news. After every game, reporters would meet him in the locker room. He already was being compared to Kareem Abdul-Jabbar, Bill Walton, Wilt Chamberlain. He played the game like men a decade older than himself, and people expected him to speak just as well.

"Moses was constantly hassled," recalls Marie Maniego, who taught Malone English at Petersburg High School and now chairs the school's

English department. "He had the natural talent to play basketball. But all the other things people wanted him to do weren't natural for him. It takes training and experience to handle interviews and to speak in public. People threw too much on him too soon."

Impatient, confused, Malone began to pull back, turning away from interviews, hiding, or when cornered, giving the bare minimum. Soon the word began to spread: Give him a basketball, but don't count on the brains.

"Moses always cherished his privacy," says Mary Malone, "I'm his mother, and he loves me, but even with me sometimes, I'd be sitting in the room with him and ask him something, and he'd hold a newspaper up in front of his face. I knew he wasn't reading it, because it would be upside down."

People close to Malone insist that having no father pushed him even more into the role of a loner. "I don't care how big a guy is, or how strong, there's some times, you know, when he's going to miss his father," says Hayes. "When you don't have a father to fall back on, that's a terrible thing. I think that was Moses' whole problem."

On the court, however, there were no problems. His junior year, Malone took Petersburg to the state championship and a 25-0 record. His senior year, he averaged 36 points, 26 rebounds and 12 blocked shots a game. Most games were romps, deteriorating into run-and-gun exhibitions for the guards and forwards. If Malone wanted the ball, he usually had to get it himself.

"The real reason Moses became a helluva rebounder is our guards could not shoot," says Hollins. "We had a play called 'Ice Cream,' and we'd just shoot it. If it misses, Moses would just tap it in. You know, so easy, like going and getting ice cream, gimme a scoop."

Petersburg's home games became the hottest tickets in town. When the high school gym could no longer hold the crowds, the games were moved to Virginia State University's 3,500-seat arena. And still people were turned away as the stands were jammed a half-hour before the tipoff. If the basketball got boring, the fans could play name-that-coach with the famous faces dotting the bleachers. North Carolina State's Norm Sloan. Virginia Commonwealth's Chuck Noe. Maryland's Lefty Driesell. It was an easy game.

The pressure Malone felt his first three seasons was nothing compared to the squeeze of his senior year. More than 250 colleges came calling, tongues wagging, and Malone began his year of playing hide-and-seek in a fishbowl. Coaches would wait outside the locker room after a game, and Moses would climb out a back window, sliding down a pole, taking off into the night. They would show up at his front door, and he'd crawl out the back, leaping off the roof to escape. The motel and rental car business in Petersburg boomed as college recruiters checked into town for days at a time. They would prowl The Heights in their sedans and on foot, spreading money around, hoping to find someone who could deliver Moses. Invariably, they returned home with nothing but empty pockets. "He would hide everywhere," says Malone's mother. "He had so many tricks to get away."

"If Mo didn't want to be found, you couldn't find him," agrees David Pair, who spent more time with Malone that year than anyone else but his mother. "He'd come here and hide on the floor of this house. When we'd be out driving and go by his house, he'd duck down in his seat and ask if anybody was there. When he was at home, we had a secret knock we'd use when we'd go to see him."

It wasn't long before the scouts knew about Pair, and they flocked to his home as well. "At first it was fun, but then it got to where I'd have to hide my car when I was at home."

Pro Hayes felt the same heat. "I'd get off work and there'd be three or four coaches at my front door. Every day. I used to bring Moses over here to give him some privacy, but when they found out where I lived, we'd both go over to Virginia State and hide out in the student center over there."

Even at school, Moses could not get away from the chase. The administrative office's phones rang so frequently that a secretary was assigned just to take his calls, which never were answered. The stacks of mail that arrived for him each day went unopened into a huge crate. His classmates gave him little relief, following him down the hallways in droves. "Moses was a friendly guy, the kids adored him, and everybody wanted to follow him," says Hayes. "He'd usually eat by himself in the cafeteria, and by the time he'd finish, there'd be 35 or 40 kids watching him eat."

Malone's social life wasn't much easier. David Pair remembers taking Malone with him to meet a friend who had several attractive nieces Malone's age. "The family lived in a trailer, and Mo had to bend over to keep from bumping his head. He sat down on the sofa, and his legs were so long, people had to step over them. We weren't there a half-hour and 100 people had showed up, wanting to see Moses. One niece was sitting next to him real close, and whenever Moses would slide down the couch, she'd slide down right next to him. Finally, he couldn't slide no more, and he looked over at me, just like that and said, 'Pair, let's go.'"

Heavy come-ons never worked with Malone, but most coaches didn't get the message, blowing their chances before they could even get their feet in his door. One local coach cozied up to Pair but made a crucial tactical error: "The man thought I was Moses' daddy."

Some coaches didn't bother beating around the bush. They came right out with offers of money, cars, and apartments. Dates were arranged during campus visits with girls who would follow up with letters and phone calls asking Malone about his decision. Becoming more jaded every day, Malone just turned away. "People who try to buy me make me very mad," he told one reporter.

When they couldn't buy him, some coaches tried buying Malone's teammates. "Coaches would try to use us to get to Moses," recalls Hollins. "I remember we were in Charlottesville for the state tournament, and I needed some film for my camera. Moses and I were together, and this guy from Detroit went down and bought us $50 worth of film. Illegal as hell, and I took it. Moses didn't give a damn. He wasn't going to that school."

If money and gifts didn't work, there were other ways to get at Malone. Like miracles. The pressure of her son's fame had given Mary Malone an ulcer, and, in a heralded visit on behalf of his university's basketball program, Oral Roberts came to the Malone home on St. Matthew Street to do his best to pray away Mrs. Malone's ailment. The treatment failed, but for a short time Malone considered going to the evangelist's university. "After he found out that he had to wear neckties all the time out there, though, that was out of the question," says Mary Malone.

In the end, after months of speculation and reports that had him going to schools from North Carolina State to the University of Houston, after being honored by the city of Petersburg with a "Moses Malone Day," after watching a box containing his uniform, photos, and a list of statistics shipped to Massachusetts for display in the National Basketball Hall of Fame, Malone gave the nod to Lefty Driesell, the bald, boisterous head coach at the University of Maryland. Malone always said he liked to watch people more than talk to them, and he liked what he saw in Lefty.

"Lefty was the type of dude who would say any damn thing he wanted to say," explains Hollins. "Moses was hearing a lot of things from Lefty that he would hear from us. I think he told Moses more bad things than he told him good. Lefty would say, 'Moses, you look shitty today,' and Moses would laugh and say, 'He's a helluva dude.'"

Malone wasn't the only person Driesell impressed. Pro Hayes still calls him "my buddy," and occasionally sends Driesell scouting reports on area talent. Mary Malone lights up when Driesell's name is mentioned: "I love him. He is straight, friendly and very nice."

When Malone finally signed a letter of intent to attend Maryland beginning in the fall of 1974, Driesell, who had vowed to make Maryland the "UCLA of the east," could almost taste his first national championship. Just one year at Maryland would be enough, according to a statement Driesell made in a Richmond newspaper. "I don't care if you never go to class," he was quoted as saying to Malone. "Hell, don't go to class. They'll kick you out after seven months, but in the meantime we'll have had a pretty good basketball team. Then, we can get you $2 million from the pros."

But even with Malone tucked safely under his arm, Driesell knew there was still one fox in the henhouse. In the third round of the ABA draft, the Utah Stars had chosen Moses Malone, making him the first high school basketball player to be drafted since Wilt Chamberlain was picked by the Philadelphia Warriors the year Malone was born. Chamberlain opted for four years at the University of Kansas, but Malone's decision, even with his signature on a letter of intent, was studded with question marks.

His year on the hot plate had shown Malone the seamy underside of bigtime college athletics. His mother had turned in Clemson to the NCAA for offering her brother cash to buy Moses a car. The University of New Mexico had gotten into dutch for giving a rented car to Nathan Dickerson. The whispered talk of money, deals and bonuses had Malone wondering if there was that much difference between the pros and college. And if not, why not take the big bucks right away instead of wasting time with under-the-table chicken feed? It wasn't as if Malone were considering going pro for the first time. He had been thinking about it for a long while.

When he was 14 or 15—no one is quite sure just when—Malone scribbled down two pledges to himself and slipped them into the yellowing pages of his grandfather's Bible, at Isaiah 64, where it is written, "... for when you did terrible things that we did not expect, you came down, and the mountains trembled before you." On one scrap of paper, he vowed to become the best high school player in the nation by the end of his junior year. On the other, he toyed with the idea of becoming the first high school player to go directly into the pros. Close friends knew about the notes, but Malone has never discussed them in public except to admit, grudgingly, that they were there. His mother respects his secret, saying nothing about Malone's prophecies, but the world and Lefty Driesell knew about the notes by the time Utah drafted him.

Malone's decision whether or not to go pro was tied by some to the very fate of amateur athletics itself. It was awaited, debated and speculated by newspapers and magazines from coast to coast. Three representatives from the Utah organization checked into a motel 15 miles north of Petersburg in August and, over the course of six days, spent $92 in quarters on tolls and put 932 miles on their rented car trying to lure Malone from Maryland with a complex multimillion-dollar contract. Advice flowed from the pages of newspapers and the mouths of friends, but the decision was Malone's alone, and that is how he made it. "Kids who come from where Moses came from struggle against odds," says Marie Maniego. "They see too much too soon, and they grow up with the ability and necessity to make choices earlier than most people."

When Malone did not appear on the Maryland campus for the first day of classes in late August, it was clear his choice had been made. Even Mary Malone was surprised. "I wanted him to go to college. I didn't even think about him going pro until he came in to the Safeway and told me to quit work, told me I didn't have to work anymore."

Mary Malone rarely gets back to The Heights these days. Her telephone number is unlisted, and only the best of friends know how to find their way to her three-story, red-brick colonial home in a well-to-do Chester neighborhood. The house and its expansive, tree-studded yard are rimmed by a black iron fence, the circular driveway protected by a heavy gate that is opened and closed by an electrical system. A white Lincoln Continental with license plates reading "1-MARY M" sits in the driveway.

The jealousy and exploitation she says she faced from some neighbors and friends when her son became rich pushed Mary Malone into isolation, but she is a happy woman, wearing jeans and a sweatshirt, relaxing in front of the television in the den where she spends most of her time at home. Photographs of Malone's high school teams, action shots of him in the NBA, portraits of his new wife Alfreda, whom he married a year ago in his mother's living room, and 3-year-old son Moses Jr. line the fireplace mantel. Amid the clutter of mail and magazines on the room's coffee table sits a .22-caliber pistol, bought on the advice of a friend. A fire crackles in the hearth, and a woman on television risks a newly won refrigerator for a shot at $5,000 as Mary Malone urges her on. The show is "The Price is Right."

When Malone arrived in Utah, acclaimed as the salvation of the ABA, he bought his mother a ranch house in Ettrick, at the edge of Petersburg. The ABA folded, Malone moved on to Houston, and he moved his mother 10 miles north to Chester. Now he is in Philadelphia, but Mary Malone is happy right where she is. Her grandson's toys are scattered across her backyard, the vestiges of a recent visit. The boy, said Malone in an early season interview will be taught "to believe in himself, so he won't be listening to what anyone says."

Mary Malone sees her son whenever she wants, even spending 11 months with him once in Houston. But he has his own life to live, she says, and the riches he has made haven't changed him, she insists. His friends in Petersburg agree. At one time, they say, his tastes ran more to women than fine wine, but now his weakness is expensive cars. When

Hollins visited him in Houston, Malone had a 6.9 Mercedes, a Porsche 928 and a Rolls Royce parked in his garage. Although the Rolls is gone now, he still owns seven automobiles.

But when it comes to the high life, Malone still lays low. His idea of a good time is playing video games or catching a movie. When he goes out to eat, he often drives his Mercedes to the nearest cafeteria or fast-food joint. "Moses will buy a Whataburger before he'll buy a filet mignon," says Hollins. "That's just the way he is."

It is no secret that illicit drugs have become as much a part of life in professional sports as airports and hotels. John Lucas, who tried to woo Malone to join him at Maryland and who was one of Malone's best friends when they were teammates in Houston, is fighting hard to come back this season from a well- publicized bout with a drug habit. But Malone, say his friends, is not interested in the trip from cornflakes to cocaine. "He don't want nothing to do with it," says Mary Malone. "He won't even talk about it."

The only monkey on Malone's back is basketball. His reputation around the league is that of a tireless worker, a relentless team player who simply wears down his opposition. To him, the game is the same one he still searches for on outdoor courts in the off-season. When he comes back to Petersburg, as he does once or twice a summer, Malone can be found on the playground. "He'll come home tired, dragging," says Pair, "but he sees a ball bounce, he has to stop and put his hand on that ball."

At the Lee Park courts, Malone will join Ed Gholson and the others in full court runs, or he'll take a younger player like Mark West, a Petersburg High graduate and center of Old Dominion University, and go one-on-one with him while a crowd looks on. After the games, he will take time to sign autographs, especially for children. "Moses has a thing about kids," says Hollins. "He would help a kid before he'd help me or a fellow ballplayer. Not with money, but with advice and with his time. He'll pick up a kid from the neighborhood and take him to Washington in his Mercedes before he'll say, 'Hey, here's $10.'"

Among children too young to have known who he was when he was playing for Petersburg High, Malone's reputation is as strong as it is among those who know him well. "He's still a hero to these kids," says Hayes. "Three buses went up to the last game in Philadelphia, and a local social club has trips planned for every game he plays in Washington."

"There's not a week since I graduated high school that Moses' name hasn't come up," says Hollins. "People who don't even like basketball will turn the tube on just to see him play. And your sports fans, you won't catch one out on the streets when a game comes on. Moses has left an impact here that will never leave. If he opened up a funeral home in this town, people would be committing suicide to get in."

But Malone owns no investments in Petersburg. His money, managed by advisors like Lee Fentress, a Washington lawyer who has been with Malone since he turned pro, is in stocks and bonds and real estate. When Malone does return to his hometown, it is quietly, without fanfare or notice. He visits his mother, his friends, and then he leaves. The city is trying to name a street after him, but neither Malone nor his mother want anything to do with it. "There's drunks and drug addicts on that street," says Mary Malone, shaking her head.

There are those who resent Malone's aloofness, his distance, his refusal to involve himself in his hometown, to donate a recreation center or a theater. "There are people in Petersburg say he owes them something," says Mary Malone. "What did Petersburg do for him? He's the one put Petersburg on the map."

It is not bitterness that guides Malone so much as a street sense developed from the time he was a child, a wariness of people looking for a soft touch. "I think there were a lot of people trading on Moses, trafficking on his greatness," says Marie Maniego. "I don't know to what extent anybody really helped him."

"There are people who resent Moses' success," adds David Pair. "They want to know why Moses doesn't give them this or that. We can't go out to eat without people hounding him, putting their hands on his shoulders and wanting him to do something for them. There was a time he'd come back here to rest, to get away from everything, but not anymore."

Malone has not forgotten where he came from, say those close to him. But he knows who his friends are, and he has developed a wisdom that is not taught in any classroom. "People still call him dumb today," says Pair. "They say he can't talk. I say he don't need to talk. He can let his money do his talking."

But it's not as simple as that. Malone's salary alone is not enough to answer his critics or to define his success. In a way, it is actually a curse, robbing him of his precious privacy. It is not his money, but something behind his brooding silence and his piercing eyes that grew up with him in the house on St. Matthew Street that answers anyone who questions his integrity or his intelligence.

""I don't let people get too close to me. That's just the way I am. And I don't worry about what people say. They can say what they want to, but they don't know Moses."

Some of the 76ers are taking the floor for warmups, but Malone stays behind, talking in quick, clipped phrases about his game, his past, his image. He has no difficulty coming up with words. It is his reluctance to share them, his protection of what is within him, that stokes the tension so familiar to Malone's inquisitors. But Malone himself is fully at ease, relaxed as he explains his place in the public eye.

"People got to understand, I was the first high school player to go to the pros. People couldn't understand that. And right now, people can't understand how I can make $13 million when they've gone to college and don't make that. I think it's a little jealousy, a little uneasiness."

Malone was no more concerned with the insecurities of the status quo when he first decided to bypass college than he is ruffled by the current cries of outrage over his stupendous salary. He knew very early that basketball was to be his life, whether he went to college or not. That understanding, he says was at the root of his historic decision.

"I was a better ball player when I was younger. I could play point guard then." He smiles and shrugs his shoulders. "Back then, college ball was too easy. And they call you on any little thing you do. You dive for a ball, you get called for a foul. I was too aggressive for the college game, and I didn't need it."

But education? Doesn't even a millionaire need that?

"I can get an education anytime, and you can learn a lot of stuff by not going to school. You can learn how people think about you. Once you get up in a role, people get a funny feeling toward you. They think you're a different person.

"I don't change just to deal with higher class people. I deal with the people I know and who I knew when I was growing up. People think because my name's Moses Malone I think I can get anything I want. My mama gave me that name when I was born. I've just given it a little beat, but I haven't changed. Right now I weigh 255. Back then I was 215. That's the only way I've changed.

"I don't regret anything I did back in '74. I had people telling me what to do, but I made up my own mind. If Moses was going to fail, it was going to be Moses' fault."

Game time, and to the eruption of thundering applause, the Philadelphia 76ers are introduced: "... from Southwest Louisiana, Andrew Toney... from Cleveland State, Franklin Edwards... from Petersburg High School, Moses Malone."

The label sticks. Here and there someone shouts, "Hey, high school boy," but the taunt is lost in a storming ovation. Philadelphia fans know their basketball, and they know who brings home the bacon.

Tonight, the job is easy. Utah is without the league's leading scorer, Adrian Dantley, and the Sixers roar off to a quick 27-point lead. Erving's game is, as always, lustrous. Ad-lib whirls, dips, scoops and slams. His every move is visible, while Malone, toiling in the lane, steadily pounds in layups and missed shots. There was fear when he arrived in Philadelphia that he could not keep up with the 76er running game, but twice this night he and Erving stage their own full court *pas de deux*, to the delight of the frenzied crowd.

The game becomes a romp, and Malone spends much of it sitting on the bench, laughing with teammates and looking looser than he ever does off the court. Playing only 39 minutes, he tops the Sixers with 32 points and pulls down 23 rebounds, twice as many as anyone else that night. For two hours, he has been at home, in his element, between the backboards. Now it is over, and the post game ritual begins. Reporters crowd around all but the lowliest 76ers. Malone, however, is in the training room, behind locked doors, where he stays for half an hour.

His waiting game pays off. Only two writers remain when he emerges, a towel wrapped around his waist. One asks him about the test of an upcoming road trip. "Test? Ain't no test," mutters Malone with amused disdain. "We do what we got to do." An easy game tonight? "Nothing's easy. Everything you do takes work. Takes a lot of work."

The writers leave, and Malone dresses. Someone's friend corners him, cuddles up next to Malone's side and has a photograph taken. Malone does not know the man, and he glares at the camera, unsmiling but patient. Outside, in the corridor, he signs two autographs, then walks away, alone.

In an essay titled "Bad Choice," printed when Malone opted to skip college, syndicated Washington columnist Carl T. Rowan wrote: "Malone will not gain the education, the self-assurance, the ability to cope in all situations — things he now needs far more desperately than a pocketful of money."

If he could have taken a look inside the Malone's refrigerator at the time, Rowan might not have scoffed so easily at the money. But more importantly, perhaps mistaking a lack of articulateness for ignorance, Rowan refused to recognize that there are many kinds of education. Growing up poor and alone, Malone learned early that talk is cheap, that glad hands and smiling faces are often the badges of hustlers. The storm he weathered during his last two years in high school, and the lessons he learned, were as valuable as any diploma he could have earned playing basketball in college. Those lessons have deepened in the professional world.

"Moses listens, and he watches, and what's wrong with that?" asks Marie Maniego. "It's not all that he doesn't know how to talk. He's just not going to let anybody take his person. He's protecting his self."

That, after all, is all he had to begin with.

February, 1983

Beyond Bull Durham

The owner is a politician, a three-time city councilman and one-time candidate for state senate who is partial to white cowboy hats.

The general manager can't tell left field from right, but she *has* learned to read a scoreboard. She, too, wears a cowboy hat, a black one.

The operations manager wears flip-flops and shorts. When he's not mowing the ball field, he's dreaming up promotional schemes, most of which have not worked. For example, the team got a good deal on its TV ads — unfortunately, they run at 2 in the morning.

The director of program sales rides a scooter to work — a push scooter. She wears barrettes and, during meetings, does headstands on the conference room couch. She's 9.

The director of beer sales is a 340-pound recovering alcoholic who goes by the name of Tiny. He has an assistant who works here because she has to — it was either this or go to jail for stealing a fire hydrant.

The grounds crew is one man, the ticket taker's son. He is the fourth grounds crew the team has had this season. The first — the general manager's ex-husband — was fired two days before the home opener.

The director of communications travels with the team, broadcasting games on a radio station whose frequency shrinks to near nothing at dusk. The first three innings or so come through loud and clear, he says. After that, you can either drive toward the station or read about the rest of the game in the morning paper.

The team's trainer has had a tough time. The home run leader is out with a separated shoulder. The best hitter has torn ligaments in his right hand. But worst of all, the clubhouse manager quit two weeks ago, so now the trainer has to do the laundry.

The players are kind of confused. They're not happy having to count coat hangers the way the general manager wants. And they don't think they should have to give her their wornout caps so she can sell them as souvenirs. They were embarrassed the night a game began and someone noticed home plate had been put in backward. But worse than all that is the pitching staff, which, unlike the rest of the ballclub, has no contracts with a major league team. The pitchers are free agents, signed and paid by the front office here. The horrendous pitching, say the players, is the reason the club won only 18 of its first 70 games, dropping 15 straight during one nightmarish stretch.

The manager has his own problems, what with the pitching situation and the injuries. And he doesn't have much experience of his own to draw on, seeing as how this is the first professional ballclub he's ever managed. He doesn't want to get into a war of words with the general manager, but they've had their battles over everything from the hats to when the players get paid. Their relationship wasn't helped when the general manager fired the third grounds crew — that was the manager's brother.

The fans don't know what to make of it all. Some have been coming out to this ballpark since it was built in 1948. They've seen winners and losers, but they've never seen anything like this. One night this season, a total of 25 people were in the stands at game time. As a tribute to their loyalty, the management introduced each one over the P.A. system, which, that night, was working.

This is the world of the Virginia Generals, arguably the worst, possibly the most woeful, and certainly one of the wackiest organizations in professional baseball.

It is early Monday afternoon. The Generals are due back from a road trip the next day, when they will open a home stand against the Salem Buccaneers. Today, the owner himself is visiting the front office.

The front office, like the wall that surrounds this stadium, is made of cinder blocks painted in Generals shades of white, blue and gold. The paint is new, but it cannot hide the fact that War Memorial Stadium, perched on a weedy lot at the industrial end of Hampton's Pembroke Avenue, is just plain old.

The war this stadium remembers is WWII. The Dodgers who first put a farm team here were in Brooklyn. Gil Hodges and Duke Snider roamed this grass. Satchel Paige once stood on that mound. Johnny Bench and Lou Piniella played here. So did Gary Carter. Over the past 40 years, with parent clubs ranging from the Dodgers to the Phillies to the Expos to the White Sox, this creaky structure has been home to one of the older and prouder minor league traditions in the nation.

But lately that pride has taken a beating. In 1983, an average of only 541 of War Memorial Stadium's 4,330 seats were filled for each home game played by the Peninsula Pilots, forerunners of the Generals. In 1984, all of 28 season tickets were sold. There was talk of the team leaving for good.

That talk caught Gil Granger's ear.

People in Williamsburg know Gil Granger. He's not quite home-grown, but he's been a local ever since he graduated from William and Mary in 1957. He raised three kids, built a nice little accounting business, bought property around town and got elected to the City Council three times. He's a Kiwanis kind of guy, described by friends as "affable, outgoing, eager to please."

But Gil Granger is not the type of guy you'd guess would be the savior of pro ball on the Peninsula. As of the end of the 1984 season, he'd never been to a game. So it seemed sort of strange when he appeared virtually out of nowhere that winter and, for $160,000, bought himself a baseball team.

It's odd to watch Granger walk around his ballpark. He swears he has no intention of giving up his team, but as he surveys the stadium, you'd swear he's ready to rid himself of the whole mess.

"It's... adequate," he says, gazing up at the weathered edifice. "We've put a lot of money into this place, but there are still some things that are the pits."

For instance, he says, the parking lot has room for only 700 cars. "When we have a crowd of 3,000," says Granger, "we're in trouble."

Fortunately — or unfortunately — that is a problem the team rarely faces. Home crowds this year have averaged a paltry 678. The real-life Durham Bulls, one of the Generals' rivals in the Carolina League, are averaging 3,800, thanks in large part to the success of the current film "Bull Durham."

Someone tells Granger the scoreboard, mounted above the center-field wall, looks pretty good with its new coat of paint and Generals logo.

"Oh, it *looks* great," says Granger. "But it doesn't work."

Eric Rosenfeld, the flip-flopped operations manager, corrects him.

"*Parts* of it work," says Rosenfeld. "balls and strikes work, but the outs don't. The innings will light up, but there's no telling what numbers will appear."

Granger turns toward the grandstands, where old seasoned bleacher boards are shored up here and there. "We didn't have to replace all of them," says Granger of the planks. "Just the ones people were falling through."

Finally he eyeballs the pigeon droppings splashed on seats throughout the stadium.

"Eric," he says, nodding toward the mess, "we've got some *work* to do before tomorrow."

In most places around the nation, bush-league baseball is booming.

Twenty million people attended minor league games last season, up 25 percent from 1981. Owners like Miles Woolf, who bought the Durham operation in 1979 for $2,500, are grinning as their clubs' values multiply — the Bulls are worth more than $1 million today. An estimated three-fourths of North America's 166 minor league clubs operate in the black.

Gil Granger, however, has seen nothing but red.

While major-league teams typically ante up for minor league players', coaches' and managers' salaries, expenses, uniforms and equipment, it is up to the host lower-league organization to provide the stadium, as well as transportation, lodging and part of the meal costs on the road.

With that standard setup, Granger's operation lost $25,000 its first season. The next, it lost $15,000. Last year it lost $45,000. This year, with the added costs of the free agents he pays for as part of a co-op arrangement with the Kansas City Royals, Granger figures to lose $100,000. Entering this season, he already had sunk almost $350,000 into his investment. Last year a group from Raleigh offered to buy the team for $500,000. Granger refused, prompting some to question his sanity.

But he seems to enjoy the confusion. When asked why he got into this business and why he refuses to get out, he sits back in a closet-sized conference room, sips a soft drink and drifts through a variety of answers, ranging from glib to seemingly sincere.

"Stupidity," he says at first, when asked what moved him to buy this baseball team. "Sheer stupidity."

Then he gets serious, citing regional loyalty: "If we ever lose baseball on the Peninsula," he says, "we'll probably never get it back."

Granger says he has plans in hand for a new stadium, perhaps near Newport News' Patrick Henry Airport. His dream ballpark would seat 8,000, he says, "with the ability to push 12." The cost, he says, would be "not an astronomical amount — basically $1.2 million."

Granger apparently has plenty of money. He pooh-poohs the price it took to buy this ballclub, saying, "I'd paid more money than that for filling stations."

He then reels off a tale about growing up in Philadelphia, watching the old A's and Phillies play and telling his wife back before they were married that he would someday own a baseball team. But he had virtually no contact with baseball between then and the day he decided to buy the Peninsula team.

Income taxes, indicates Granger in an offhand way, are perhaps one reason he won't let go: "If I sell for $500,000, that's $150,000 I've gotta pay taxes on. Why give the government that money? What will they do with it, send it to Iran?"

But the most telling of Granger's reasons is his children. As he talks about them, it begins to sound as if this team might ultimately amount to little more than a legacy for his kids.

"None of my children will ever be a CPA," says Granger. "That's not in their nature. But I think the baseball business is a nice business, an interesting one to get them involved in."

And that may have been what prompted this announcement last winter:

The new front office manager of the new 1988 Virginia Generals would be Gil Granger's 29-year-old daughter, Gilinda.

Gilinda Granger is the first to admit her background is not exactly that of a budding baseball executive.

"Last year I learned how to read a scoreboard," she says. "This year I learned how to read stats. And I know the names of the positions now, although I'm still not sure about right or left field. Is that facing the outfield or looking in?"

Granger's office is cluttered with boxes of used balls and old baseball hats — all of which she plans to recycle. Many of the baseballs are ones she retrieved from kids who gather outside the stadium at game time to catch fouls.

"Those kids aren't there for sentimental reasons, they're out there for money," she says, describing the kids selling stray balls back to her employees for 50 cents apiece.

"Those balls cost me $5.25 each," she says. "It costs me between $12,000 and $18,000 a season just for baseballs. That's the price of a *car*. So every time one of those kids takes a ball, he's basically taking a taillight off my car.

"People think I'm being crude about this," she says, tipping back the brim of her black hat, "but that's the stand I'm taking. And I *have* saved $8,000 in balls this year.

"I may not know baseball," she says, "but I know business."

Actually Granger's business background is somewhat sketchy. After graduating from high school and attending college awhile, she came back to Williamsburg, ran a hot dog shop, bought a camera store, met and married a Navy man in Norfolk named Roger Phillipe, sold the camera store and moved to a farm on the Eastern Shore, then moved to Virginia Beach where she worked as a live-in nanny. Somwhere in there, she also got into another line of work — selling synthetic drugs.

"At one point I decided I was going to make money on my own and do whatever I could to make it," she explains. "I wanted to be somebody besides Gil Granger's daughter. In Williamsburg I was always Gil Granger's daughter."

When she and Phillipe were charged in 1982 with distribution of marijuana, Phillipe pleaded guilty. She did not. The two were married that spring, and two days after their wedding, Phillipe was sentenced to nine days in jail. Granger got 30, which she spent writing wedding thank-yous. Now, she has a framed certificate signed in February by Gov. Gerald Baliles, removing "political disabilities" resulting from her conviction. Granger says she's proud of the pardon and sorry for her past.

"I was not selling illegal drugs," she says, "but I was walking a very thin line. I was found guilty of crossing over that line. I was stupid, and I've never come near that line again."

Neither, she says, will anyone in her organization. This year, says Granger, the Virginia Generals are the only team she knows of in the Carolina League that has a policy of drug testing.

Granger is ready to hand the governor's pardon right alongside her autographed photo of Cincinnati Reds owner Marge Schott. Schott, a controversial figure herself, is one of only three women executives in major league baseball. Granger is one of only five in the minors. It seemed natural that the two should meet, which they did, says Granger, in Dallas last winter. And when things got rough early this season, Granger flew to Cincinnati to meet with her mentor again.

"I needed some motivation," she says. "Kansas City was not pleased with what they were hearing about me. And I was catching a lot of flak around here."

Only someone like Schott, says Granger, could understand her problems: "There's a lot of things we both have in common — feeling left out by the old boys network."

The moment Granger says she remembers best from that visit was sitting with Schott at a Reds game and watching her fine outfielder Eric Davis $50 for tossing a baseball to fans.

"That made me feel so good," says Granger, eyeing her boxes of balls. "I can't *tell* you how good I felt."

It is Tuesday afternoon, and the Virginia Generals are trickling onto the field. Some pitchers are jogging out in right field. A couple of infielders are playing pepper by the dugout. Manager Joe Breeden is out by the mound chatting with an instructional coach from Kansas City. Things look tidy, sharp, organized... *professional*.

"Yeah, that's the way it's supposed to be," says trainer Jim Stricek, sitting in the stands, where a crew of kids wearing Virginia Generals T-shirts are scrubbing pigeon droppings off the bleachers.

"To people who are around this game," says Stricek, "baseball is a religion. The field is a cathedral. The clubhouse is a confessional".

Then he pauses and glances in the direction of Gilinda Granger's office.

"And *her*?" he says. "She should be persecuted for blasphemy."

"She knows nothing about this game," continues Stricek, who at 31 is looking to a career in the big leagues. "The things she's tried to do are a mockery. To be honest with you, we're the laughingstock of the Carolina League. This team plays better and is more comfortable on the road, where there are less distractions. Everywhere we go, people want to hear the latest Gilinda story."

Infielder Deric Ladnier, who leads the team in home runs despite being sidelined with a separated shoulder, has plenty of Gilinda stories. The blond 23-year-old fully expects to be among the 10 to 20 percent of bush-league players who make it to the bigs. He was signed three years ago out of the University of Mississippi, where he played against the likes of Bo Jackson and Will Clark. In his Florida high school days, Ladnier was in a top-flight league that featured a pitcher named Dwight Gooden. Ladnier has come a long way from high school—but he didn't expect it to be a long way *down*.

"Odd?" he says of the Generals' organization. "This is about as odd as it gets."

Vacant bleachers. A field that was hardly in better shape than the gravel parking lot when the season began. And a general manager who, rather than concede a rainout, has leaped on the field during a thunderstorm and joined the 10-year-old kids struggling with the tarp. These things — along with the foul ball chasing and the hat-collecting and the hanger-counting — says Ladnier, are "embarrassing" for the players.

"It's gone from 'Well, let's give her a chance'," he says of Granger, "to, 'There's no way.'"

Outfielder Pete Alborano, the only Virginia General selected to this year's Carolina League all-star team, says he can't believe what he's seen this season. He spent last summer at Eugene, Ore., in the Northwest League, where 2,000 fans would show up for batting practice and 6,000 would watch the games. Alborano says he was "scared" when he saw the setup here.

"It wasn't what I expected," says the 22-year-old Brooklyn native. "People just seem like they fly in and out of here. From the field crews to the pitchers, everything's so confusing...

"When I was at the all-star game, I got the feeling everyone looks at us as a Mickey Mouse operation."

One person who sees it that way is Dave Rosenfield, general manager of Norfolk's AAA Tidewater Tides — one step away from the major league Mets. Rosenfield has had his eye on the Peninsula operation for years, fronting a group of investors interested in buying the Class A club across the water.

"With the proper operation," says Rosenfield, "The Peninsula could support a Class A club very well. I'm certainly willing to put my name and other people's money where my mouth is."

But, says Rosenfield, he hesitates to call the current Peninsula baseball organization professional.

"It's an *abortion*," says Rosenfield. "As long as Gil Granger lets his daughter run that operation, it will never succeed."

At game time Tuesday night, 455 bodies are in the bleachers. Grandstand tickets for Virginia Generals games are $4—50 cents higher than Tides tickets and $1 more than it costs to see the major league Royals. But few fans on the Peninsula actually pay full freight — there are plenty of discounts, family packages and promotional gimmicks that slice the price.

"*Anybody* can get in for $1.50," says Gilinda Granger, noting the discount price for showing up an hour early. "All they have to do is watch batting practice."

Nobody showed for batting practice, but by game time, Elton Futrell and Leroy Quick are settled into their seats, two of the few actual fans among this year's 922 season ticket holders — most season tickets are bought by local businesses and few of those seats are actually filled with bodies. Both Futrell and Quick, retired from Newport News Shipbuilding, have been coming to this ballpark for 40 years. Both have their names painted on their seats. But as he watches Salem score three runs in the top of the first inning, Quick looks like he's about ready to take his name off that chair.

"I don't know what the holdback on them is," he says, watching a catcher's errant throw sail into center field. "But I just haven't seen the ball being played like it should. Last night they won two games up in Price William. And now look at them."

Futrell is a bit more forgiving.

"I've seen 'em all," he says, fingering the cowbell he's been ringing the past 40 years, "and this is the poorest club I've ever seen here. There's some that says it's the management, but I don't know about that. Me, I'm just a fan of baseball. I come out, win or lose. I don't care about anything else but the game on the field."

The game on the field does not go well this night. The Generals commit four errors, adding to their league-leading total. The final score is 6-1, Salem. The players trudge back to the clubhouse. Gilinda Granger is in the front office, counting receipts. And Herbert "Tiny" Woolston is in his beer room, drawing drafts for the last of the evening's customers.

"The people that come in here do think this is a really different year," says the former Army sergeant and Air Force mechanic who was a fan here for 20 years before Gilinda Granger asked him if he'd like to tend bar this summer.

"They talk about the management not knowing what they're doing," he says. But Tiny is not ready to pass judgment on the woman who gave him his job.

"People always look for a place to put the blame," he says, pulling the tips out of his jar, "when things are going bad."

But somehow, down here in Tiny's Place, underneath these old right field stands, with the green ballfield glowing out there under those white lights, with a cool drink in hand and the sound of crickets drifting in from the darkness beyond, all the problems disappear and the timeless magic of an empty minor league stadium on a summer night takes over.

Somehow, for the moment, things don't seem that bad at all.

August 14, 1988

150 MPH for God, Country and STP

Nine o'clock Sunday morning and the boys in the bus are already up and at 'em. Hell, half of them never even bothered sleeping last night. They didn't drive down from Titusville, Pa., 14 of them in a yellow school bus stocked with Pabst Blue Ribbon and fried chicken, to waste time sleeping, by god. No sir, thank you, they spent most of the evening howling at the moon, cranking Hank Williams Jr. on the eight-track and raising a toast every hour on the hour to King Richard.

That's right, King Richard. The words are right there on the side of the bus, written in elegant black letters, a nice contrast to the man-sized number 43 painted in white on the bus's midsection. The boys have been down since Friday afternoon, parked in the overnight campground set up beyond the grandstands of the Richmond Fairgrounds Raceway. They watched the small-timers take it around the track at Saturday's Late Model Sportsman Eastern 150, but today they'll get what they came for. In four hours the hotdogs, the Grand National big boys, will fire it up for the Richmond 400, stop number two on the 31-race NASCAR circuit. In four hours, Richard Petty will pull off his fancy black Stetson, the one with the peacock feathers hanging from the back, strap on his helmet, toss away his half-smoked cigar, the little thin kind he's been smoking for years, and climb through the side window of his aquamarine-and-orange Pontiac #43 while the boys in the bus, along with 23,000 other men, women and children jammed along, around and inside the raceway's half-mile asphalt track, go absolutely wild, unleashing a roar for the King and looking for that green flag.

But right now the boys are catching their breath in a sea of motor homes. All around them, row upon row of vans, campers and station wagons have turned the fenced, muddy field into a mini-Woodstock,

1980's Southern-style. Confederate flags, hoisted from the back doors of Winnebagos, ripple in the stiff morning breeze. The RV license plates read California, Texas, Massachusetts, but the bumper stickers say even more: Drive Like Hell — You'll Get There; God Bless America; When the Green Flag Drops, the Bullshit Stops.

Already the traffic is backed out on to Laburnum Avenue and beyond, a mass of restless, idling engines. Plenty of pickups and Corvettes, for sure, but there are just as many VWs and station wagons. The wives and kids, aunts and uncles, and grandma herself, they're all here, skipping church for a good seat, slapping down $22 a head for a ticket, filing past the Goody's girl with her free samples of headache powder, turning away from the corn dogs and french fries till later, settling down in the wooden bleachers with a seat cushion and a transistor radio, waiting for a race that is still four hours away, passing the time by leafing through the free Richard Petty comic book honoring this, his 900th NASCAR start, and admiring the Richard Petty T-shirts they're giving away at the gate.

Down below, beyond the barbed wire fence that rings the track and keeps cans bottles or over-enthusiastic fans from landing on the raceway, inside the steel-girder guardrails that separate the infield from the racetrack itself and that mark the pit area into which wounded, disabled cars will dive all afternoon, are the automobiles, the crews and the drivers.

Darting through air heavy with fumes from gas, oil and hot rubber, PR men in nylon jackets — *everyone* is wearing a nylon jacket — jockey to get their driver, their crew, their product in front of the nearest microphone or camera. Every jacket, every hat, everything that can carry a patch or a decal, from the yellow hood of Darrell Waltrip's Pepsi Challenger Chevrolet to the rear pocket of those white hotpants on the leggy blonde handing out free samples of Skoal tobacco, is branded with the logos of the American marketplace. Every fender is a billboard on which Hurst shifters, Valvoline motor oil, Champion spark plugs and Purolator filters share advertising space with Gatorade, Piedmont Airlines, Pet Dairy products, Hardee's burgers, Miller beer and Wrangler jeans. And towering over it all, like Zeus surveying Olympus, up there, above the raceway's first turn, as big as a house, looms a gargantuan pack of Winston cigarettes.

It is, after all, the good graces and thick wallets of the people at R. J. Reynolds Tobacco Company that bring America the NASCAR Winston Cup Grand National series, that enable Harry Gant, Neil Bonnett, Cale Yarborough and Lake Speed (yes, that's the name his mama gave him) to strap themselves in at Daytona in February and push through Richmond and Martinsville, Talladega, Ala.; Darlington, S.C.; Atlanta, Ga.; Charlotte, North Wilkesboro and Rockingham, N.C.;

Nashville and Bristol, Tenn.; Dover, Del., and Brooklyn, Mich., until they take the final checkered flag of the season in November at Riverside, Calif. That's nine months of superspeedway and short track Sunday afternoons filled with bumper-to-bumper 150 m.p.h. chases in the name of God, Country and STP.

It's not quite what the boys up in the hollows of Carolina and Virginia had in mind 50 years ago when they spent their weekdays outrunning the law with trunkloads of homemade whiskey and their weekends proving whose car was fastest around the cow pasture. It's not exactly what Bill France had in mind when he moved to Daytona Beach, Fla., in 1933 and found the local speed freaks gunning their stock cars north on the hard-packed beach, running their tires through the surf to cool them off, cutting left through a gap in the sand dunes, left again down Highway A1A and a final left back to the beach. By 1948, France had organized enough promoters, drivers and businessmen to launch the National Association for Stock Car Auto Racing and to hold its inaugural race in Daytona. But France could never have dreamed then, with a field full of home-engineered cars and a $3,000 purse, of today's corporate-style racing teams and the more than $1 million awarded at this year's Daytona 500.

It wasn't just faster cars, bigger crowds or better races that shot NASCAR from a rough and rowdy, loosely knit series of go-arounds in the 50s to today's megabuck, slickly packaged string of nationally televised events. It was the government, or more specifically, the Federal Trade Commission that gave NASCAR its ticket to Treasure Island.

When the FTC decided in the late 60s that cigarettes could indeed turn a person's lungs black and crusty, it pulled the tobacco companies' ads off television and radio, leaving the makers of Salems and Marlboros gasping for their advertising breath. But someone down there in the North Carolina corporate offices of R.J. Reynolds looked out his back window and noticed the thousands, no, the *millions* of everyday people, hard-working people with hard-earned paychecks, flocking out to those racetracks every weekend to see drivers like Junior Johnson and Ned Jarrett bang fenders, and most of those people were sure as hell smoking cigarettes, and what better place to unfurl the Winston banner than right there, right over the entrance to the racetrack, and before you could think twice, Bill France and his automobile racers were shaking hands with the people at R.J. Reynolds, and the Winston Cup series was born.

That was in 1970. Up until then, the sponsorship auto racing had gotten had come from the manufacturers of Detroit, who were at best skittish, and from auto-related corporations like Union Oil and

Goodyear. But with Winston's move into the field, every damn product from 7-Eleven to Mountain Dew began showing up on the hoods and fenders of racecars, united by a simple gospel: What wins Sunday sells Monday.

The money poured in, and the cars went faster, and the fans loved it. But there was a problem. In the old days, the best drivers were the ones who could fight as well with their fists as with their Fords, men who didn't especially go looking for trouble but who wouldn't back away from it either, on the track or off, and who were damned if anyone was going to tell them it might look better if they maybe wiped some of that grease out from under their fingernails.

The backers with the big money liked a winner, sure, but they were looking for more than just wins. They needed someone who could handle himself in front of a camera, who could carry himself at a cocktail party, who could appear between races at shopping malls and car shows and do more than chew tobacco and spit. We're talking *image* here, and after all, who wants a greaseball selling Dentyne?

So the drivers found themselves in another race — the race for sponsors. And other things being fairly equal, the ace in the hole for an up-and-coming driver was not necessarily his knowledge of gear ratios but how pretty, how presentable he could be. Most of the roughnecks fell by the wayside.

But they are not all gone. There is still room for that crackling independence and fiery temper that can make a special kind of legend out of even a so-so driver.

Just take a look at the Eastern 150, that Saturday afternoon prelude to the Sunday shootout at Richmond. This is a stop on the 32-race Budweiser Series for the Late Model Sportsman drivers — the up-and-comers or the almost-but-never-quite-made- its, the last notch of racing before the big time. These cars have sponsors, too, but for the most part they're smaller outfits, auto parts stores, garages or steak houses that pitch in a few thousand a year to help out a local boy. But even here there is some big money, the kind behind Dale Jarrett's red-white-and-blue Pet Dairy Pontiac LeMans, and when he got pushed into the wall Saturday afternoon by Wayne Patterson's Chevrolet, his car so crumpled it would take two tow trucks to pick it up off the track, well, that was more than Dale could take, and that's why he climbed out right there on the racetrack like a man walking onto a freeway, waving his arms at Patterson's car on the next lap, forcing Patterson to dive into the pit and sprinting after him. He would have pulled Patterson right out of that Chevy and given him a licking if he hadn't been collared by a crowd of peacemakers. Jarrett's father, Ned, who was up in the press box working color for the television people must have thought he was back in the old days again, and Tommy Ellis must have shaken his head and laughed, thankful for once he wasn't in the middle of a fistfight.

You see, if there was one man you'd expect to see in a brawl out there on Saturday, it would be Tommy Ellis, Richmond's native son and 1981 Late Model Sportsman national champion. Ellis has been racing the Late Model circuit since 1970, when he was a 23-year-old rookie. He made his name at Richmond's Southside Speedway, where he was known as "Terrible Tommy." His aggressiveness got him victories, but it also got him penalties.

The bad boy label has stuck, and although he claims he resents it, the yellowed photos and clippings of 10 years of on-track fights taped to the office door next to his garage south of Richmond suggest that Ellis is just a little bit proud of that reputation, too.

If you don't like the girlie magazines spread across his desk, if you don't like George Jones roaring out of the garage's stereo speakers so loud you can't hear yourself think, if you don't like the red Corvette with TWE-12 plates sitting in the driveway around front or the blood-red 1979 Pontiac Grand Am waiting in the garage for a new engine, if you were expecting something shinier than a cinderblock garage perched on a tire- strewn lot next door to the house he was raised in, the house his daddy still lives in, if you've got questions about why a man would stick himself in Southside Richmond when the only way to make the big time is to move out to where it's happening, to North Carolina, if you wonder why a man would spend Wednesday through Sunday of every week on the road to races between Maine and Florida and the other two days working from dawn to midnight on an engine that could blow on the first lap for a reason no one can figure out, if you can't understand why a man would do this year in and year out, pulling in $100,000 in a good year and spending every cent of it on tires, engines and cheap motel rooms with little or no hope of ever breaking through to the big leagues, well then Tommy Ellis doesn't really have any time to waste with you.

"Time has passed me by," he says, wiping his walrus moustache with a thick forearm and leaning over the $16,000, 355-cubic-inch Hoehns and Eanes engine hanging by a chain from his garage ceiling. The Pontiac shell sitting in the background goes for $20,000 without the engine. "It used to be if you had talent, that was the most important thing, but it's certainly not that way anymore."

There's no way a big-name sponsor is going to gamble on a man nicknamed "Terrible," but Ellis still has something to race for. "I make a living," he says, thanks to friends who volunteer as his pit crew on weekends and to a local boilermaker who pitches in sponsor money each year. But don't get the idea that Tommy Ellis has mellowed. The temper is still there. When his car hit the wall during a morning practice run before the Eastern 150 and it limped into the pits with a mangled rear fender, Ellis attacked the mass of twisted metal with his bare hands, ripping shreds of steel from the bumper in a fury of frustration. And when the repaired Pontiac blew its engine on lap 102 of that afternoon's race after running second all day, Ellis didn't quit. He came back two weeks later to win the Mountain Dew 400 at Hickory, N.C.

By 11 Sunday morning the cars, the drivers and the fans are ready for the Richmond 400 to begin. But it's still two hours until the green flag, and a lull settles over the raceway. Even Ray Melton, the press box public-address man who's been serenading the crowd with never-ending promos for everything from Terry Labonte souvenir placemats to next weekend's race down at Hampton, is taking a break. And down on pit row, Brother Bill Baird is testing his microphone for the morning service.

Brother Bill is the official chaplain for the NASCAR Winston Cup Series. For five years now, he's traveled with the drivers from the beginning to the end of the season, giving them an opportunity to get together with God the morning of a race. It's a grass-roots kind of religion, a personal contact with God that NASCAR drivers use to mix the Promised Land with a Pontiac.

"Ninety-five percent of these guys are religious," says Baird, a former tackle with the Minnesota Vikings, as he adjusts the sawhorses around which his congregation will soon stand. "This is their way of saying this is what God means in their lives. Like Cale says, when you cross the start and finish line at Daytona, you don't know if you're going to come back."

Beyond Baird, inside yet another barbed-wire fence, is the infield. It's been a morninglong picnic for the folks down here. Over by the fence at the second turn, a heavy man with a thick beard is popping a couple of Schaeffers for him and his buddy.

"I like the sound, man, the sound of them motors," says the beard. "I like to hear 'em rip. It's the rumble of them cars. You feel it in your body, and that's what it's all about."

"And the ladies, don't forget the ladies," reminds his friend, taking a heavy hit from his Schaeffer.

The sound. It's a roar that shakes the earth and doesn't let up until the last car crosses the finish line. These cars are nothing but pure power, thin sheet metal bodies wrapped around only the bare essentials — a 600-horsepower engine, a network of heavy steel roll bars, a deep bucket seat padded on the right side to hold the driver against the two-and-a-half Gs of pressure he'll feel taking it into the turns, a short-wave radio for communication with the pit crew, a fire extinguisher, a 22-gallon gas tank and the driver. Thirty-eight hundred pounds of streamlined machine riding on four superwide, inner-lined, $560-a-set Goodyear Eagle racing tires. No headlights, no doors, no side windows.

The first few trips around the track are like a parade, the pack, restrained by a pace car, running in an orderly procession of twos, building up speed for the green flag, revving their engines, bursting into short weaving motions to warm up their tires. But when the green flag drops, any kind of order is forgotten. The cars, now just flashes of color, rocket into a fight for the groove, that precious fast lane that gets them around the track the quickest. Before long, except for the four or five leaders, it's almost impossible to tell who is running where.

For the most part, the pit crews watch, wait and count laps, exploding into frenzied activity when their man pulls off the track. The jack man shoots one side of the car into the air, two men with air wrenches blast the lug nuts off while the tire man waits to throw two new Eagles on, the gas man rams a can into the rear tank, the windshield gets a wipe from a pole-handled squeegee, the new tires are on, a second can of gas is emptied, and the car shoots away, burning rubber down pit lane — all in about 20 seconds.

In a sport where a tenth of a second can mean the difference between first- and second-place money, a man's mere position on pit row can make him a winner. The top qualifier, the man with the pole position and a crack-drilled, paid team of 15 crew members, gets the first slot on pit row, closest to the exit. The second fastest qualifier gets number two, and so on down the line to the back of the pack, which is where Buddy Arrington usually sets up with his crew of four or five blue-jeaned volunteers.

Buddy Arrington is the last of the independents, a survivor. Some of the less kind people on the circuit call men like Arrington "strokers," giving them credit for little more than filling out the field. But within the subculture of stock car auto racing, where the Allisons, Yarboroughs, Waltrips and Pettys command the moneyed upper crust, Buddy Arrington is a working class hero.

Born in 1940 and raised on a tobacco farm in Franklin County, Arrington grew up "racing up and down the road, like everybody." At 14 he quit farming and went to work at a service station in Martinsville. A Chrysler dealership followed that, then another service station, and finally another dealership back in Rocky Mount in 1964. That's when Chrysler offered Arrington a truckload of parts if he'd take his Dodge on the Grand National circuit. Chrysler later pulled out, and NASCAR has grown up, but Buddy Arrington is still running a Dodge, and he's still putting his own engines together in the garage he built next to his used car lot on the 20 acres he owns north of Martinsville.

Arrington looks like a holdover from the 1950s, his sideburns clipped just so, his thick brown hair rising in an Elvis-style pompadour from his forehead, the simple black-framed sunglasses, the white socks, the cowboy boots.

In the far corner of the garage, Arrington's son Joey is dabbing a little oil on a new set of valves. Joey is the only full-time help Arrington has. When they make the twice-a-season trip to Michigan, Joey and Buddy share the 16 hours of driving each way. But when they go out to California, Buddy, who has worn a heavy back brace with metal stays ever since a 1969 bustup on the wall at Daytona, has to fly and Joey drives the three-day, cross-country trip alone. Buddy would rather not have to fool with the long runs, but he has no choice. He makes his money on the NASCAR point system, which gives a man credit for every race he finishes. It's not the winner's purse Arrington looks at when he crosses the starting line — he's never won in 20 years on the circuit. It's finishing and picking up the points. Through the first five races of this season, he stood 17th in points and totaled $27,195 in earnings. Last year he finished seventh in the final point standings, and he stands 13th on NASCAR's all-time points list.

"If you're into racing independently, and you're not there at the end, you go home with nothing. I work all the time to do it. I don't have time to go to meetings and go to parties and get drunk. I'm not made like that and that's probably why I haven't got a sponsor. If that's what it takes to get one, they can all have it."

The only way a man working out of his own small garage can compete is living hand-to-mouth and making every penny count. "I do what it takes to keep racing," says Arrington, who took in almost $200,000 last year and spent every cent to keep himself rolling. Most other operations shell out at least $500,000 without sweating. Richard Petty's operation figures its per-race expenses at about $30,000 and a season's total costs at close to $1 million.

Arrington stays on the track through a yard-sale approach to his inventory. Other crews might run through as many as 30 tires in one afternoon. Arrington rarely uses half that many, and the tires he runs on come from someone else's car. "I scrounge around and buy $20 used tires from the Woods boys or Petty or who it might be."

It's still a thrill to get that green flag, says Arrington, but it's basically a job, money, another day's work. He claims he can win with the right breaks — "My car's as good as any car running" — but when it comes down to that moment in a race when a man has to take the decisive chance, to risk all or nothing, a possible blown engine, a ruined rear end, or victory, Arrington invariably holds back. "Happens all the time.

You have to hold back and finish. If you go for it and don't make it, you're hurt. Riding, finishing and making lap money. That's what any independent's got to do."

Exit Buddy Arrington, enter Ricky Rudd. Two sides of the NAS-CAR coin. The last of the old guard giving way to the new breed. Ricky Rudd wasn't exactly born with a silver spoon in his mouth, but his road from racing go-karts to piloting the red-white-and-blue Piedmont Airlines Chevrolet #3 was about as smooth as you can get. Ricky Rudd is one of NASCAR's best bankrolled, most successful stock car drivers, with nothing but glamour, money and top five finishes expected of him in the coming years. Rudd is 26.

He's paid his dues—of sorts. At 8, he was racing go-karts professionally, running the "outlaw," non-sanctioned circuit around his Chesapeake home, shooting his 60-pound body around one-third mile ovals at 70 m.p.h. and stealing the purse from grown men. His father was an ex-dirt track stock car racer himself back in the 50s before turning to an auto parts and body shop business. He did all the engine work for his boy's karts, while Ricky rolled into his teens, joined the International Kart Federation—kind of a miniature NASCAR—raced larger tracks at faster speeds and pocketed a couple of national championships. At 15 he began toying with motorcross racing, having the same kind of success with dirt bikes that go-karting had given him, and at 18 he felt "kind of faded out." So where does a burned-out teen-age champion turn?

With the help of a family friend, an ex-Grand National driver named Bill Champion, 18-year-old Ricky Rudd, the sandy-haired boy with the All-American looks, found himself in the lineup at Rockingham in 1975, revving engines with the big boys. "I thought I was going to win everything there was," he remembers. "But I had a right rude awakening."

Rude to the tune of a tenth-place-finish. It wasn't what he was used to, but it wasn't disaster either. In 1977, he drove his 1975 Chevy Malibu to the Rookie of the Year crown. After one more year as an independent came the breakthrough—two seasons of short dances with Junie Donlavey's Truxmore operation and the DiGard Gatorade team, then the 1982 hookup with Piedmont.

Backed by one of the best racing teams in the business — Richard Childress's Winston-Salem outfit — Rudd roared out of the blocks this season, capturing the pole position in four of NASCAR's first six races. He recently moved down to Charlotte from Chesapeake, to be closer to the team's operation, but he's really only needed at the racetrack, behind the steering wheel. "I don't know the first thing about engines," he admits. "I don't even know what makes one run." All Rudd has to do is fly to a race (on Piedmont, of course), drive the car, show up once in a while at Piedmont executive meetings and conventions, make a few personal appearances and mix in at the cocktail parties thrown at the racetracks.

There's always the chance that comfort so easy come could just as well be easy go. Rudd found that out back in 1980 when Junie Donlavey let him know one day that Jody Ridley was taking his place. The same thing happened the next year when the Gatorade team brought in Bobby Allison and bumped Rudd to the role of backup driver. "That's racing," he shrugs. "Sometimes you show up at the track and somebody's in your seat. It's not what's right or wrong. It's just a matter of finances."

By the time the checkered flag dropped on the Richmond 400, 2 hours, 43 minutes and 26 seconds after the first green, Ricky Rudd's Chevy was already loaded back in the Piedmont tractor-trailer. It had only lasted 177 laps this day. Arrington finished the race on lap 380, good for 20th place and $2,400. Richard Petty ran eighth, and Bobby Allison edged out Dale Earnhardt to grab the $23,725 first prize and a Miller shower in the winner's circle.

Out in the parking lot, the long process of emptying had begun, and even the boys in the bus started packing it up.

And out at the main gate, white-haired, wizened Henry Crawford counted the thick wad of bills he'd pulled in selling patches and belt buckles.

"Well over a thousand," nodded Henry. "Not a bad day."

July, 1983

Saturday's Hero: A Beat

So when the sun of October slopes in late afternoon, the children scurry home from school, make footballs out of stuffed socks, they leap and dash in the powerful winds and scream with delight. Fires are burning everywhere, the air is sharp and lyrical with the smell of smoke. There are great steaming suppers to be eaten in the kitchens of home as the raw October gloom gathers outside, and something flares far off.

—Jack Kerouac
The Town and the City

Gloom is gathering as Duke Chiungos wheels his Lincoln through Lowell, Mass. The Merrimack River, choppy in the brisk morning breeze, looks as wicked as the gray clouds tumbling in from the east. Chiungos glances down at the roiling water then up at the rolling sky. He turns toward Edward D. Cawley Memorial Field. Halfway there, he slows.

"See that?" he says, nodding at an empty lot surrounded by the downtown's dreary redbrick buildings. A century ago they housed the mills that made this small New England city a giant among the nation's industrial centers. But now the dark buildings are only monuments to the past, some transformed into museums and restaurants, others abandoned. On the lot where a factory once stood, there is a ring of polished granite blocks and some benches. A small sign hanging from a railing reads **JACK KEROUAC COMMEMORATIVE PARK**.

Kerouac — the man whose reckless living and breathless prose captured the essence of the Beat Generation, the writer whose books mirrored the manic urgency of Eisenhower-era wanderers and became bibles to the searchers of the '60s. Excerpts from his books — *Doctor Sax, Maggie Cassidy, The Town and the City, Vanity of Duluoz, Lonesome Traveler* and, of course, *On the Road*, the novel that vaulted Kerouac from obscurity to fame — are chiseled into the granite blocks on this lot. The benches are empty.

"Plenty of people in this town didn't want that park," says Chiungos, a commercial realtor, as he stops at a traffic light and looks at the lot. "*They* say Jack was nothing but a drunk. But then a lot of people around here just don't have it in their heads that he's a celebrity, recognized all over the world".

The light changes, and Chiungos eases into the town's midmorning traffic, talking about Kerouac — not the man who was crowned king of the Beats, but the boy Chiungos and his buddies called Zagg because of his moves in the backfield. It might surprise the drifters who still stuff copies of *On the Road* into their backpacks as they set out to find America, but it was football that shaped Kerouac's life, cut him loose from Lowell and launched him into literary legend.

The boy who walked the mile and a half home with Chiungos from Lowell High's practices on fall afternoons 51 years ago was not a world-renowned author, nor was he a drunk shunned by the city where he was born and would be buried. Before he met Allen Ginsberg and William Burroughs; before his cross-country jaunts in drive-away Chevys and empty boxcars; before the jazz, the dope, the manic prose and finally the fame; before he became tormented by the success he sought and drank himself to death; before all that, Jack Kerouac was, purely and simply, a football star.

He was a big enough star to draw college scouts to look at him. Frank Leahy, the Boston College coach at the time, watched Kerouac run for the winning touchdown in the 1938 Lowell-Lawrence Thanksgiving Day game, and then was invited over to the Kerouac home for the holiday meal. Later, Leahy put his public-relations man, a young guy named Billy Sullivan, on the case. Sullivan's uncles owned the Lowell printshop where Leo Kerouac, Jack's father worked.

But the younger Kerouac turned his back on Boston College to become an Ivy Leaguer, a halfback for Columbia. Leahy moved on to Notre Dame. Sullivan went on to become a pro football mogul, founder of the New England Patriots. And the elder Kerouac, he was fired after his son announced he was heading for school in New York City.

In the fall of 1939 the dispatches from New York began arriving in Lowell describing the hometown hero's exploits. First he played at Horace Mann prep school, to which Columbia sent him for a year of seasoning. The next fall he joined the Columbia freshman team. The Lions' varsity coach, Lou Little, hailed his new halfback as a future star, comparing Kerouac to Columbia legend Sid Luckman, who graduated in 1939.

"This Kerouac was all-Massachusetts State in high school," Little told the *Spectator*, the university's newspaper, in the spring of 1941, "and he's shown great promise here at Columbia. He's short, but husky and very fast."

This was a story they could understand back in Lowell, the kind of all-American glory that hits home in a blue-collar town built on the virtues of hard work and hope. But the next year, Kerouac inexplicably forsook it all. In his second season at Columbia, he quit football, quit college altogether. The stream of novels that were to follow did little to explain that act to the folks back home.

"Here we are," Chiungos says, pulling up to the empty football stadium at the east end of town. These are the same bleachers that were filled with 14,000 fans 51 years ago, when Chuingos anchored the offensive line, and Kerouac was the fastest man on the state's second-ranked team. Chiunges, too, avoided Kerouac at the end. The dingy saloons, the embarrassing stumbling and foul-mouthed boisterousness that marked Kerouac's final days — Chiungos steered clear of all that. "He was a little disappointed because I never wanted to see him those last years," says Chiungos. "But the places he was going, that just wasn't my style, and I really didn't want to see Jack like that."

Chiungos is 67, the same age Kerouac would be. Twenty years have passed since Kerouac collapsed in a bungalow in Florida on an October morning, his stomach hemorrhaging after he had drunk a can of Falstaff beer while watching *The Galloping Gourmet* on television. He died the next morning in a St. Petersburg hospital. Chiungos stands up for the schoolmate he once blocked for. "A lot of people remember the end," says Chiungos, "but not many remember the beginning."

He was publicized as a great "climax runner" in the newspapers. Instantly he had hundreds of friends, students and teachers alike, and he hardly knew what to do about it all. In the company of his fellow teammates he soon learned the knack of limping and swaggering through the halls of the school in all the glory of a famous hero.
—The Town and the City

The Town and the City was Kerouac's first book, published in 1950, seven years before *On the Road*. In it, Kerouac tells the story of a boy growing up in a gloomy New England town, playing ball on the sandlots, starring in school, dreaming of becoming a college athlete and seeing that dream briefly come true before it falls down around him in the early years of World War II. He is left aimless and empty, at the side of a highway headed west.

The first chapters of the author's life story are the same. They can be seen in rough outline in ghostly fragments of *The Lowell Sun*. These are stored on microfilm in the basement of the downtown public library — the library where Kerouac went when he played hooky from high school and read the works of William Shakespeare. On the half-century-old pages of the *Sun's* sports sections, Kerouac is a boy again.

Here he is, in the summer of 1937, a 15-year-old pitcher for the Pawtucketville junior league baseball team. The team is dead last, 1-8. The box score shows Kerouac was shelled in an 8-4 loss, yielding five hits and four walks in the first two innings. He did better at the plate, batting cleanup, getting two of Pawtucketville's four hits. In the group photo, Kerouac, wearing a sleeveless T-shirt and jeans (the league had no uniforms), looks sullen.

That October, he is listed as one of the two youngest players on Lowell High's varsity football roster. At 5'8", 155 pounds, he is also one of the smallest. It takes the *Sun* a few tries to get the new kid's name right: "Leo Kerouac turned in some real nice football yesterday afternoon and may see some action in the Lowell high backfield against Manchester," says one piece. "Leo Kerouac seems to be well on the way to becoming an excellent ball carrier," says another. And there he is, as Jack, later that season, "knifing" for a four-yard score in a B-squad game.

Then it is 1938, and Kerouac makes headlines as a starter on what promises to be one of the strongest teams in Lowell's history. After the season opener, the *Sun* columnist chooses to highlight the halfback: "Young Kerouac has the legs and the style. He looks like a football player."

But as the autumn wears on, Kerouac is in and out of the starting lineup, scoring three touchdowns against Worcester Classical one week but then seeing only spot duty against Manchester the next. At mid-season his role is defined in another *Sun* story: "Jack Kerouac, Lowell's speed-king, will be used as a 'situation' ball carrier... one of the fastest school boy backs in the state is expected to play a major part in Lowell's offense tomorrow."

After six games Lowell is undefeated and unscored upon, and ranked second in the state, and Kerouac is seeing action as its first — and usually only — man off the bench. His coach, Tom Keady, calls him the squad's "climax runner." However, when the team drops three straight games, Kerouac's name is hardly mentioned. Nevertheless, going into the season finale, the Thanksgiving Day matchup against archrival Lawrence High, he is Lowell's second-leading scorer, with five touchdowns. He begins that game, as usual, on the bench. Then, in the second half, before 14,000 fans, he scores the only touchdown in an 8-0 win. The next day's account of Kerouac's run, beneath a photo of the grimacing halfback lunging toward the end zone, is brief: "With the ball on the Lawrence 14, Zoukis faded back to the 21 and tossed a neat pass to Jack Kerouac who grabbed off the leather on the Lawrence nine and outsmarted one Lawrence secondary man to score right at the corner."

A dozen years later, through the freedom of fiction, Kerouac described the play as it must have felt to him, transforming a simple score into an epic journey in *The Town and the City:*

Another Galloway player paused, twisted, reached out for the ball, barely grasped it in his fingers, turned and went plummeting downfield along the sidelines. The roaring of the crowd surged and grew thunderous, the Martin mother jumped up on her seat to see, and she saw a figure racing down the sidelines, shaking off tacklers with a squirming motion, plunging through others with a striding determination, tripping, stumbling, staggering on half fallen and half running, straightening out once more, plodding, faking, yet suddenly approaching the goal line in a drunken weary run, staggered aside by another lunging figure, momentarily stopping, then carrying on again, striding to the line falling, with a dark figure smashing into it, now wavering on bent knees, now finally driving over and rolling in the end zone triumphantly.

Eighteen years later Kerouac was still rerunning that same play in *Vanity of Duluoz*, published in 1968, only a year before he died:

Second half they figure they might need me and put me in. (Maybe they figure I looked awful bad in that Nashua game and nobody'll care.) At one point I am almost loose, but some kid from Lawrence just barely trips me with a meaty Italian hand. But a few plays later Kelakis flips me a 3-yard lob over the outside end's hands and I take this ball and turn down the sidelines and bash and drive head down, head up, pause, move on, Downing throws a beautiful block, somebody else too, bumping I go, 18 yards and just make it to the goal line where a Lawrence guy hits me and hangs on but I just jump out of his arms and over on my face with the game's only touchdown.

In fact and in fiction, that moment meant as much to Kerouac as any in his life. No matter how far he strayed, in life or in literature, he kept coming back to that Thanksgiving Day game against Lawrence in 1938. It earned him his scholarship to college. It also made him the kind of local hero that his literary career never could. Except for *On the Road*, none of Kerouac's novels was a major financial success. Even that book was attacked both for its content and its breathless, run-on style, which Kerouac labeled "spontaneous prose." Some critics had less flattering descriptions of it:

"Verbal goofballs," said *Saturday Review*.

"Like a slob running a temperature," said *The Hudson Review*.

"That's not writing," said Truman Capote on David Susskind's TV show. "It's *typing*."

The attacks stung. Kerouac was famous when he died at 47 — his obituary was headlined in *The New York Times* — but he was miserable. His friends still wonder, as they did then, if Kerouac was ever as happy as he was on the football field.

Sam Samaras runs the liquor store where Kerouac was a regular during his last years in Lowell. But the two men go back further than that, back to the Saturday mornings in the mid- 1930s when Samaras would take his gang of Greek buddies across the river and challenge Kerouac and his French-Canadian pals to a football game. kerouac's team was so strong they ran ads in the *Sun* challenging all comers.

"Man, it was rough," says Samaras, sitting on a case of beer in the back room of his store and recalling those sandlot Saturdays. "Nobody had helmets. A couple of guys had jerseys, that's all. this was a time when the toughest guy ruled, you know what I mean?

"But the thing about Kerouac is he wasn't a fighter; he wasn't belligerent. Still, he could take a blow. No matter how hard you hit him, he'd get up and congratulate you.

"And fast? He was *dangerous*. You had to hit him early, because once he got out of the backfield he was gone. Couldn't catch him. One time — this wasn't in a game against us — he scored nine touchdowns. *Nine* touchdowns. I think he wrote about that in one of his books."

Kerouac did, in *Vanity of Duluoz:*

"... we won 60-0, after missing 3 points after, I thought from that morning on, I would be scoring touchdowns like that all my life and never be touched or tackled...."

Samaras is 68. Many of the boys he mentions who played in those pickup games are now dead. But across town, in archives at the University of Lowell, some of their voices are preserved on tape among the 300 hours of interviews recorded in the 1970s by a writer named Gerald Nicosia, whose book *Memory Babe* is considered the best of the many biographies of Kerouac. On those tapes some of Kerouac's closest boyhood friends—men named G.J. Apostolos, Scotty Beaulieu and Skippy Roberge—focus on what sports meant to Kerouac. And to all of them. Like the *Sun* stories on microfilm, the voices are scattered snippets, fragmented echoes of the past.

"He was good at *everything*," says one voice.

"Strong as a goddam bull," says another.

"Right here, right in his thighs, that's where he had it."

"What a build."

"And what a *sister*!"

Laughter and the sounds of the men pouring themselves another round of drinks. Then Samaras's voice can be distinguished: "He wasn't, I don't know, he wasn't *hungry* enough. He wasn't the kind of guy who was real gung ho. He wouldn't *hurt* anybody."

A silent pause, the clinking of glasses.

"Apparently," someone says, "he wanted to be a writer."

"Had to be."

... although I also know everybody in the world's had his own troubles, you'll understand that my particular form of anguish came from being too sensitive to all the lunkheads I had to deal with just so I could get to be a high school football star, a college student pouring coffee and washing dishes and scrimmaging till dark and reading Homer's Iliad *in three days all at the same time, and God help me, a WRITER whose very "success," far from being a happy triumph as of old, was the sign of doom Himself.*

—Vanity of Duluoz

By the time Kerouac reached high school, he was torn in the way he would be until the end. He was driven to devour books and, as he wrote in *Vanity of Duluoz*, "to end up on a campus somewhere smoking a pipe, with a button-down sweater, like Bing Crosby serenading a coed in the moonlight." But another part of him bristled at the ridicule he got from friends for wanting to be different from then. The torment drove him to a priest.

The Rev. Armand Morissette recalls the first time he met Kerouac. It was in the same front room of St. Jean Baptiste Rectory in Lowell where Father Spike — as the 79-year-old priest has been called all his adult life — meets visitors today. He still writes a regular column for *Le Journal de Lowell*, Lowell's French-language newspaper, as he has for 50 years. He still speaks with a thick French accent. And he still takes people curious about Kerouac to the Rainbow Cafe, a bar around the corner, where Kerouac's picture hangs in a place of honor above the bottles.

"I had only been a priest about three years," says Father Spike of his first encounter with Kerouac, in 1937. "He looked very upset, and he says, 'My name is Kerouac, Jack Kerouac.' I knew his family, but I did not know him.

"So I says, 'What's the matter with you? You look so upset.'

"And he says, 'Everybody's laughing at me. I want to be a writer, I want to be a poet, and they're laughing at me. They all me a sissy.'

"So I says, '*I'm* not laughing.' I says, 'To be a writer is a great, wonderful and influential thing, a very important thing.' But, I told him, to be a writer he would have to go to the university, and his parents had not much money.

"'Well,' he says, 'I'll play football; I'll get a scholarship. And I'll show them I'm not a sissy.'

"'Fine,' I says. And that's what he did. I remember when he made the touchball in the big game—you know, the point. Oh, boy, I mean he was the *hero*. Lots of headlines. Just like Doug Flutie, you know?"

It is the 1938 Lowell-Lawrence game that Father Spike remembers. But that game was still two seasons away when Kerouac first went to see him. The strange thing is that for all his fabled speed, Kerouac never became a fixture in coach Keady's lineup. "Jack was tremendous," says Chiungos, who was a two-year varsity veteran by the time Kerouac joined the squad as a junior. "But Keady was the kind of coach who when he had his mind made up on a starting team, that's the way it stayed.

"Rough and tough, that's the way he coached, but then that was the era. Jack was something special when he had room to run, but all we had were these moth-eaten plays, you know, bulling through the line for four or five yards. It was a game of brute strength, a fairly simple game. We'd practice 15 plays during the week, then use about four in the game. Jack, he was a breakaway player, and they weren't used to that. It was like Jack was just ahead of his time, in a way."

Kerouac did not take being benched in stride. Something was simmering inside him. Chiungos sensed it long before Kerouac wrote about it.

"Jack harbored a great deal of hostility toward this town, or toward some of the bigger people in this town," says Chiungos. "It seemed he didn't think some of the people in authority were fair in the way they dispensed things, whether it was the businesses who hired and fired his dad or the coach who didn't play him enough. It was like he didn't think the world was fair. He was sensitive, and he would remember. He wouldn't say too much about it, but he would *remember*."

Morning, breakfasts, saltpeter so we wouldn't get horny, showers, taping, aching muscles, hot September sun tacklings of silly dummies held by assistant coaches and idiots with cameras taking our pictures dodging this way and that.

What were the chances of Columbia this year? Nothing, as far as I could see...

—Vanity of Duluoz

Kerouac stayed in the Sun's headlines after his climactic Thanksgiving Day touchdown, spending the winter of his senior year on the school's indoor track team, sprinting, hurdling, running twice in the Boston Garden and becoming Lowell's leading point-scorer. But as far as his classmates were concerned, he had already moved beyond Lowell High. He was bound for Columbia.

"We were all so proud," says Charlie Kirkiles, who was a sprinter on the track team and who stops in most mornings at Samaras's store for a sip and some small talk. "We were all just ordinary kids. We were poor. We didn't have big ideas about life. So when Jack got that scholarship, I mean, how many kids did that from Lowell High? Who ever heard of one of *us* going to Columbia? We thought it couldn't happen to a nicer guy."

Kerouac spent the 1939-40 school year at Horace Mann in the Bronx. He roamed the city, discovering jazz and writing profiles of Glenn Miller and Count Basie for the high school paper. He wrote fiction as well, publishing two short stories in the school's literary magazine. But what he did best was run with the football.

The 1940 Horace Mann yearbook describes Kerouac as "A brilliant back," detailing his November 1939 performance against the rival Tome School in the kind of Homeric terms the young Kerouac might have written himself: "Kerouac turned in one of the most remarkable individual performances ever seen on the Maroon and White gridiron. The fast-stepping back sparked the game with his brilliant broken-field running. Midway in the first quarter, he returned a Tome punt 72 yards for the lone touchdown; a little later, he dashed sixty-five yards before being pulled down on the Tome fourteen; and near the end of the game, he added the finishing touch to his dazzling exhibition, by breaking away for a gain of twenty-nine yards."

Hyperbole about Kerouac wasn't confined to his classmates. According to a *New York Hearld Tribune* report of that same game, "The visiting squad formed a vague background for the brilliant running of Kerouac."

The profile beneath Kerouac's yearbook photo reads as if he had achieved his Bing Crosby dream: "Brain and brawn found a happy combination in Jack, a newcomer to school this year. A brilliant back in football, he also won his spurs as a *Record* reporter and a leading *Quarterly* contributor. Was an outfielder on the Varsity baseball nine."

When he arrived at Columbia in the fall of 1940, it seemed that Kerouac had finally found his niche, quickly establishing himself on the freshman team. In its report on an opening loss to Rutgers, the campus newspaper called Kerouac "probably the best back on the field." That brought varsity coach Little out to the next game, which was against St. Benedict's prep school. Little was accompanied by the Dartmouth coach, Earl Blaik. Little and Blaik saw the kid from Lowell return the opening kickoff 90 yards. After an ensuing punt return, the coaches watched Kerouac limp to the sideline.

Little was skeptical of the injury and forced Kerouac to practice during the week. By the next game, against Princeton, Kerouac was in too much pain to play. A doctor's report, which was mentioned in that week's *Columbia Spectator* under the headline KEROUAC LOST TO YEARLING GRID TEAM, reads: "Their hopes darkened by the news that Jack Kerouac, star back, will be out with a leg injury for the rest of the season, Coach Ralph Furey's Freshman gridiron charges practiced in the rain yesterday afternoon."

His right tibia was broken, but Kerouac hardly cared. "I went to Columbia because I wanted to dig New York and become a big journalist in the big city beat," says Jack Duluoz, the protagonist in *Vanity of Duluoz*. The broken leg was actually a blessing to someone who still had training-table privileges: "... I enjoyed the leisure, the steaks, the ice cream, the honor, and for the first time in my life at Columbia began to study at my own behest the complete awed wide-eyed world of Thomas Wolfe."

He also took in the New York nightlife and entertained William F. Buckley Jr. and some friends from Horace Mann. He stayed involved enough in school to run for — and win — the vice- presidency of his class. As for football, he was bitter that Little had doubted his injury. Still, he was ready to play. A *Spectator* story that spring quoted Little as predicting his would-be sophomore would "tear up the turf."

"We're planning on using him at wingback, where his speed will tell," said Little. "Can he go to his left on the reverse? I'll say he can!"

But when the 1941 season began, even with his roster depleted by prewar enlistments, Little did not start Kerouac. Years later, Kerouac blamed his benching on the KF-79, a trick play that had made Little's career when he used it to upset Stanford in the 1934 Rose Bowl. Kerouac considered the play — and the coach — a fossil. To Kerouac that bowl win was ancient history. "He hadn't done anything noteworthy since with his team," wrote Kerouac of the fictional coach Lou Libble in *Vanity of Duluoz*. But apparently the play was still a favorite of Little's in 1941, and Kerouac could not run it.

"I began to see that good old Lu Libble wasn't going to start me," Kerouac wrote in *Vanity of Duluoz*. "He insulted me in front of everybody again by saying, 'You're not such a hot runner, you can't handle the KT-79 reverse deception.'"

Once again Kerouac felt cheated. At Lowell High, he had kept playing the game. At Columbia, he quit. Kerouac came home that fall and eventually found a job writing sports for the *Sun*. His only bylined story during the three months he was with the newspaper was an account of a Lowell High basketball game. His name was misspelled as "Jack Korouac.":

... the Kirk Streeters poured out on the floor for the second half of the game with renewed gusto. Before a few seconds had elapsed, Tommy Petroules dropped in the tying basket. This was the precursor of a new and vigorous Lowell high attack. The Red and Gray five began to function beautifully, sporting an iron-clad defense, all the while passing and shooting with rare skill. Lawo, Ciszek, and Petroules were splitting the twine from all parts of the floor, while the Lawrence hoopsters were barely able to get near enough for scoring attempts...

The final score read Lowell 32, Lawrence 21, and a grateful ovation was tendered the lads by the victory-minded spectators.

"I really didn't think he was much of a writer," says George Mc-Guane, whose desk was near Kerouac's. McGuane retired a decade ago after 42 years with the *Sun*. A former AFL official and author of a pictorial history of the New England Patriots, the 75-year-old McGuane operates the clock at all Patriot home games, and he plays golf several times a week. Occasionally, he also holds court for visitors who are curious about Kerouac.

"He wasn't that sociable," McGuane says. "He'd come in, sit down at his desk and start typing, just typing away, typing all the time. He was feverish that way. But I could never figure out what the hell he was writing.

"I knew he'd been a good football player, and I was aware of him as a good-looking Greek — that's what I thought he was, Greek. To me he was this nice-looking kid who came from Lowell. How the hell did I know he'd do all these things later on?"

Kerouac quit the *Sun* and became a merchant seaman, sailing on a supply ship across the Atlantic. When he returned from that trip in October 1942, a telegram from Little was waiting, inviting him back to Columbia. Kerouac went, but only long enough to sit on the bench against Army. After leaving Columbia for good, he started working on his novel *The Town and the City* and hooked up with a group that included Ginsberg, who was a Columbia student at the time, and Burroughs, who would later be given the title for his most famous novel, *Naked Lunch*, by Kerouac.

For the next several years, Kerouac and his friends, along with a shifting cast of visitors, lived the bohemian life, sampling the jazz and drug subcultures of the city. When a grammar school dropout and reform-school veteran from Denver named Neal Cassady dropped in on the group in 1946, Kerouac was spellbound. Here was a man who had hitchhiked cross-country, who was living the wild life. Cassady once thumbed more than 1,000 miles just to see a Notre Dame football game. Kerouac was an actual football star, the kind of athlete Cassady had always wanted to be. The two became fast friends, and in 1949 they undertook the cross-country adventures that would be chronicled in *On the Road.*

But before Kerouac totally broke away from Lowell, he returned for one more stab at conformity, in 1950, when *The Town and the City* was published. It was a conventional novel, containing nothing like the fireworks of *On the Road.* Kerouac played the role of conventional author, coming home to Lowell for a book signing at a department store. This wasn't quite what his friends had expected of him, but at least he was the kind of writer they recognized.

"He looked beautiful," recalls Chiungos. "He had on this green velour jacket, sitting there signing autographs for the book. He looked great, just like a real writer."

Father Spike was there too. "I went and bought a book and was standing in line for the autograph," he says. "And Jack looks up and shouts at me, 'Aha! I *told* you!'"

"I says to him afterward, 'Jack, that's a very nice book. Very well written.'"

But critically and commercially *The Town and the City* hardly caused a ripple. Not until *On the Road* was published would America take notice — even as Lowell turned away from him.

"His life-style by then was something else," says Chiungos. "And this is what I think is what a lot of people in Lowell held against Jack."

Samaras thinks of the guy who greeted him back in the '60s when he delivered the bottles of Scotch Kerouac ordered over the phone during his last years in Lowell. "The minute I walked in the door, he'd get down like this," says Samaras, dropping into a three-point stance. "He'd say, 'Hit me, Sam, go ahead and *hit* me!'"

"He looked like a bum," says Samaras, shaking his head. "But he wasn't a bum. No way in hell was he a bum."

Father Spike thinks of the funeral at which he performed Mass before Kerouac was buried in Edson cemetery on the south side of town. The service, held in St. Jean Baptist Church, drew a mostly out-of-town audience. "Maybe 30 people were there from Lowell," says Father Spike. "It's like Christ said — a prophet is not honored in his own village. It's always like that."

October 23, 1989

Senior Scout

Almost four decades of beating the bushes from Maine to Florida, and all Harry Postove has to show for it is a plaque with his name tacked to a cinder-block wall outside the Tidewater Tides Metropolitan Memorial Park. That and a tiny house in Norfolk just off Colley Avenue, a short stroll from the Steak 'N Egg.

The place is only a few blocks from Wood Street, where Postove was born 72 years ago. Its bedroom is filled with yellowed note cards bearing the verdicts on backwoods baseball players, thousands of faceless pitchers and forgotten shortstops who never made it out of town but who for one magic evening had a scout sitting up there in the stands watching them.

The scout was Harry Postove.

There is more in this house. There is a living room strewn with clippings from countless sports pages. On the mantel sits a gallery of dusty-framed snapshots of Postove's brothers and sisters, of his father, a tailor from Poland, and of his mother. One of his four brothers played in the Giants' farm system before the war, but in the photograph on the mantel, the brother is wearing the hospital robe of a wounded veteran, not the pinstripes of a baseball player.

Flanking Postove's musty fireplace are three bats, leaning at odd angles against the bricks like weary sentries. One is a tight-grained, shellacked Adirondack. Screwed on its head is a small metal plaque commemorating the 53rd All-Star baseball game in Montreal in 1982, and inscribed at the top of the bat is Harry Postove's name.

Another bat is black, a Hillerich & Bradsby model dated 1973 and inscribed with the signatures of the National League champion New York Mets. Koosman, Seaver, Staub, McGraw, the then-aged Mays.

The last bat is another charcoal-hued H&B, this one dated 1959 and bearing the names of the American League Champion Chicago White Sox. Early Wynn, Nellie Fox and company. When that bat was lathed, Harry Postove was the chief White Sox scout on the East Coast, already a veteran of 13 years with a stopwatch and a notebook.

Today, He's been at it 38 years and counting.

Add it up.

Four years with the Cubs. Seventeen with the White Sox. Three with the Royals. Five with the Mets. Seven with Montreal. And two with Oakland, the club whose card he currently carries.

It's fall now, with the days getting shorter, cooler. The ballparks of the AAA International League, Postove's minor league stomping ground, are empty, echoing. The high school fields in Virginia and North Carolina, where Postove roams in fair weather, are ruled by weeds.

The only action for Postove this time of year is in the empty bleachers of the scattered colleges holding fall workouts for a month or two before the cold drives them inside. He might be over at Old Dominion University's practice today, down at Chapel Hill tomorrow afternoon to catch a University of North Carolina scrimmage and up to tiny Louisburg College for a night game.

The athletes Postove will be watching are new-age. The bats they swing are aluminum, the grass they run on is most likely synthetic. They are as familiar with contracts, clauses and computers as they are with a slider or a scroogie. But when Harry Postove unfolds his metal chair, pulls out his notebook and loosens up his stopwatch, it may as well be 1947. And there's only one thing he's looking for.

"I don't want to hear no ifs or buts. All I want to know is can he or can he not play."

As a boy growing up in Norfolk, Harry Postove could not play.

When he got out of Maury High in 1930, he'd done his best on several Boys Club teams, but now it was time to put aside childish things and find a job.

The job he took was selling papers. That led to a copy boy slot with the old Norfolk Ledger-Dispatch. And that led to writing a bit of high school sports, then a bit more, and pretty soon Postove's byline was slugged assistant sports editor. Old-timers still recall the time Postove took the results of a local dog show from a woman over the phone and changed the word "bitch" to "ditch" throughout the article.

"I thought she was cussing, see?" he explains.

When the war came, Postove became a recreation director for the Navy, organizing ball teams for the Norfolk Naval Training Station and Naval Air Station. The players who came and went through Norfolk during the war years had names like Pee Wee Reese and Phil Rizzuto, Bob Feller and Dom Dimaggio. " You had to be a big leaguer to make those teams," recalls Postove. "That gave me the jump on evaluating ballplayers. I seen what it took, and what you had to do to play."

When the war ended and the ballplayers flocked back to the game, there was nothing for Postove to do but follow them. In 1946 he was hired as general manager of the Cubs' Class B farm club in Shelby, N.C.

"I was just giving in to baseball, that's all," he shrugs, running a hand through his still ample, coal-black hair. "I had no idea I was going to be a scout."

When the Cubs' scout for the mid-Atlantic region left in 1947, Postove was offered the job, "and that was it."

Springtime in Florida, catching the Dodgers in Vero Beach or the Red Sox in Winter Haven or the Twins in Orlando. Then back home to Norfolk and the Chevy that carried him to every high school and college game within a one- or two-state radius of the Mason-Dixon line — "Chevrolet oughta give me a car, because I would not drive anything else." His annual cycle became as rhythmic as the budding and withering of leaves.

The fleabag hotels, the ramshackle minor league ballparks, the night-long drives from one state to another, the hot rumors of a can't-miss prospect who turned out to be nothing but another slow farm boy beating up on fat country fastballs — for decades, Postove lived the life of the scout, learning his trade by trial and error.

He learned what to look out for in a pitcher, that it isn't enough to throw 93-mph aspirins. "A lot of guys throw fast, but they're straight. You judge a pitcher by his velocity *and* whether his ball is alive, whether it's *moving*."

He learned to recognize arms, speed, bat contact, power. And even if a player had all of these, if he was a natural, a Mays, an Aaron, a Musial, there was still no telling if he had what it takes to ride those gifts to the top.

"There are very few God-given ballplayers, the ones who have got everything going for them. Most of the ballplayers I signed had to *make* themselves into players. A lot of clubs use the word 'definite,' but as far as I'm concerned there's no such thing as a definite, no sure thing.

"What hurts a scout is a ballplayer that doesn't keep at it, that doesn't keep helping himself *after* he's signed."

It hurts, says Postove, because a scout is judged by the fortunes of the athletes he signs. The clubs are no more patient with ifs and buts than are the scouts.

"They leave you on your own, and the results tell the story."

Postove's story is highlighted by two names: Junior Gilliam and Luis Aparicio.

He signed Gilliam for the Cubs in 1949 after spotting the young second baseman playing for the Baltimore Elite Giants black baseball club. "He wasn't that impressive in the particular things he did, but the first thing I noticed was he was the first one on the field and the last one to leave. He really hustled."

The Cubs released Gilliam in the spring, "to save a few dollars," grunts Postove. He watched helplessly as the Dodgers picked the kid up the next season and nurtured him into one of the better known names of the game. The next time Postove saw Gilliam was at the end of the 1959 regular season, against none other than Chicago. "There he was out there against the Cubs, beating them to death. And I felt great, because I had been right."

The way the Cubs saw it in 1950, he had lost them the $5,000 it cost to sign Gilliam, and Postove was given the boot. That experience could have been one reason he developed into one of the least easily impressed scouts in the business. It's a reputation he still has. Dave Rosenfield, general manager of the Tides, has watched Postove scout for the last 23 years, and besides describing him as "a total devotee of baseball" and "a workaholic," Rosenfield calls Postove "a harsh grader."

"I've always been a tough judge," Postove says proudly. "I've always kept my sights high, and that's the secret of scouting. If you sign the guy, and he don't develop, you're held responsible. You're staking your job on it every time you sign a ballplayer.

"Now, you've got scouts that are signers, and they've got a whole lot of players in the minor leagues, but that's not the answer. The object is you're supposed to sign a major league prospect, and you might scout all your life and be lucky if you get a man to the major leagues."

Luis Aparicio not only made it to the majors, but this past summer he was inducted into the Hall of Fame at Cooperstown, N.Y. The tiny shortstop with the golden glove was Postove's most famous find. In a frayed folder he pulls out of his back room, Postove keeps a set of faded clippings from a Caracas, Venezuela, newspaper detailing in Spanish the visit of "Senor Harry Postovie," the scout from America. Postove was supposedly in town to keep tabs on White Sox shortstop Chico Carrasquel, who was playing in the off season for the Caracas team. But he was actually more interested in Carrasquel's backup, a bug of an infielder named Aparicio. The Cleveland Indians had sniffed out

Aparicio but decided against his size. And that opened the way for Postove's coup.

"Sure, I was worried about his size, but he did everything," says Postove, pulling out the very notebook page he'd written on during his South America trip. "I've got X's all over this card, and that's good."

A find like Aparicio, along with lesser-known names like J.C. Martin, Joe Hicks, Bruce Howard and Al Weis, who all made it to the White Sox under Harry Postove's name, gave him the job security a scout rarely enjoys. From 1951 through 1967, Postove labored for the Sox, but when an illness cut short his contract with Chicago in 1967, Postove emerged from the hospital jobless, having to prove himself all over again. And the game itself — the owners, the players and the financial structure — was a different one than he had married 20 years earlier.

"Baseball used to pay its way," explains Postove, "and it could depend on itself for survival, but it's not that way anymore."

The men who own today's baseball teams, notes Postove, are millionaires who earned their bucks in other businesses. The San Diego Padres are founded on Ray Kroc's Big Macs, the Montreal Expos owe their existence to Seagram's whiskey, St. Louis' bankroll flows from the suds of Budweiser and Detroit was paid for with pizza.

"I wouldn't say these are bona fide baseball people," says Postove. And with the era of free-agent signings and arbitration, where ballplayers are free to put themselves on sale to the highest bidder, the game's financial structure has become a top-heavy one, with record salaries going to the players while the clubs are forced to trim the budget elsewhere. Two of the first things to go during an organization's belt-tightening are the scouts and the minor league clubs themselves.

""When I started with the Cubs," says Postove, "we had 15 farm teams, and that was a small number then. Now you won't find an organization with more than six. Back then you could sign players and take a chance on 'em, let 'em play a little while, give 'em a chance to develop before they get released.

"I'll tell you what they're looking for today — and they're not going to get it — is quicker results. Branch Rickey used to say it, and it's true: It takes four to six years for a player to develop to major league level. And it takes four or five years for a scout to learn his territory, and the ball clubs don't want to wait.

"Scouts are getting cut right and left. They're the first to go, but it doesn't surprise me. I knew one thing from the start. It's a cold-blooded business."

Postove's 1947 salary with the Cubs was $4,000. Twenty years later, at the end of his White Sox tenure, he says he was not making much more than $10,000. Today he makes "enough to get along," but he has no hope of a pension.

"The players have one of the best pension plans anywhere, and at one time they had a chance to vote the scouts in on it, and they didn't do it." So he rents the upper floor of his house to a medical-school student "to help pay the bills."

"You eat up a lot of expenses," he notes, looking on the bright side of a scout's meager pay, but he admits he never would have made a career out of scouting if he hadn't stayed single — "I never sat still long enough to get married" — and if he hadn't had his father's house to live in during the early years. once he committed himself to the game, he says, there was really no other choice but to stick with it. And his needs became few.

"I was always used to not making money," he explains. "Remember, I worked for a newspaper."

In the slower months of September and October, after he's through catching the playoffs and World Series on the tube — he attributes the recent rise of the Cubs and Mets and the perennial success of the Dodgers to "their belief in scouts" — he mixes in a couple of days of golf with his college fall ball scouting. Then there are the slow months of winter "to rest up" and "maybe visit some friends in Florida" before the bats start cracking again in March.

Postove doesn't like to glamorize his profession, he refuses to crow about the finds he's made, and although he may once have worshipped the game, "it's just a job" to him now.

The A's may be his last stop, he says. "I think I'm phasing out. If I lost this job, I don't know if I'd go for another one."

But despite it all, in the face of nearsighted owners, money-hungry ballplayers and a system that all but ignores the contributions of the bird dogs and scouts who bring in the talent, Postove still believes in the game that defines his life.

"What you can do if my name is brought up and somebody asks, 'What does he know about baseball?' is you can say, 'He's still working, isn't he?'"

Harry Postove is still working.

September 26, 1984

II. PRIVATE WARS

The Sniper

The sun lay low in the Vietnamese sky. Steam rose from the damp jungle mulch. The only sound in the sweltering stillness was the buzzing of flies and gnats as they swarmed above Carlos Hathcock's body, collecting on his neck, probing the corners of his eyes, digging into the creases of his mouth. His knees and elbows were blistered and bleeding. His pants were soaked with urine. But Hathcock felt nothing. He had moved beyond feeling. He had climbed into "the bubble," and he was ready for the kill.

For two days Hathcock and his partner Johnny Burke had crawled through ferns, mud and rotting leaves, silent as snakes, stalking their prey, a lone North Vietnamese Army sniper. For two days the Asian had eluded their sight, hunting them as they hunted him, sniper on sniper. And now it had come to this, the two Marines lying flat on their stomachs, their eyes trained on the tree line across a grassy clearing.

Burke saw nothing. But Hathcock, his body frozen, his right eye glued to the telescopic sight of Winchester, his mind locked in on the hunt, caught a flash, a quick glint of angled sunlight bouncing off a point in the foliage.

He needed nothing more. In an instant the cross hairs of his scope were on the point of light, and he squeezed the trigger.

Only when he reached the dead man's body did Hathcock realize that the NVA soldier, too, had been zeroed in for the kill. The point of light had been the lens of the Asian's rifle scope. Hathcock's bullet had whistled cleanly into that lens, entering the man's head through his eye.

Hathcock was alive for one reason: he had fired first.

One shot. One kill.

That is the sniper's creed, and no man in any war embodied it more than Gunnery Sgt. Carlos Norman Hathcock II. During two tours in Vietnam, he was credited with 93 confirmed kills. By Hathcock's own count, jotted in the dog-eared notebook he carried in his shirt pocket on each mission, the number was actually three times that. But some bodies were carried away by the enemy and others were obliterated by ensuing artillery fire. And some of Hathcock's kills were simply too extraordinary for his commanding officers to believe.

It was hard to believe a man could live in the Vietnamese jungle for days at a time, creeping through areas controlled by the Viet Cong, stalking and shooting unsuspecting enemy soldiers from distances that were rarely less than three football fields and were sometimes as far as 1 1/2 miles.

It was how Hathcock fought — his stealth and style as well as his shooting — that made him a legend not only among his own troops but among the enemy. His only show of bravado was the tiny white feather he wore tucked into the band of his camouflage bush hat. After he and a fellow sniper pinned down 200 North Vietnamese Army regulars in a rice paddy for three days, the enraged NVA offered a bounty of three years' pay to any soldier who could find and kill the American they called "Long Tra'ng"— White Feather.

No one collected that reward. It was a freak land-mine explosion in 1969 that put Carlos Hathcock out of action. The blast left him badly burned. Six years later he discovered he had multiple sclerosis. Now he is retired, living with his wife Jo in suburban Virginia Beach.

On a wintry weekday morning, a breeze tinkles the chimes hanging in front of the Hathcock's modest brick house. The street is silent. Children are in school. Adults are at work. Jo Hathcock is out shopping, and her husband is inside the house, behind drawn living room curtains, alone.

There is little to suggest that the small gaunt man sitting in this darkened room is considered a living legend by the U.S. Marine Corps, which each year presents the Carlos Hathcock Award to its top marksman. A book about Hathcock titled "Marine Sniper" was published in September. He gets phone calls and letters from people he has never met, people who have read the book and want to thank him for his heroism in Vietnam.

But Hathcock does not feel like a hero.

"It was just a job," he says, getting up to turn off the television. "I was a Marine. I did what I was ordered to do, and I did it the best I possibly could."

He moves slowly, painfully, grunting when he rises, wincing when he walks. He looks older than 44. The war wounds and multiple sclerosis that forced his retirement in 1979 have taken their toll. On a cold wet day like this, just climbing out of bed is a painful struggle.

"You never can tell what's going to happen with this disease," he says. "When you wake up in the morning, it's 'I'm alive again.' Then you see if you can walk."

There is no self-pity in Hathcock's voice. No introspection. No drama. He is as straightforward and matter- of-fact about his illness as he is about the science of sniping. And to him it is a science, one he began studying as a boy growing up in rural Arkansas.

He hunted rabbits and squirrels then, pretending they were Japanese soldiers and he was John Wayne. He cried when he watched Duke die in "The Sands of Iwo Jima," and he swore he would become a Marine. On his 17th birthday he did just that, enlisting at the recruiter's office in Little Rock. He was small — 140 pounds — but as the Marines soon found out, he was uncanny with a rifle. By the time he finished a three-year stint at Cherry Point, N.C., he had won Marine Corps, interservice and national shooting championships, including the 1965 Wimbledon Cup, in which he outlasted 2,600 of the nation's top civilian and military marksmen for long-distance shooting's most prestigious prize.

In the final round of that match, Hathcock demonstrated nerves as steady as his aim. The shooters were given three minutes to fire a single round at a target 1,000 yards away. At that distance, a bullet rises to the height of a three-story building during its trajectory. As a steady breeze blew across the shooting range, Hathcock heard his competitors fire their shots within the first minute. He chose to wait, counting on the breeze to stop. For more than two minutes he held his fire. With 15 seconds left, the pennants fluttering overhead suddenly dipped. Hathcock seized the moment, squeezed the trigger... and won by 4 inches.

He had been in the bubble that day, in that special place where nothing exists but the target seen through the tube mounted on a rifle. That, and the wind. And the head. And the humidity. And anything else that might affect the flight of a bullet. Even as a 12-year-old with a .22 in his hands, tromping through the Arkansas woods, Hathcock had been able to climb into the bubble. Once he got to Vietnam, he would live there.

Hathcock arrived in Vietnam in 1966, a year after winning the Wimbledon. He had been trained as a sniper, but he was assigned as a military policeman, guarding remote POW compounds outside Chu Lai. Itching for action, he volunteered for reconnaissance patrols. But he felt uneasy surrounded by men who knew little or nothing about the outdoors. They were sloppy. Unsafe.

"I figured I'd be better off operating by myself," says Hathcock. "Then it came on me one day I had a real good M-14. So I asked if I could go out and do something."

That afternoon he got his chance. His unit was on a hill. Arriving helicopters had been bothered by shooting from the valley. Hathcock slipped outside the compound and hid in a group of rocks. Soon a boy appeared 300 yards away, herding some water buffalo across a field. Hathcock watched. The boy stopped and turned toward a thicket. Hathcock waited. The boy talked to the foliage. Then, as he turned to move on, a man with a rifle crept out of the bushes, moving to escape among the animals.

"He didn't get far," says Hathcock.

Then he nods.

"That was a good off-the-rack M-14."

It was dawn, somewhere near the border between Laos and North Vietnam. Hathcock wasn't sure which country he was in. He only knew that his target was sleeping in a building 800 yards away. The man was a North Vietnamese general, someone U.S. intelligence officers wanted dead. After Hathcock had been briefed and shown aerial photographs, he knew he might not come back from this one.

The compound was in the middle of an old rubber plantation, surrounded by nothing but 2,000 yards of flat, open field. It had taken Hathcock four days and nights to inch 1,200 yards through the foot-high grass. Several times NVA patrols had passed close enough to smell him. He had come eye-to-eye with a deadly bamboo viper, freezing until the serpent slithered on. He had eaten nothing. His only nourishment had been several capfuls of water. His body ached, but now he was within range. As the sun rose, he readied his weapon.

He gently unfolded a small piece of cloth and laid it beneath the rifle's muzzle. Gases would spew from the Winchester's muzzle as it fired, and the cloth would keep them from kicking up dust and giving his position away.

He gauged the wind by watching how the trees rustled, how smoke drifted from the soldiers' cooking fires, how the grass and weeds between him and his target waved, how the heat mirage rippling in the air tilted with the breeze.

When a white sedan approached the house's entrance, Hathcock's muscles tightened and his mind began factoring. The general stepped into the morning light, surrounded by a group of officers. Hathcock breathed steadily, waited until the officers stepped aside, then planted a single, fatal round in the general's chest.

The confused soldiers had no idea from which direction the shot had come. They had hundreds of acres to search. By nightfall Hathcock had crawled back into the safety of the jungle.

"That was a classic," says Hathcock, lighting a Salem and settling into an easy chair.

But solo missions like the shooting of the general were rare. The bulk of Hathcock's work was done closer to U.S. positions and with a partner. During his first six months operating alone around Chu Lai — "Free-lancing is what it was" — Hathcock had collected 14 kills, enough to convince his superiors there was a role for the sniper in Vietnam. A training program was organized, and Carlos Hathcock became the chief among five instructors on a hill south of Da Nang. There were no blackboards in this school. The classroom was the jungle, and the grading was pass/fail.

"In this shooting match," he told his students, "second place is a body bag."

The basic role of the sniper was to protect U.S. infantry units in the field from Viet Cong in the forest — "To back the hamburgers away," as Hathcock puts it. The snipers worked in two-man teams, alternating as observer and shooter, patrolling the perimeter around American troops. The Marine snipers chose their targets carefully, hunting for enemy machine gun and mortar crews and, especially, for officers.

"You take away the leader," says Hathcock, "you got nothin' but a mob."

Viet Cong leaders, says Hathcock, almost always carried pistols. If no pistol could be seen, Hathcock would simply wait for someone to start pointing. "Leaders," he says with a slight smile, "love to point."

Once he had his target in sight, Hathcock liked to keep at least 300 yards between himself and his prey. "Any closer than that, and they can shoot *back*," he says. "Just hose the area down."

More often than not, a sniper outing meant several days living in the jungle, and preparation was vital. "There's more to it," says Hathcock "than a person with a pretty rifle going out into the woods."

His own routine began with putting his Salems away — "The enemy can smell you as well as see you."

He would fill two canteens with water and stock his pack with C-ration cans of cheese, crackers and, especially, peanut butter — "To stop you up so you don't have to go potty."

He would load five rounds in his Winchester Model 70 .30-06 bolt-action rifle — "A good stick, a real good stick."

And he would slide 80 more rounds into a bandolier strapped around his waist — Hathcock rarely broke into that bandolier, noting with pride the cost-effectiveness of snipers.

"They say an average of something like 50,000 rounds were fired for each kill made by a line trooper in Vietnam," he says. "The average for a sniper was 1.3."

Hathcock preferred the craft of the single shot to the saturation spray of typical jungle combat. There was something cleaner about it, something more controlled. He liked to be in control, but he was never cocky.

"I always had butterflies. I was scared to death all the time. Anybody tells you different, stay away from him. He's a fool."

Unlike movie images of World War II snipers perched in palm trees, Hathcock stayed on the ground. "Good snipers do not climb trees," he grunts. "You go up a tree, you gotta come *down* a tree."

It was important, says Hathcock, to keep on the move, never shooting from the same spot twice. "If they find your position," he says, "they can call in the big stuff."

Hathcock always had an escape route planned, and on long- range missions like the shooting of the general, his plans depended on detailed information gathered by what he calls "the super spooks" — the CIA. He is uncomfortable discussing the organization, but as an example of its power, he recalls his first intelligence-directed kill.

The target was a French interrogator working for the North Vietnamese. Hathcock was told when the Frenchman would appear, where he would walk, even what he would be wearing. Then Hathcock and his partner were helicoptered at night nearly two hours north and dropped in the jungle with a map. They made their way to the shooting site by dawn. Then they waited.

"Sure enough," says Hathcock, "here he comes, walking down the path they said he would, smoking the pipe they said he'd be smoking, wearing exactly what they said he was going to wear."

As he describes the kill itself, Hathcock slips into steeliness, choosing his words as carefully as he would aim his rifle.

"The shot was good."

He pauses a beat.

"The shot was deadly."

While he was in the field, Hathcock commanded a neat, ordered world. The hunt was nothing but a sequence of logical acts leading to a clean, precise conclusion. It was only when he was back among other people, among soldiers who fought a different, more chaotic war, that things got messy. Some of those soldiers called Hathcock a murderer and an assassin. He was stung, but he understood.

"The word sniper's always been a bad word in anybody's language," he says. "It's a job nobody wants. The sniper wears the black hat. He hides and kills from ambush. Good guys don't hide."

But to Hathcock, a hunt in the jungle was basically no different from one in the Arkansas woods. The targets even reacted the same when hit. He remembers being fascinated after he shot his first humans. "They would roll in a ball and flip-floppy on the ground," he recalls, "just like rabbits."

When he talks of bodies and bullets, Hathcock is detached, almost clinical. Emotions don't disturb his words. And there is no pleasure in his discussion of death.

"I didn't enjoy the killing," he says. "What I enjoyed was the thought of pitting myself against another living, breathing, thinking human being."

The killing, says Hathcock, was simply a consequence of the hunt. And the enemy he stalked in Vietnam, he notes, was the same one his fellow Marines went after in their own ways.

"I have no guilt," he says. "It was a job, *my* job. Just like an artillery man had his job—except he didn't look people in the face when he shot 'em."

Only once did Hathcock relish the kill itself. The target was a female NVA officer the Marines at Hathcock's base camp called Apache. The woman commanded a platoon of enemy snipers who had terrorized the base for months, and she was known for her horribly sadistic torture of captured U.S. soldiers.

"I really wanted that woman," says Hathcock. "She was an animal."

When he finally shot her — not once but twice, "for good measure" — he and his partner broke down and cried.

"That," says Hathcock, pursing his lips, "was a good day."

When Hathcock finished his first tour of Vietnam in 1967, he retired and came home to his wife and baby boy in North Carolina. Until she had read a newspaper story about her husband's exploits, Jo had no idea what exactly he was doing in Vietnam. She was shocked by the story, and Hathcock decided it was time to come home. He tried working as an electrician, but after a visit to Camp LeJeune, where he was surrounded by his "shooting compadres," he could not stay a civilian.

"Right then," he says, "I realized how far out I was away from my element."

So, 22 days after he retired, Hathcock re-enlisted. He joined the Marine Corps national rifle team in Quantico, Va., and two years later, he was shipped back to Vietnam. The return was a rude jolt.

"It was an entirely different war, like daylight and dark."

Back on the same hillside where he had trained his first teams of hunters, he found Marine snipers wearing buttons on their hats and jewelry with their dogtags.

"It seemed like everything we'd done had disappeared," says Hathcock.

The enemy, too, had changed.

"Instead of untrained South Vietnamese communists, we were fighting hard-core NVA units. They didn't hit and run. They hit and stayed."

Hathcock had notched 86 confirmed kills during his first tour. This time he got seven before a halftrack on which he was perched rolled across a 500-pound mine. The explosion blew Hathcock to the ground and sent flames 40 feet high.

With his uniform on fire and skin hanging ragged and black from his arms, Hathcock climbed back on the burning vehicle and pulled away six Marines before he collapsed.

He spent the next six months in an Army burn center in San Antonio, Texas, with Jo at his side. In 1970 he joined the Marine Corps Rifle Team in Quantico, but he could not handle a weapon. His burns would not allow him to strap on a shooting jacket, much lest twist the tight leather sling of an M-14 around his wrist. He could not endure direct sunlight, so he stood in the shade, wearing long-sleeved shirts, a wide-brimmed campaign hat and white gloves on his burn-scarred hands.

By 1975, when he was stationed on a submarine tender in Spain, doctors determined it wasn't Hathcock's burns that made his legs so weak he could not climb the ship's ladders. It was multiple sclerosis.

And still he hung on, returning to Quantico, where he tried to shoot again. His scars would split open, soaking his sweatshirt with blood, but he would not leave the range until his fellow Marines pulled him away. By 1979 he was passing out from the combination of wounds and MS. Doctors said he could take no more.

In April of that year — 55 days short of 20 years service — Carlos Hathcock was retired from the Marine Corps with 100 percent disability.

"I was bitter, really bitter. I thought they had just thrown me out to pasture."

Hathcock is seated in a room in the back of his house, a room he calls "the bunker." It is tiny, with small windows up near the ceiling. For a full year, Hathcock lived in this room, "sitting here like a slug, looking at nothing, reliving the war, my career, my life."

As he speaks, his eyes shine with wetness.

"I felt I wasn't of any use to anyone."

Only when Jo threatened to leave him did Hathcock pull himself out of his stupor. He tried tinkering in the yard, but the heat and stress were too much. Then he began taking walks by the waterfront, and one day he wandered into a tackle shop near Virginia Beach's Lake Whitehurst.

He liked what he saw — an array of fishing gear as intricate as his rifles. And men talking about their boats and lures in tones Hathcock recognized — the same tones he had used when teaching his Marine students about shooting. He came back to the shop the next day. And the next. And soon he was helping out with odd jobs, becoming fast friends with the store's owner, Steve McCarver.

"I was getting back into life again," says Hathcock. "Doing something. Helping somebody."

He pulled his Marine mementoes — weapons, trophies, medals, photos — out of their boxes and turned the bunker into a personal museum. Before long he was hanging citations of another sort beside his shooting awards — fishing citations. These days, when the weather is warm, Carlos Hathcock can most likely be found with a pole in his hand, hunting catfish and carp.

"They say I've got to avoid stress with this disease," he says. "Got to do things I enjoy. And I can handle sittin' on a riverbank waitin' for the cat to bite."

When his son enlisted in the Marines four years ago, then signed up for six more, Hathcock beamed. "I'm glad to see that."

When a Marine writer called him in 1984 about doing the book, Hathcock was stunned. "I'm still in awe that people thought enough of the job I did to actually write a book."

When he and Jo were summoned to Washington last summer and he was awarded an "exceptional leadership" trophy at a black-tie Marine Corps banquet, he was "shocked."

And when a member of the Norfolk Police Department Emergency Response Team called last year asking him to teach sniper techniques to a four-member rescue squad, Hathcock leaped at the chance. Now he spends at least one day a week sharing the secrets it took him a lifetime to learn.

"I've got this head full of... *stuff*," he says, leaning forward and rubbing his legs. He squeezes his eyes shut, then relaxes and sits back. "I just want to help people."

But he no longer shoots. The last time he tried was two autumns ago, when he went hunting with some friends. He enjoyed the familiar feel of walking in the woods. The sounds and smells brought him back to his boyhood. But when it came time to use his rifle, he could not do it.

"When it came down to pulling the trigger and taking the life of a poor wild animal..."

Hathcock pulls his Windbreaker tight around the collar and shakes his head.

"I just couldn't. I quit right there that day."

It was just a scrap of paper, something someone scribbled down for Hathcock while he was still in the Marines. He doesn't know where the paper is now, but the words are etched in his mind:

There is no hunting like the hunting of a man, and those who have hunted armed men long enough and liked it, never care for anything else thereafter. —Ernest Hemingway

March 22, 1987

Bloods

Then they came around the corner again. This time they unloaded this B-40 rocket directly into the bunker. I was facing them. Gillis was covering my back.

We were lifted straight up into the air. The blast blew out his eardrums. They tell me I must've had my mouth open, because all the fillings were blown out of my teeth.

When I fell, I landed on mu side and I dropped the weapon. It got so much sand in it that it jammed. I got the sand out. I just took the clip and shook it. And I started firing. And firing. And firing.

—Luther C. Benton, III, from "Bloods"

It's been 17 years since that August night in 1967, 17 Veterans Days since Hospital Corpsman Luke Benton earned a Purple Heart and a Bronze Star for killing what the government claimed were 47 Viet Cong during a firefight at a provincial hospital 20 miles from Da Nang.

Benton doesn't talk much about his year "in country." He's no more than the Rev. Benton, associate minister at Portsmouth's Ebenezer Baptist Church, to all but the close friends and family who know about the medals mounted and framed in his den and the jagged, twisted tailfin of that B-40 rocket sitting on the shelf in the TV room.

"I don't have any problems talking about it," says Benton, "if anybody asks."

More people are bound to be asking, now that a book called "Bloods" has hit the nation's stores. "Bloods" is a look at the Vietnam War though the eyes of 20 black veterans. Wallace Terry, who spent two years as deputy chief of Time magazine's Saigon bureau, taped more than 300 hours of interviews with 50 veterans before producing the book that

Walter Cronkite says "fills a yawning gap in the record of our Vietnam experience." One of the 20 men whose words fill the pages of "Bloods" is Luke Benton.

Time magazine calls the book, which went on sale in August, "superb." The New York Times described it as "powerful and disturbing." The Washington Post says it is "a raised fist." In its pages are the first-person memories, questions, bitterness and thankfulness of black veterans whose backgrounds and voices are as distinct as their individual wartime experiences.

Nearly a decade after the evacuation of Saigon, the Vietnam War has carved its own section in bookstores. Films like "Coming Home" and "Apocalypse Now" signaled a media onslaught for a topic that sat virtually untouched for years. The nation needed time to sort out its emotional and moral confusion about Vietnam, to allow its wounds to at least partially heal. Now the topic is touchable and Vietnam, in its own heartbreaking way, has become hot property for societal psychoanalysts, sages and storytellers.

Until "Bloods," one story that wasn't told was that of the black man in Vietnam. He died in disproportionate numbers early in the war; while 10 percent of the nation's population was black, 23 percent of its Vietnam fatalities were of color. He bore arms against a non-white nation while his own country was embroiled in bitter civil rights battles. In 1965, America's front lines in Vietnam were so filled with blacks — as many as 60 percent — that the soldiers called it Soulville. They grappled with the sight of Confederate flags, burned crosses and Ku Klux Klan costumes scattered among their white comrades. And when they returned to the States, "The Big PX," they faced an unemployment rate for black veterans that is today more than double that for whites.

Benton had no idea what Terry was planning when the Washington, D.C., journalist called him early last year. A cousin of Benton's had referred Benton to Terry, and in July '83, Benton met him at Norfolk International Airport, spent the day speaking into his tape recorder and saw him off that evening. That was the last Benton heard of the project until he found a complimentary copy of the book in his mailbox three months ago. He is as surprised that the book is selling out at local bookstores as he was to find that the man who had blown in and out of Norfolk one day last summer had really taken his words and put them between hard covers.

Surprised, but not excited. His only misgiving about the book is Terry's precise re-creation of the speakers' diction. Benton is upset with the fact that he sounds "uneducated" in the book. Perhaps because of this, he is meticulously careful to phrase his thoughts now.

"It's just a piece of me in there," says the 42-year-old preacher and health department employee, fingering the book's pages. "It's not the best piece, but as far as the world might be concerned, it's probably the most exciting piece."

I was a sailor's sailor. I always did my duty and then some. Perfect military bearing. Immaculate all the time. On this ship I worked in the pharmacy, and I was probably the cleanest person around. When we picked up the Gemini 10 space capsule, someone said, "We need to have a medical person open the door." They came and got me.

Everything about Luke Benton is clipped and precise. The trees around his Lake Forest brick ranch are carefully trimmed, the branches neatly stacked by the curb, the pine needles raked into tidy piles. When Benton takes a seat at his backyard patio table, he first wipes the bench with a napkin. His tan three- piece suit is sharply cut, his brown polka-dotted tie knotted just so. His pencil-thin mustache is sharply sculpted at right angles, as carefully arranged as his words.

Benton says he's always been innately neat. It was natural that he became a hospital corpsman when he joined the Navy after graduating from I.C. Norcom High School.

When he arrived in Vietnam in 1966 to teach the villagers of Hoi An how to take care of their medical needs, it was natural that he became obsessed with the never-ending struggle of cleaning out the garbage the villagers insisted on dumping in an open well.

It was natural that he would not stand for the flea-infested village dog a white sailor tried to bring into his bunk room. Nor did Benton stand for the racial slur he heard when he asked the sailor to take the dog away. "The dog went," nods Benton, "and he did, too."

And it's natural that Benton works today as a sanitarian for the Norfolk Health Department, inspecting and issuing permits to restaurants.

"I can walk in and look around," he says, "and in just a few seconds I can point out the problem areas. It's second nature, instinct, to me."

It's an instinct born in the Portsmouth ghetto where he grew up and nurtured in the knee-jerk tension of Vietnam.

I had been there maybe two months when I went in the marketplace. I was wearing black pajamas. I was real thin then, 116 pounds. And though I was 6 feet, I could be mistaken for them, especially in the dark.

They had a lot of Chinese in the area that were shop owners. And the money people were the Chinese. They were sellin' fish, vegetables, all kinds of stuff.

There were some soldiers walkin' around and some policemen. For some reason I just didn't get into crowds. Well, this guy just walked into this crowd, and he just pulled the string and the (bomb) blew up. And when he blew up, there were other little things on him that flew away that later blew up. Really six different explosions. It was just a mass of mess out there. Blood and guts all over.

In Vietnam, Benton had little trouble fitting in and moving around in a hostile environment. "I learned that right here," he says, describing his boyhood days in Portsmouth's Douglas Park and his walks to school through the adjoining white neighborhood of Academy Park.

"My white brothers taught me about being able to survive under adverse conditions, and my black brothers taught me, too, because not all of them were my friends."

There were other lessons. About drugs, for instance. "In the ghetto that I lived in, you saw people OD-ing in the street, and that was before drugs were a recognized problem in America. I was seeing the end of what drugs do before I saw the beginning."

So Benton never did try drugs. He was a small boy "with a flashy temper," and his vice was violence. He knew how to fight, and when he finished high school, he took a cue from an uncle, an ex-Navy man, and joined the service, where he spent four unremarkable years measured by high marks for neatness on his fitness reports and occasional scraps.

"I was not a perfectly good guy. I did what everybody else did, you know what I mean? I drank and smoked, just like all the other guys."

When he got out of the Navy after those four years, he was ready to beat the world. "I was a hot-shot military man, figuring I'd go out and get me a job."

But the jobs weren't there. The best he got was advice during one interview. "The man told me, 'If I was you, I'd go back in the Navy.'"

I asked a group of young [Vietnamese] men, "Why aren't y'all fighting for the liberty of your country? Are you crazy?" They rode around on the Suzukis and Hondas all the time.

They said, "You crazy? Our Soldiers not trained good enough to fight Viet Cong or NVA."

They said, "Why should we do it anyway if the Americans are gonna do it? If the Marines are gonna come? We really idiotic to do that. And it won't make any difference anyway."

Like most of the veterans in "Bloods," Benton has mixed feelings about America's involvement in Vietnam. He went in gung-ho to stop Communism, became jaded and cynical about the rationale behind the war, now calls himself a "dummy" for his initial innocence and yet remains fiercely protective of his patriotism.

"I was patriotic then, and I am now. If you want to live in freedom, then somebody has got to go out and ensure that freedom, even if it means a little bit of dirtiness. God never said that there would not be any war."

He wasn't in Hoi An long before the theme of liberating South Vietnam began to sound silly to him. "It didn't matter to them who ran the country. They were poor, and they weren't going to get any better, no matter who ran the country, because the country did not have the resources to support itself."

America's role was not as selfless as he had first thought: "I see it now as an economic venture that cost a lot of lives. Somebody got rich."

The officers above him, says Benton, were subtly racist, denying him privileges routinely granted the men around him — the unrestricted use of a jeep, for instance — and they often gave orders that made little sense. "Sometimes you have to appease the giant," he shrugs. "I mean, you can't hit him and knock him upside the head. He'll destroy you. So what you do is you appease him. You do what is necessary."

And what was necessary was continuing to be a sailor's sailor.

"I had a duty to do, and I did what I had to do."

I just opened up on a pack of 'em with this M-4 grease gun that shot not only through them but through the building and through the slot machines. Iron slot machines. It just tore them all to pieces. It just blows a hole through you that just can't be imagined.

By now planes swooped over in the area, 'cause the whole area was under attack. And they dropped in the flares that illuminated the area. Shadows would move across, and I would shoot whatever moved. I shot shadows moving. We had ducks and chickens and dogs. And they were all just shot up. Everything that moved, I engaged in fire.

We had two boxes of grenades. We threw them all out. Just pull the pins, throw the hand grenades. It's like in a mad panic. Throw 'em and throw 'em and throw 'em.

I think I was just makin' it on an animal instinct of survival.

But then I prayed.

"Have you ever died before?"

Benton is leaning forward, fixing his gaze on the surface of the manmade lake rippling behind his home.

"If you've been close enough to death, you don't forget. I mean, when you see people die, and I'm not proud of it, but when you have actually killed people, if there's any good or any worth in you at all, you just cannot forget it. The look on their faces, the look in their eyes, whether or not they yelled or screamed, how long they yelled or screamed. Whether it was dark or light."

Benton says God talked to him that night. He says God also spoke to him in two calmer moments while he was in Vietnam, one before and one after the nighttime battle. He is a Baptist minister today, but his was not an instant conversion, a pact made with God in a hail of bullets. It took him 14 years to make his move. In the meantime, Benton became bad news, a walking gun barrel with a hair trigger.

"I was violent, all the time. I put that spiritual experience completely out of my mind."

He fell in love with his .38-caliber Smith & Wesson, carrying it wherever he went. He told Terry of a poker game in which he thought someone was cheating. Benton told the man he should be ashamed of himself. Then he calmly pulled out his pistol and fired. Luckily, the man had moved. "If he hadn't, I would've killed him."

When he returned home in May of 1968, Benton was wired. "Things were not the way I expected them to be. I was kind of an animal. I lived ridiculously. I carried a gun, and I didn't take crap off anybody."

He had no need or desire to seek out the company of other veterans. He joined an American Legion post only because he frequented its bar so often that he was forced to sign up or quit coming.

Soon after getting back from Vietnam, he ran into an old friend who bought him a drink over some puzzling words: "He said, 'When you get through drinking that drink, I want you to leave, and I'll talk to you in maybe a year and a half, because I don't want to be around you. Until then, you'll be nothing but trouble.'"

"And," adds Benton, "he was right."

At home, with wife Jackie and three children, Keith, Brian and Candace, now 21, 19 and 14, the days were tense. "After you've been gone for a year, and you haven't been with your mate, and you're young and you go through experiences like that, you're going to have problems. There's no getting around it."

Benton stayed in the Navy for 13 more years, continuing to struggle with the violent legacy of that August night in Vietnam and with the voices that continued to whisper to him about God.

They said I killed 47 of them. I don't really believe it. They always exaggerated the body count. The whole thing in Vietnam was how many people you kill. I saw about 25 bodies in my position.

At the time, I thought I should have at least gotten the Silver Star. But they gave me a Bronze Star. For holding them off even when we were being overrun and for keeping on fighting after the bunker was blown up. Especially me being a sailor. And a hospital corpsman at that.

Everybody said they couldn't believe what I did. I guess because I was black. When you're white and you think that no good can come out of black people, when you think that black men are cowards who run scared, yellin' "Massa save me," then I guess they would be amazed.

"Sure, I got a Purple Heart hanging in there, and my kids think it's wonderful their dad's got a Purple Heart," says Benton, his voice sounding less bitter than the words themselves. "But if their dad don't provide food for them, the Purple Heart doesn't mean very much."

Neither, he says, do the rows of ribbons given him by the Vietnamese.

"Those were no big deal. The country doesn't even *exist* anymore."

Noting the fudged kill count, Benton says, "At that point I realized it was all a sham, anyway, just a big lie. And the sooner I could get out and get away from that place, the better I'd be."

Of the racism, he says, "I'm not blaming America, and I'm not blaming what America believes in. What I have to blame is the individuals I had to deal with."

On the subject of being a veteran, not just of Vietnam but of any war, Benton's thoughts are well-defined, his words carefully chosen.

"Maybe I'm living in the past, but I feel that if you've served your country, it means that whatever is necessary to be done to preserve this way of life, you're willing to do it. The people who do that ought to be rewarded in some special way. To see a veteran without a job, as far as I'm concerned, is absurd."

As far as he's concerned, every day should be Veterans Day, in terms not just of remembering but of helping the ex-military man.

"I've served America well. I've upheld my end of the contract. I did 20 years and one day. Marching in a parade is not something I need to do."

I believe that a man, even a preacher, cannot preach beyond his experience. How can an individual tell you how the Lord helped him to get over the crisis in life if he hasn't had a certain amount of experience in order to be able to relate to the people he's preaching to?

America hurt so many young men by putting them over in Vietnam to be introduced to prostitution, gamblin', drinkin', drugs. To fear. To terror. To killin'. To they own death.

I think God meant for me to overcome those things.

"I don't think for a second that I'm paying God back because I didn't die or anything like that. I was under no duress, no psychological strain at all when I accepted my calling. It was not a desperate grasp."

It was in 1981 that Benton preached his first sermon at Ebenezer Baptist. Since then he has earned a bachelor's degree in religion from Baltimore's National Theological Seminary and College and he is currently studying for a master's in divinity from Florida's Gulf Coast Seminary. When he's not working his job with the health department, he's studying the Bible, working with several home-centered Bible study groups, helping direct the choir of Joy, a Suffolk gospel group, and carrying out his duties as assistant minister at Ebenezer Baptist, where the pastor is the Rev. Dr. Ben. A. Beamer, former vice mayor of Portsmouth.

"I always had a low esteem for preachers," says Benton. "I always considered them to be weak, namby-pamby kind of guys. You just push 'em over. Nothin' to 'em, you know. You smack 'em on one cheek, and they turn the other. I was not about to be that kind of person."

When he did make the move to the church, it was not to the pulpit. He rarely preaches on Sunday, choosing instead to take his ministry to people's homes on weeknights and Saturdays. "I do it in an underground fashion. I'm a radical, but I'm a survivor."

The trip from war veteran to a man of God is far from complete, admits Benton. "I still don't know if I could turn the other cheek if a man walked up to me and knocked the heck out of me."

But his days are more settled than they used to be.

"When I first came back, my wife said I'd get up whenever she came into the bedroom. I wouldn't wake up; I'd *get* up. But today, you could drop a bomb down the block, and it *might* wake me up."

Critics have praised "Bloods." Readers have hailed its significance. Andrew Young writes, "It should be read by every man, woman and child in every corner of the world."

But Luke Benton couldn't really care less. He hasn't even read the book yet.

"I'm not very carnal," he shrugs. "I see it as an honor, and it's wonderful, thank you, but it's not something I want to dwell on.

"It might," he suggests, "mean something to my grandchildren."

November 11, 1984

The War In Kay Hamlin

She has a hard time with the memories. They drift inside like patches of fog, edgeless images she can't quite hold. They never take shape enough to hold, but neither will they go away. They simply hover. Hover and haunt. Like the boy in the rain.

It was November, she thinks, but she's not sure. November, 1966. Somewhere in the Quang Tri province, in Vietnam.

It was night. It was raining. Not the hot steamy rain that fell to the south, but a cold rain, a thick, sodden rain.

The fighting had been heavy for three days, sending a steady flow of casualties into the medical tent. Bodies in pieces, boys screaming with pain, screaming for their mothers, the medics pushing the portable radio as loud as it could go, trying to drown the din of death with the Beach Boys.

She can hear it now.

"Dying like that is never quiet."

It was all she could do to move from one body to the next, deciding which could be saved, which could wait, which had no hope. Nearer than she ever dreamed she would be to death, she did her best to keep her distance.

"You never wanted to get too close, never wanted to look at their faces too much, never wanted to know their names."

She closes her eyes.

"But this kid, he was so quiet. He was just different."

He had a chest wound. It sometimes seemed all they saw were chest wounds, she and the surgeon and the eight medics who formed the team.

There was no front line in Vietnam, but their job was to seek the heat, to come as close as they could to the chaos, to save the lives not already lost.

She can see it now.

"These were fresh hits, brand new, five minutes after being blown to pieces."

The kid could be saved. That's what she was hoping as she carried him out into the night, into the rain. The evac helicopter was nowhere in sight.

She's there.

"I was squatting, pulling my poncho over his head, trying to keep him dry, balancing his IV's on my shoulders."

The helicopter was taking forever. Then the boy spoke.

"He just kind of looked up at me and said, 'Tell my mom I love her.'"

She's silent.

"Then he died."

A long silence.

She's coming back.

"I don't know who he was, when it was, where it was. And I wish more than anything I could have found his mother and let her know what he said."

Now she's here, she's back.

"I dream about that," she says. "I still see his face."

She reaches for her cup of tea.

"That was Vietnam for me."

Kay Hamlin is an emergency room nurse. A career nurse.

"When I think of myself as a person," she says, "I think of myself as a nurse. That is my identity, who I am."

For the past 16 years, she has worked nowhere but in the ER. In California, then in Iowa and, for the past six years, at Sentara Leigh in Virginia Beach, she has always sought the hottest spot in the hospital. The emergency room has always been that place. She knows there are those who would wonder why any of the 15,000 women who went to Vietnam — most as nurses — would want to come close to a place that might remind them of that horror.

"A lot didn't," says Hamlin. "A lot of nurses came back wanting nothing to do with nursing, period, let alone emergency room nursing."

But just as many came home with a habit only a combat vet could understand.

"We came back speed junkies," says Hamlin. "We like—we *need*— the adrenalin, that rush. A critical patient comes through the door, a trauma, and everything just kicks in. Everything gets clear—crystal clear and focused."

It is early on an autumn evening. Rain is sweeping past the living room window of Hamlin's comfortable Kempsville home. She lives alone, with one daughter in Pittsburgh, a son in college in North Carolina and another daughter in grad school in New Zealand, where Hamlin was born 44 years ago.

She has poured two cups of tea and is settled into an easy chair. She's small — 4-foot-11, 96 pounds. She's wearing jeans and a sweater, looking less imposing than she does in her office, where, as head nurse for the emergency department, she supervises a staff of 47. There is a trace of a British accent when she talks. But right now she's having trouble talking at all. Some of her own nurses have no idea she was in Vietnam.

"It's something I don't bring up." she says. "A lot of people just don't seem to understand."

What they don't understand, she says, is why anyone would have volunteered for Vietnam, and why a woman would want to go to war — especially that one.

"It had nothing to do with believing in the war itself," she says. "We went because we felt it was the only thing we could do to help. We went because we were *nurses*."

For Hamlin, the reasons ran even deeper. She sets her teacup aside and fetches a photograph. It was taken in 1919, in New Zealand. Three men in military uniforms are surrounded by women and a child. One of the men is Hamlin's father. The others are her uncles. All three had just come home from the war.

"That's my Uncle Jack," she says, pointing at a tense figure with troubled eyes. "He was shot through the head at Gallipoli. He never got over it. I remember they built him a special house on the farm, with no windows in it. That's where he would go to be alone."

She moves her finger to a wavy-haired figure perched on a chair.

"That's Uncle Cecil," she says. "He was gassed in the Argonne. He lived for the next 20 years, but he wasn't able to walk.

"Mustard gas," she says. "The Agent Orange of World War I."

Then she moves to her father. His is the happiest face in the photo.

"My uncles were enlisted men, my father was the officer," she says, almost as an accusation. "He always said that was the last of the gentlemen's wars. He was in the air force. They flew around in the sky and dueled."

She sets the photo down.

"It was a different war for him than for them."

Through their memories, it became her war, too. As did the next one, in which two of her cousins — including the child in the photo — became prisoners of the Japanese.

"They survived," she says, "but one committed suicide right after it was over."

Hamlin wanted to be a doctor, but her family could not afford it. When she chose to be a nurse, her mother was upset.

"I remember her saying nursing was nothing but emptying bedpans and why would I want to do that?"

She finished nursing school in 1965. Within a year volunteers were being gathered for a combined Australian/New Zealand force to support U.S. troops in Vietnam. Among the first expedition of 600 were three New Zealand nurses. One was Hamlin.

"I suppose maybe I was trying to prove something," she says, "that I wasn't just sitting at home knitting mittens."

As Leigh's ER head nurse, Hamlin has to handle paperwork more than patients. She triages problems more than people. Although she keeps her scrubs close at hand, her standard uniform is a business suit or dress.

"It's hard," she says. "It's hard not to hop right in."

Hamlin says her staff treats anywhere from 70 to 100 patients a day. They budgeted for 29,000 ER patients this year. Already they have seen 33,000. Those kinds of numbers, along with an industry-wide nursing shortage, put even more pressure on the people in the trenches.

"The profession is under duress right now," she says. "There is a shortage, and it's easy to blame nurses for many problems. Nurses are overwhelmed, underpaid and pushed to the limit in many places. It is not the easiest job in the world, and it's harder when you have to do even more with less."

Her words are matter of fact, without complaint. Hamlin has no patience with complaints. She remembers how she felt when she first stepped on an ER floor after coming back from Vietnam.

"It was real difficult," she says, "seeing people coming in and screaming and yelling because they hurt their big toe."

Her outrage eased with time. She realized nothing can be compared to war. Although many things die in combat, one of them cannot be compassion — not for a nurse.

"I believe so strongly in this profession," says Hamlin. "People look at it and don't understand it's so much more than emptying bedpans and changing sheets. It's seeing patients as whole people, as people who come in the door with so many emotional and physical problems.

"They may come in with an ankle sprain, but it may turn out their ankle's sprained because they're homeless and living on the street, or they're being abused.

"That's where we call in other resources. We don't necessarily just send them home. We may get them to a shelter, get them free medicine, chip in and pay for a meal, pay for a cab. Physicians don't do these things. That's not their job.

"These are things nurses do."

The most important year in Hamlin's life remains a blur.

"I just don't have a concept," she says of her time in Vietnam. "Days, nights, weeks all fade into one another. You get so tunneled into making it through the day, you lose any sense of names or places."

When she went to Vietnam, Hamlin weighed 120 pounds. When she came home, she weighed 89. The first thing she did when she got back was resign. The next was to marry. Her husband, an American sailor, brought her Stateside. "Then," she says, "*he* went to Vietnam."

The marriage did not last long. They had two children, and he came home from Vietnam an alcoholic. "He had his own problems," she says, "but I had two babies. We didn't need that."

In 1971 she was divorced, leaving her a single mother with a New Zealand nursing license not accepted in her new country. So she went to California, enrolled in nursing school, "started from scratch."

Looking back, she wonders if her desperate straits didn't save her sanity — even her life. The pain of what she'd seen and felt, the nightmares, the boy in the rain—these things kept their distance while she put her life in order.

"None of that started for a while," she says. "I'm a firm believer that the body takes care of itself first, sometimes in strange ways, before it can let the mind back in."

By the time she moved to Iowa in the mid-'70s, Hamlin's life was secure — solid enough for the past to begin seeping through. She began having nightmares. When she awoke, the first thing she reached for was food.

"Most everyone I know who came back had some crutch they used," she says. "Mine was eating. I'd wake up in the night and instead of having a drink, I'd eat my way through the refrigerator."

Even now she is too embarrassed to say how large she grew. She does say she "at least doubled" her weight. Finally, she says, she simply decided to stop.

Now her body is back to itself. A second marriage is over. But the rawness of Vietnam remains. Two years ago she visited the Vietnam Veterans Memorial in Washington for the first time. She was devastated.

"I looked at that wall and thought, how many of you died in front of me, or in my arms?"

The current project to build a Vietnam Women's Memorial brings the same response from Hamlin that every male veteran felt when The Wall went up.

"It's about time," she says. "I think there needs to be some acknowledgment that nurses were in Vietnam, that we served, we participated, and just because we didn't die in great numbers, we still came back with scars.

"And we made a contribution. There are an awful lot of veterans who are alive today because of things we did."

There are so many things that still raise the war in Kay Hamlin, that bring back the boy in the rain.

"It's strange," she says. "Sometimes smells trigger memories more than anything. Like the smell of blood.

"Or sounds," she says. "The Beach Boys. God, we used to crank that radio up."

Just last month Hamlin went to Washington for the national convention of the 17,700-member Emergency Nurses Association. She is president-elect of the 100-member Tidewater ENR. There she heard stories from nurses in emergency rooms in cities like New York, Washington and Chicago.

"War stories," she says. "They're seeing 20 to 30 victims of shooting and gang violence, drug violence, every day. I thought, God, it's Vietnam all over again."

She needs the reminders, says Hamlin, enough of the tension to bring on the rush. But she doesn't need to return to war. "The horror," she says of those cities, "would be too much."

So would the anger, which smolders inside with her memories.

"The waste of lives," she says. "So many 17-, 18-, 19-year- old babies. I wasn't much older. But they were babies."

She's drifting back again.

"You take a boot off, and a foot comes off with it, and you look at this kid's face and he can hardly shave."

She snaps back.

She takes a sip of tea.

"I look at my son now, he's the same age as those kids were, and I watch him sleep and say, dear God, not ever again."

Today, Oct. 4, 1989, is the first National Emergency Nurses Day.

Brotherhood of the Bike

Sandman stands alone. Outside by the trees he stares into a bonfire, gazing at showers of sparks as they leap like tracer bullets toward the midnight sky.

In the house the others are partying hard, Hank Williams Jr. pumping out of the stereo, the brothers climbing on tables and howling at the night, the women earning drinks by baring their breasts at the bar.

Sandman likes it better out here, by the woods. This is where the bikes are, two dozen of them, parked in a circle like chrome horses, their sleek bodies glinting in the firelight. Harleys, each and every one.

Sandman rides nothing else. Nor do his brothers. It is Harleys that pull them together — Harleys and Vietnam.

In Nam, Sandman and his brothers wore grunt green, mud brown and blood red. Now they wear a different set of colors: the dirty blue denim and black leather vests that are the badge of bikers.

These bikers belong to the Vietnam Veterans Motorcycle club.

They are not outlaws. They are not what law-abiding bikers fearfully call One Percenters. They are not what federal authorities call dangerous motorcycle gangs.

They just look that way.

With their ponytails and long shaggy beards, with small weapons — buck knives and wooden clubs — hanging from their belts, with spurs latched to their heavy boots, and most of all with that raw, rumbling, terrifying roar that comes only from a Harley, the Vietnam Vets could easily be lumped with the Pagans, or the Bandidos, or Hell's Angels or any of the handful of hardcore biker gangs classified by law enforcement authorities as organized criminals.

But Sandman is no criminal. Neither is he simply a "citizen"—the biker term for more mainstream motorcycle enthusiasts. Sandman works for the federal government in Washington, but he will never be mainstream. He was in Vietnam too long. Seven years, to be exact, only four of which are marked on his vest because the rest were spent in parts of Southeast Asia Sandman still won't talk about. Americans weren't supposed to be there then.

Seven years, and when he was discharged in '69, Sandman still stayed, sliding over to Thailand for a year-and-a-half "on my own." After that he had business in El Salvador — as a mercenary — before he wound up in a downtown Washington apartment, looking out his window at protest marchers and trying to figure out where he fit in.

Sandman was in Vietnam—so deep that at 43 he is still climbing out.

Which is why he is here this autumn night, by this fire in this field in Virginia Beach, joining members of the state's three VVMC chapters — Lynchburg, Richmond and Virginia Beach — and his own Northern Virginia-based Washington brothers for a weekend of hell-raising, bike-riding... and soul-searching.

"This is my way out," says Sandman, nodding toward the cluster of Harleys.

"Getting out on that bike," he says, "is the one thing that makes me feel comfortable. When I'm there, I'm in my own little world."

The biker world.

In the eyes of Middle America, it is scattered packs of bearded hellions roaring down interstates or rumbling up to intersections, revving their engines while the station wagons around them roll up the windows and lock the doors.

In the eyes of Hollywood, it is Marlon Brando in "The Wild One," or Peter Fonda in "Easy Rider," or a B-film of terror titled "Hell's Angels on Wheels."

In the pages of magazines like Iron Horse and Outlaw Biker, it is a raunchy landscape of defilement and debauchery, of tattooed men and women hellbent on obscenity and outrage.

The Vietnam Vets are regulars on those pages, fifths of Jack Daniel's clutched in their hands, their fingers fondling topless girlfriends, their legs wrapped around the Panhead engine of a Harley-Davidson motorcycle.

There is no telling exactly how many there are. The club's printed bylaws urge members to keep a "low vis." When they do appear in public — a lone rider idling at a stoplight, a dozen or so descending on a local POW-MIA event, 5,000 of them from across the country

converging on Washington D.C. this past Memorial Day weekend —
the air is tinged with fear and loathing.

But there is nothing to fear from the VVMC, according to Rick
Lybarger, the club's Virginia state president, who on a recent weekday
afternoon was in the back yard of the Virginia Beach chapter's clubhouse, shouting "Beer me!" at the women inside and pulling a piece of
paper from his wallet by way of introduction.

"It's a poem," said Lybarger, a 6-3, 220-pound former semipro
football player from Ohio who spent 1969 as a Marine in Vietnam. He
was clean-shaven then, but now, at 37, he has a braided ponytail and a
bushy beard. The poem is one he wrote for his father, a construction
worker, bar bouncer and biker who went by the name Bazooka. His
father, says Lybarger, first propped him on a Harley when he was 3.

"Right then I knew that's what I wanted to do the rest of my life,"
he says.

And he has done it. Through stints in the Marines and the Navy,
through a broken marriage, through an electrician's career that landed
him his current steady job with a local company, and through all the
other stages of his life represented by the snapshots and snippets he
keeps stored in a shoebox, Lybarger has always had his Harleys. He's
been through seven of them, but he is quick to note that there's a
difference between owning a Harley and being a biker.

"Not all people that ride motorcycles are bikers," says Lybarger.

"Being a Vietnam vet doesn't make you a biker, either," he says.

He folds the poem and slips it back into his wallet.

"My old man was a biker," he says, "which means he did what he
damn well pleased and got away with it as long as he could."

Yoda figured he couldn't get away with it much longer.

It was the summer of 1970, and Yoda was young — 19. He was
strong — at 5-1 and 115 pounds, he could bench press 235. And he was
tough — three times in three years he had been hit by bullets, and each
time he had climbed back on his Harley, a 1928 Flathead with a shotgun
mounted on the side.

But Yoda was beginning to wonder how long his luck would hold
out.

He had bought his first bike at 15. A year later he was riding with
the Warlords, one of the larger clubs in St. Louis. When the Warlords
rallied for a run, more than 300 bikes would show up.

It was 1968 when Yoda joined, and most of the Warlords were
military veterans, "Some just comin' out of Nam," says Yoda, "others
left over from Korea." All, says Yoda, were prepared to "go down on
Front Street" — his way of describing a man taking a stand. With the

Warlords in the late '60s, says Yoda, taking a stand often meant gunplay.

"This was the real deal, real heavy," he says, describing shootouts in bars, "demolitions" in clubhouses and a particularly large "gunfight" in Kansas.

"Yeah, people died," Yoda says of the Kansas battle. "But I was used to that. I had a lot of friends who died standing next to me in a bar or something. You'd get sprayed with the blood and the guts, so I was used to that."

But by 1970 Yoda had had enough. "Time was moving slow," he says. "Every minute was like a year.

So Yoda set aside his bandolier of bullets and his Bowie knife and rode his Harley down to the nearest Navy recruiter. "Maybe," he thought, "they'd get me back on track."

They did. Yoda was a Navy diver until 1978. Then he joined the Army, where he became a paratrooper and graduated first in his class at special forces school. In 1981 he returned to the Navy, where he is now a SEAL diver. All along he has kept his Harleys. At 37 he is still a biker, but Yoda is older and wiser than the young Warlord of 20 years ago.

"I like to deal with people who have already proven themselves, who aren't on an egotistical macho trip," he says. And that, says Yoda, is what drew him to the Vietnam Vets club after he arrived in Norfolk in 1983. Today he is the Virginia Beach chapter's president.

"Being in a group like this is about unity, but more than that it's about truth," he says. Although he was never in Vietnam, Yoda's eyes gleam with the same mix of menace and wisdom as Sandman's.

"A lot of this is simply being able to look a man in the eye and not have him bullshit you," he says. "A big part of riding these bikes is showing who you really are, no act. Just you, stripped down, showing your reality for what it is."

For the Vietnam Vets, says Yoda, reality is a particular blend of age and experience that is beyond most bikers.

"Here," he says of the VVMC, "I'm dealing with a mature biker, somebody I know is not gonna put me out on Front Street for a humbug.

"We don't steal bikes, we don't deal drugs, we don't sell women and we're not into territorial claims, like saying, 'Virginia Beach is *ours*!'

"That's not what we're about," says Yoda.

"If you're gonna go down on Front Street with this group," he says, "it's gonna be for something real."

It is hard to pinpoint the beginnings of the Vietnam Veterans Motorcycle Club. There is no national headquarters, no press office, no published statistics, no printed history. Except for their occasional forays into the public eye — mostly at POW-MIA-related events — they keep to themselves. And they don't like to talk about their numbers. They'd rather have outsiders — the police, the public, other clubs — guess.

"That's just common sense," says Yoda. "That's just older school thinking, especially if you grew up the way I did."

Lybarger is more willing to share some sketchy figures. He says he joined 400 brothers at the club's national meeting last August. Other gatherings, he says, in places like Sturgis, S.D. — "A good biker town," he says — have drawn as many as 1,500 VVMC members. Then there was that Memorial Day blowout in Washington.

"It's gotten to the point," says Lybarger, "Where every major city has a chapter."

The local chapter has about 10 members, says Lybarger. There were even fewer when he discovered them in 1985. Lybarger was one year out of the Navy then, riding his Harley down a street in the Ocean View section of Norfolk when he passed a man wearing VVMC colors. He flagged the man down and asked about the club. At first, answers did not come easily.

"Anybody that approaches this club," explains Lybarger, "the first thing we do is find out their intent."

After a while, Lybarger found out that the Virginia Beach chapter had been formed earlier that year. Nationally, the group had coalesced in the early '80s. But its seeds were sown a decade before that, as pockets of bike-riding Vietnam vets came back from the war and sprouted across the country. Some had been bikers before they went to Vietnam. Others became bikers while they were there. Either way, they came home to the highway with a vengeance.

"The concept of freedom is important," says Yoda. "The need for that sense of freedom and the closeness people achieve in the military under stressful conditions are what draw us together."

The club is open to any man with military service between 1962 and 1975. Those who actually did duty in Vietnam are "combat" vets; those who did not are "era" vets. Both are eligible, but they must own more than a military record. They must also own a motorcycle — "an *American* motorcycle," says Lybarger. Which means either a bike made by the Indian Motorcycle Co., which folded in 1954, or a Harley-Davidson. The Virginia Beach chapter rides only Harleys, for reasons that go beyond mere patriotism.

"You can't explain it in words," says Lybarger of the Harley's allure. "Unless you feel it when you ride it, there's nothin' to say."

Locally, the club's membership ranges from active duty military men, to a couple of electricians like Lybarger, to the unemployed. The Richmond chapter includes a banker. The Washington chapter is filled with federal employees. Some are married family men. Many are single. Most are divorced.

"This is as much about an attitude as it is about bikes," says Lybarger. But he has a hard time defining the essence of that attitude. He uses terms like freedom, brotherhood and family—terms common to any bike club. But there is more to this one.

There is something peculiar to this group that bonds them to their bikes—something peculiar to the impact of Vietnam. When it is suggested that this is a generation of vets unlike any this nation has seen before, that many of them are seized by a mixture of anger, aggression, frustration and outrage unknown to veterans of other wars, and that for some of these men there is no better way to blow off the pressure than to climb on a massive Harley-Davidson motorcycle and open the throttle, Lybarger nods.

"That's not a bad explanation," he says.

"But then," he adds, "there are some brothers who just need to talk."

"And then," he adds, "there are some brothers who don't need anything."

Pete needs to talk.

As Sandman stands by the fire, Pete sits on the porch, drinking a Bud. Pete is what the club calls a "prospect," somewhat like a fraternity pledge, although the brothers cringe at the analogy. Neither are they comfortable with comparisons to other clubs. They are aware of the degrading, even unmentionable indignities some biker groups heap upon their prospects. But the VVMC, says Lybarger, asks nothing more of its prospective members "than to show you're a man about your business and you're a brother."

Pete is a brother. He lost his right leg to a mortar round on Thanksgiving day, 1969. "We'd just finished a hot meal and gone out on patrol," he recalls. He's 39 now, drawing 100 percent disability and, despite the amputation, still riding his Harley Superglide.

"The shift's on the left," says Pete, tapping the prosthesis on his right leg, "so I get along real good."

Pete's been riding motorcycles for years, but it was something else that drew him to this club — something he couldn't find among the World War II and Korean War vets at the VFW Hall, and something he knew he would never find among other motorcycle clubs.

"Being a combat vet, you need somebody to relate to," he says. "People who haven't been in combat can listen to you, listen real hard, but they can't understand. Like my wife — my second one. She's 13 years younger than me, and I basically don't ever talk to her about it. And those other veterans, it's not the same. This was a different war, a different place."

Pete shrugs, takes a swallow of beer and smiles.

"Everybody who's been to Vietnam gets the blues once in a while," he says. "It's good to have a place to let it out."

Breeze agrees. He's one of Sandman's brothers in the Washington chapter. With his thick curly hair tied back by a bandanna and those captain's bars on his denim vest, Breeze's officemates up at the Internal Revenue Service would hardly recognize him.

Breeze was in Vietnam in '67 and '68 — "Artillery," he says. "A gun bunny." He's seen a lot of change in America since he came back — most of it too late and too sudden. The recent explosion of interest in the war — what some skeptics are calling Vietnam Chic — leaves Breeze cold.

"Yeah," he says, "it's almost *in* to be a Vietnam veteran these days. And it wasn't that long ago nobody wanted to *see* you."

Breeze looks around at his brothers and notes that most of them are divorced, including his buddy Joker. Joker has two sons, one he calls Spare Parts and the other Sparkplug. The boys aren't here, but a 4-year-old named Clint has found Joker's lap. Clint, whose mother is a guest at the party, wears a Harley-Davidson T-shirt.

"Most Vietnam veterans have been through more than one wife," says Breeze. "The reason for that is the same reason most of us need this club. Some of the guys have lost wives *because* of the club — their wives see them open up more to the brothers than they can to them, and they resent that."

Their motorcycles are one thing that sets them apart from other Vietnam vet groups, says Breeze — "We need something stronger," he says. And one thing that sets them apart from other motorcycle groups, he adds, is their age. The youngest member of the Virginia Beach chapter is 31. The oldest is 43. The average age is 38. Breeze looks around, shakes his head and grins.

"If we'd gotten together like this when we were 20 years old," he says, "Lord knows what trouble we'd have gotten into."

According to local law enforcement authorities, the Vietnam Vets club has given no one here any trouble. Federal and local officials say they know of the club but have no record of any wrongdoing. Club members themselves say they will not tolerate crime. And they police themselves to prove it. Last year, says Lybarger, one member of the Virginia Beach chapter was run off the road by an automobile. The enraged brother pulled a gun and came up shooting.

"He was loco," says Lybarger. "We pulled his patch."

They do carry legal weapons. They do look tough. If they're going to ride the way they want, says Breeze, they have no choice.

"It's a defense, a deterrent," he says, explaining the posture. "The easiest way to keep 99 percent of the people off our backs is to intimidate them."

There have been scraps with other clubs, like the trip Yoda and Lybarger took last year to Charleston, S.C., where they helped the VVMC chapter there face down a challenge from a rival gang.

"Sometimes it gets to be cowboys and Indians," says Yoda. Sandman uses a similar analogy to explain his own needs.

"I think I was born way too late," he says. "To me, my bike is like a horse. When I'm on it, I've got the wind in my face, the horse under my ass, spurs on my boots. A hundred years ago I would have felt more at home. A hundred years ago there weren't so many laws. You had to depend on yourself then.

"To a true biker," he says, "that's what this all means — independence and freedom of choice.

"But true bikers — the ones who camp in the woods, who go on long runs — we're the last of a breed."

As are Vietnam vets in general, notes Lybarger.

"We're a limited edition," he says. "There's only so many of us, and it's only gonna last so long, because the Vietnam vet is fading fast, running out of time."

There will be no more generations of Vietnam vets. That is this club's curse. But in a way, it is also the bond that is their curious blessing, the tie that binds them together and sets them apart.

"We have the one thing no other bike club has," says Sandman, walking toward his Harley.

"We have Vietnam."

October 2, 1988

The Shadow of Death

When the odd little woman with the foreign accent first arrived in Highland County four years ago, few of the farmers and hunters among these hills and hollows paid much attention. She didn't seem the type to take over that run-down farm up over Bullpasture Mountain, but the sounds of digging, sawing and hammering that began echoing from the property's pine-studded glens were good sounds, the sounds of hard, honest work.

It's true the trucks and vans that began winding up the road along the Cowpasture River were a little strange. They had out-of-state tags — some from as far away as California. And the drivers looked like, well, hippies. They slept in tepees up on that farm. At dusk they trickled out of the woods, gathering for a communal meal and singing songs as the sun slid into West Virginia.

Still, these newcomers were bringing life to a dead place. Sheep appeared in the farm's meadows. Chickens roamed the yard. And that woman, she was actually canning her own fruit and vegetables, knitting her own sweaters, hoeing her own garden.

But then word got around that there was more going on up there than farming. Down at Ronald Miller's store in the village of Head Waters, there was talk that these new folks planned to build an airstrip in the valley, that they were going to be flying in people from around the world. Sick people, dying people.

Miller's wife, Carolyn, who ran the post office in her husband's store, was getting hundreds of letters addressed to this woman every day — more letters than the whole town of 80 received in a week. But

Carolyn Miller didn't mind. After all, the folks who came down to pick up the mail and a few supplies were so polite. They didn't seem like troublemakers.

Until someone mentioned the babies.

It is a warm spring day in 1987, and Elisabeth Kubler-Ross has stopped to bask in the bloom of the farm she calls her "Shanti Nilaya" — Sanskrit for "home of peace." The tiny silver-haired doctor gazes at the breeze-stoked valley below her and sighs.

"They are good neighbors," she says, her gravelly Swiss-German accent crunching her consonants. She nods her head, shrugs her thin shoulders and sucks on a cigarette.

Her words are kind, in spite of the nails and broken glass that have been sprinkled on her driveway in the dead of night. In spite of the hateful letters slipped in her mountainside mailbox by unseen visitors. In spite of the telephone call she received Christmas Eve, telling her the Ku Klux Klan was going to burn her off her property.

"They are good neighbors," she repeats.

Then she pauses.

"As long," she says, "as you don't talk about AIDS."

Babies with AIDS.

When it was announced in 1985 that the Elisabeth Kubler-Ross Center being built on a 300-acre western Virginia farm was not only planning to conduct workshops for terminally ill patients, suicidal Vietnam veterans and parents of murdered children, but also intended to build a hospice to care for infants with AIDS, this rural county exploded.

Wary tolerance turned to violent hostility.

Meetings were called among the county's tiny towns. Petitions were circulated. Local government officials suddenly blocked the Center's requests for building permits. And Kubler- Ross' Shanti Nilaya became a battleground.

"Why in Highland County?" shouted an angry voice at a public hearing in 1985. "Why are you imposing this disease on us? This is the wrong place to bring the disease."

Kubler-Ross had not thought so in 1983. When she moved her death-and-dying workshop headquarters from San Diego to Highland County that year, she explained the move in terms of isolation:

"I need a place in the boonies for this kind of work," she said. "You have a hundred people working very intensively, you know, with a lot of sobbing and crying and screaming. You have to be in a place where you don't disturb your neighbors."

That has turned out to be impossible. Even in Virginia's least populated county, where sheep outnumber people five to one, no neighbor is beyond the shadow of death — especially when the shadow is as horrifying as AIDS.

But then it is fear, not AIDS, that has always been Kubler-Ross' biggest foe. And so, although she announced in August that she no longer plans to build an AIDS infant hospice in Highland County, she is not leaving her farm. She has spent her life teaching people how to deal with what she calls "unfinished business," and there is plenty of that right outside her front door.

"Fear, shame and guilt are man's biggest enemy," says the doctor, stepping into her rustic home. "My whole life's work has been to help people with these things, and it's not coincidence that I get into a community where they are rampant."

To watch her tend the steaming pots covering her kitchen stove, it is not easy imagining this 60-year-old woman as a world figure, as a globe-trotting center of controversy, as a person whom critics have called "a death 'n' dying junkie" and a morbid "Queen of Death."

As she chats with the birds who come to tap at her windows, she pulls a half-dozen loaves of bread out of her oven, forces pound cake and coffee on a visitor and makes it easy to believe her when she dismisses herself as nothing but "a Swiss hillbilly."

Yet even in this domestic clutter there are clues to the contrary. The pile of books, boxes and letters spilling off the kitchen table, for example, are just some of what she calls "my AIDS stuff" — research for her latest book. Due to be published in October, it will be her 12th, furthering her position as the world's leading authority on thanatology — the study of death. The working title is "The Challenge of AIDS."

There are 50 more manuscripts stacked in a back room, all written by other people, all on some aspect of dying, all waiting for review and the Elisabeth Kubler-Ross stamp of approval.

Even the dozens of dolls covering the bed and shelves of an upstairs room are a link to the dark side. They were sent from people around the world, destined to be delivered to babies dying of AIDS. Two of the dolls, notes Kubler-Ross, were handmade by a young Swiss girl. When asked where the girl is, the doctor is matter-of-fact: "She is dead." The girl had cancer. She was 12.

It is people like this whom Kubler-Ross visits when she travels to the 24 or so week-long death-and-dying workshops she directs each year at sites around the globe. A week earlier, she had been in Australia and New Zealand. Now she is home for five days. Then she will be off to Louisiana, New York, California, New Mexico and, in June, England. Each workshop costs the 80 or so participants $550 apiece.

The 20 lectures Kubler-Ross delivers each year bring a standard fee of $5,000 each. The money all goes toward the $55,000 a month she says it costs the center to sustain its worldwide operations. It also covers the costs of the needy who cannot afford her workshop fees.

"Almost all cancer and AIDS patients are poor or become poor because of the cost of their care," she says. "It's important that these people aren't discriminated against just because they can't pay."

It is for these people that Kubler-Ross spends her rare spare moments knitting scarves like the one she picks up as she takes a seat in her living room. Sun streams through a stained- glass window. The place is festooned with trophies from her travels. Weavings hang from hand-hewn wooden beams. African and Indian carvings are perched on dark antique furniture. Animal skins are draped on well-worn sofas and chairs. The room has the look and feel of a lived-in cabin—even though Kubler-Ross is here no more than six days at a time, five times a year.

"If I didn't have this place," she says, lighting another in a non-stop chain of Marlboros, "I would not last."

Her work boots are muddy from a morning spent hauling and spreading manure on the yard. Her jeans and sweater hang from her frail 5-foot frame. She has been on the go since dawn, but she is far from weary. When she is on her farm, the more she works the more she beams.

Especially when she is alone. During most of the year, a crew of volunteers moves into the property's farmhouse, down the lane from her hillside chalet. They work the livestock, the fields of alfalfa and the gardens. But in the winter they move out, and Kubler-Ross is left with her precious privacy.

"We were snowed in three days last month," she says, "and that was heaven. Nobody got up here, nobody."

In better weather, she is assailed by unannounced pilgrims who appear at her front door. Some have even come out of the steep woods behind her home, hiking in from the west.

"They claim they are lost," she grunts. Then she shakes her head.

"When I wasn't here this last time, people came and just walked into the house to look at it, like a, what is it, a tourist attraction.

"After that, I started locking up."

But there is no locking out the mountain of mail on her dining room table. "That's yesterday's, she says, nodding toward an over-flowing crate of letters. "Every day it's a box."

They come in all languages, scribbled pleas for help and advice. As she has done for two decades now, Kubler-Ross answers as many as she can personally. There is no choice, she says.

"You get a letter of desperation from a mother whose one and only child is dying of cancer, you'd answer too," she says.

She sorts her mail into boxes marked Super Urgent, Very Urgent, Urgent, Not So Urgent and For Your Pleasure Only. The latter, she says, are a rare treat.

"We had in one workshop six parents of children who were murdered. One father had three children murdered. Those people need a lot of help, and those letters you answer first. That's the Super Urgent."

The bulk of the mail, she says, is from children and adults who are counting the days until they or someone dear to them will die. "You can't wait too long with them. Because you don't know how close to death they are, and they all have their unfinished business."

Unfinished business — the phrase peppers Kubler-Ross' conversation. She has dedicated her life to helping people tie their emotional loose ends. Dangling feelings of remorse and regret are never more exposed and painful than when a person suddenly peers over the precipice of death. Over the last two decades, Kubler-Ross has sorted and defined those feelings, dragging dying from the realm of taboo into the mainstream of her profession, softening skeptics with her resolve and results. Today, if a dying man is able to have his family surround him during his last days in a hospice, if a medical student is taught the now-classic five stages of dying, if clergy and counselors have more to offer a terminally ill patient than empty words and rigid dogma, it is because of this former country doctor from Switzerland who shook the medical and religious establishments with the publication of her 1969 bestseller "On Death and Dying."

Now she has almost a cult status among people connected to death. In her workshops and lectures she is deluged by tragedy and sorrow. But at home, she would rather raise her vegetables. That is why the vans and tepees that followed her here in 1983 have vanished. The volunteers who now work on the farm and on the workshop-building construction are carefully screened by the eight-person staff at the center's administrative headquarters in Head Waters. The groupies are long gone.

"They were manic depressives and schizophrenics, psychopaths and flaky people," says Kubler-Ross, waving her hand and shaking her head. "I don't like trailers and vans and flaky people. They don't come for the farming. They come because they are very needy people who want to be in contact with me. And that I don't need.

"This is my healthy place where I come to recharge my battery. I can't run a psychiatric unit here. People who come here have to be grounded and workaholics. Otherwise it's not my cup of tea."

She is a stern taskmaster, shooing outsiders away from the volunteers at work in her fields. "If they talk to reporters," she says, "they would never get any work done." But Kubler-Ross demands no more of the people around her than she does of herself. She sleeps five hours a night, cooks pots of food for the people around her but eats little herself, smokes cigarette after cigarette...

"Yes, yes," she nods. "And I enjoy my coffee. And I don't eat brown rice and vegetables. I don't meditate. I don't do anything right."

She pauses.

"Except, when I get negative, I work on it."

In the end, she says, all her work comes around to attitude and outlook. The message is simple, but it is not easy convincing a man whose wife murdered his three children with a sledgehammer to think positively.

"You have never seen a human being like this," she says of the father, who was dragged to one of her lectures by a friend. "He was like a zombie. He had no life energy in him."

She talked with the man after the lecture, persuading him to attend a workshop. "I mean, he had to come. He would not have survived. And by divine manipulation, which some people call coincidence, a mother was in that workshop whose child was brutally raped and murdered... They really helped each other."

The stories are rerun over and over. One heartbreak after another. And yet Kubler-Ross says she does not drown in the sea of sorrow around her.

"All I want to do is to try and figure out how to give these people some life back," she says. "And then I see them a year later and they come and hug me and laugh and smile and are living again. And that keeps you going."

At the same time as she has tended to her patients, Kubler-Ross has also worked through her own share of personal pain. When she began talking in the mid-1970s about near-death patients who had contact with afterlife "spirits" and about her own "spontaneous" out-of-body experiences, she was ridiculed by the medical community that had been so slow to accept her initial work with the dying. Her husband of 22 years, whom she had met in medical school in Zurich, divorced her. When a subsequent sex scandal surfaced surrounding a colleague in San Diego, the story was trumpeted in the pages of national magazines, with Kubler-Ross' name prominently displayed. Although she had nothing to do with the scandal, her reputation was marred.

Yet she endures, tending to her own unfinished business as she tells her patients to tend to theirs. She and her ex-husband, for instance, are still close. They and their two grown children spent Christmas with his new wife and 3-year-old: "My kids and his kids and the two wives. We cooked together and had a nice time.

"We've always been good friends," she says of her ex-husband. "We were married 22 years. You don't just suddenly become an enemy. It wasn't easy, but it's so much nicer. That's just another thing that people have to learn.

"The big art that I go around teaching is don't get negative. When you get negative, you become totally drained.

"It's not always easy," she adds. "And yes, you are allowed to get pissed off."

Then she smiles.

"But only for 15 seconds."

She has counted the seconds often in the last two years. But for a woman who has spent her life leaning into the windstorm of controversy, the local furor over AIDS is really no surprise.

"I think by now I'm shockproof," she says. "You know, I have one thing after the other. Twenty years ago, when I started to work with dying cancer patients, I was treated the same way. They spit in my face... And then 10 years later, the same medical institutions gave me honorary doctorate degrees. It is the same with AIDS."

The 27 babies she had lined up for her proposed infant hospice have found homes with foster families across the country—none in Virginia. Inspired by Kubler-Ross' efforts, two Catholic churches in California and Texas have opened infant AIDS hospices — "I am their godmother," she smiles. And she predicts hospices for adults with AIDS are the next movement on the death- and-dying horizon.

"Right now we have a minimum of 2 million carriers of AIDS in this country," she says. "In 10 months, 10 percent will have the whole disease. In another 10 months, 400,000 will have it, then in 10 months it will double again, and in another 10 months it will be 1.6 million.

"But what does this country do to plan? I mean a real plan. How are you going to take care of 1.6 million patients who need care? Nurturing them, keeping them comfortable, pain-free, change their beds, their diapers. They become blind. They become mentally disturbed. They have every central nervous system pathology. They have diarrhea. They vomit.

"They need loving, tender care. And you can't put them all in hospitals. And the hospices are not going to be able to take care of them because they would have no room for their cancer patients.

"We need a real plan, and we need to do it now, before we're so overloaded that people go crazy. You need to train an army of volunteers who know how to take care of such very sick patients. You need home health care, you need people who go to their homes and cook them a soft meal that they can swallow.

"It's like the elderly, except that these people are much more sick. An elderly person you can put in a comfortable chair and you have the television and you have some people that talk to them and touch them.

But these are people who can barely lift their head, and if you're going to end up with a million of these young people, you better get ready now."

She takes a deep breath, and lights another cigarette.

"What I wanted to do, and it would have been so simple, is to start with a prototype AIDS baby hospice, and give them a real lovely home in a healthy environment like this farm, and they would at least have a year and a half or two years of life, of real life. Healthy fresh air, home-cooked vegetables, you know, a healthy environment.

"Right now, they're kept in hospital rooms in pediatric units. They are vulnerable to every bug that comes into the hospital. It's the sickest environment for a child who has no immune system.

"And they only keep them there for experimentation and money. That to me is the biggest American disgrace. It's all money. A 2-year-old I know of was in the hospital eight months, and they were paid $240,000. For a little child who barely ate anything and didn't need much, you know, medical attention. What this child needs is hugs, love, nurturing and one love object that they can relate to and perhaps have some bonding with."

Asked about the parents of that 2-year-old, Kubler-Ross winces.

"They were not available."

She stubs out her cigarette, lights another.

"There are lots of them that way.

"There are lots of mothers who have been married many years who don't know that the husbands are bisexual. Then the child is born who has AIDS, and then they try to trace back where the AIDS came from and then the father has to confess. And the wives are very resentful, most of them. They reject the child and the husband. And the husband is at such a level that he doesn't know how to take care of this baby."

It's hard to say how many of these babies there are, says Kubler-Ross. Estimates are about 1,000 right now, but "that's very low," she says. "Because most of them keep the babies hidden away, and they will never ever let it be known that their child has AIDS. Especially if they live in places like Virginia and Tennessee and Georgia, you know, where they're not allowed to go to church anymore, where they are ostracized. Anywhere where fundamentalists live, they view that this is God's punishment."

Kubler-Ross rises and moves outside, back into the sunshine flooding her front porch. A Swiss flag hanging from a pole in the sloping front meadow gently riffles in the breeze. She describes one of the letters she recently pulled from the pile on her dining room table. It was from the mother of a 3-year-old with AIDS. The woman was desperate. She was willing to pay for advice. But, like so many of the mothers who send their cries to Kubler-Ross, the woman was not willing to sign the letter, and it became just another anonymous howl in a secret storm.

"It's heartbreaking," says Kubler-Ross. "I would have hopped in the car and brought the mother and the baby here in this house. It's a big house. I can house lots of children on my farm."

She suddenly stops and shakes her head. She realizes she has gotten carried away. She will build her center here — smaller than the one originally planned. She will train counselors here. She will have short sessions with the broken and dying — one-day and three-day workshops. But she cannot house even one child on this farm. And no one with AIDS.

"They would burn me down," she says.

She listens to the silence of the pines around her.

"Most people are decent people," she says, "if you don't threaten them. But if they are threatened, it brings out the worst in them, the absolute worst."

April 5, 1987

A Death in the Family

Tommy has been dead a month now, but Delma Lee still calls him, late at night. That's when she dials the Tidewater AIDS Crisis Task Force and listens to her son's voice on the answering machine.

In the daytime, Delma Lee sits in her den and watches Tommy on TV. She's got two videocasettes to choose from. She prefers the one taped in March, when Tommy appeared on a local news program. He looks good on that tape. Healthy, happy, upbeat. When the interviewer asks him what he sees ahead for himself, Tommy answers eagerly.

"A good future, a long future," he says. "I look forward to the day that the cure for AIDS comes around. The day that happens is going to be the greatest day of my life."

The other tape was made four months later, when Tommy appeared on an AIDS telethon. He's thinner. Weaker. Sadder. The disease has taken its toll. The scab covering the lower half of his face glistens under the studio lights and makes it difficult for him to talk. He's lost weight, strength, and — most of all — hope.

"I'm more up and down like a roller coaster," he tells the interviewer. "I don't think I'm as positive as I used to be."

Three months later, at age 25, Tommy Wright was dead.

The urn that holds his ashes still sits in Delma Lee's den, next to a photograph of Tommy in his Air Force uniform. Those ashes will be buried a week from Friday — the day after Thanksgiving.

Delma Lee thanks God that Tommy found Jesus before he died. She sits in her living room, a Bible on the coffee table, gospel sheet music on the organ, and describes Tommy's accepting the Lord as "the one good thing that came out of all this."

But still and all, Delma Lee — along with her husband and daughter and son and so many others who knew and loved Tommy at the end — hasn't been able to close the book on the death of her oldest son. Tommy is gone, but the pain and the questions linger.

"We're supposed to learn from all things in our life," says Delma Lee. "But I just don't know how we're supposed to learn from *this*."

Delma Lee began learning about AIDS in the spring of 1985. That's when Tommy called her from South Carolina, in tears.

It was the kind of call she'd gotten so many times before. Ever since he'd been old enough to move out of the house, Tommy had drifted in and out of his parents' lives, in and out of jobs, in and out of town. When he'd run out of money, out there on the road somewhere, he'd call home for help, and Delma Lee would take him back in. Then it would start all over again. The arguing, the tempers. Tommy and his father would explode, and they'd throw him out again.

But this time was different. This time Tommy was calling about more than money. He'd been tested while giving blood in Charleston, and the result had come back HIV-positive. The AIDS virus was inside him.

"I really didn't know what he was talking about," says Delma Lee. "AIDS was just something I'd seen in the headlines. Why read about it? It wasn't affecting me."

The Wrights had no reason to think something like AIDS would ever affect them. From all appearances, Delma Lee and her husband Tom had built a textbook life together. They'd met at a Virginia Beach skating rink back in 1961. Delma Lee was a Norfolk native, graduated from Maury High School, working for VEPCO. Tom was a young sailor from the hills of central Virginia. They married that year, spent the better part of two decades living a Navy family's life, raised three children and finally settled in Virginia Beach after Tom retired in 1977.

They still live in that same house, on a quiet suburban corner. An American flag hangs on the front patio. Tom's collection of baseball caps, bearing slogans about fishing and Fords, hangs in the den. Twenty-two-year-old Cheri and her husband live nearby. Sixteen-year-old Jimmy — a high school sophomore, a member of Naval Junior ROTC — lives upstairs.

This is, from all appearances, a house of solid values, the home of a solid family. But there were problems in this house. Problems with Tommy. And they began long before he called home about AIDS.

"It would have been easy to turn our backs on Tommy," says his mother, "after all we'd been through with him."

Delma Lee cries as she does her remembering. Tom clenches and unclenches his hands as he does his. They blame themselves for Tommy's troubles, which tormented their household from the time he was a little boy. The Navy, says Delma Lee, kept Tommy's father away from the house too often. When Tom did come home, she says, they would fight over how to discipline him. By the time Tommy finished first grade, school psychologists were telling the Wrights he was hyperactive.

"He wasn't hyperactive," says Tom. "He was just confused."

The confusion apparently never went away. Tommy became "a loner," says Delma Lee. "He got into some weird things."

Before he finished junior high, Tommy had been arrested once for breaking into and ransacking a home and another time for arson. He had spent time at a psychiatric center in Portsmouth and at a detention center in Chesapeake.

When he entered Kempsville High School, things seemed to fall in place. Tommy joined the local Demolay chapter, rising from chaplain to master councilor. He was chosen "beau" of the local Job's Daughters. Delma Lee was proud of that. She had been a Job's Daughter herself.

"He had lots of girlfriends," says Delma Lee. "He and all the Jobeys would go out dancing. He was finally involved with some decent people."

Both his junior and senior years at Kempsville, Tommy was elected vice-president of his class. He seemed to have pulled himself together. But at home, says Delma Lee, there were still the same problems. Arguments, fights. Tommy's temper flashes.

"I couldn't control him," says Tom. "He'd go out, do whatever he wanted, and give us a batch of lip when he'd come home."

"I couldn't wait until he was 18. So he could leave."

Tommy did leave, after graduating in the spring of 1980. But he kept coming back. He worked a string of jobs — tending the counter at Wendy's, driving a cement truck, waiting tables. "But nothing was leading anywhere," says Delma Lee.

Then Tommy tried college. He went for a semester to Tidewater Community College. And that, says Delma Lee, is where "he met this guy."

Delma Lee had "an instinct" about her son's new college friend, but she kept it to herself until another of the family fights sent Tommy toward the door. That's when he turned and told her — "Defiantly," recalls Delma Lee — that he was gay.

"I thought," she says, "What have we got facing us now?"

In many ways, it was harder for the Wrights to deal with their son's homosexuality than it was to later deal with his AIDS. When they talk about the disease, the Wrights are talking about tragedy. When they talk about homosexuality, they are talking about sin.

Delma Lee's Bible told her how to respond to a gay son. "I knew it was wrong, him being like this," she says.

"But," she adds. "He was still my son."

To Tom Wright, however, the sin was not so much defying the word of God as defying the code of manhood he'd learned in the hard-working hills where he grew up and in the ships' boiler rooms where he worked for 20 years. He talks openly about AIDS, but Tom Wright leaves it to his wife to discuss Tommy's gayness.

He won't even talk about it," says Delma Lee. "It just turns his stomach."

When Tommy moved with his friend into an apartment in Norfolk's Ghent neighborhood and invited his family to visit his new home, Delma Lee went. Her husband stayed home.

"He wouldn't set foot near there," she says. "He totally discarded the fact he had this son. He wanted nobody to know about this."

When Tommy enlisted in the Air Force in 1983 — "To try straightening out his life," says Delma Lee — the whole family prayed it was a change that would make Tommy happy. But a year later he was arrested while on liberty in Okinawa — "He had a knife on him or something like that," says Delma Lee — and the Air Force gave him a general discharge. He came home, tried training as a manager at a Pic 'n Pay shoe store, gave that up and headed for Charleston.

"He had no idea what he was going to do down there," says Delma Lee. "That's just Tommy. He hitchhiked."

Then came the phone call about AIDS and Tommy's trip home in MAy of 1985.

By the time Tommy walked through the door, Delma Lee had read enough to know that the disease could only be spread through body fluids (primarily blood or semen), that she and her family were safe, that they could hug and kiss Tommy — if he'd let them.

That summer she learned more. She learned that although Tommy had the virus, he did not yet have the disease. She read that scientists guess maybe a third of the people who carry the HIV virus will develop AIDS in the next few years. All she and her family could do was hope Tommy wasn't one of those people.

For a while, it seemed he wasn't.

Tommy was "feeling fine," when he came home, says Delma Lee. He stayed a month, then he got restless again. At night, he'd stand in front of the house, looking up at the stars.

"Tommy always loved to look at stars," says Delma Lee.

When he decided to take off for Florida two months after coming back from Charleston, she wasn't surprised.

"Apparently," says Delma Lee, "you can really see some stars down there."

Things seemed to go well for Tommy in Florida. He wound up in Fort Lauderdale, moved in with a priest and a doctor, and seemed happy. But then, in the summer of 1986, he started coughing. A hacking cough. It wouldn't go away. And in September, the doctor called Delma Lee.

"He told us he thought Tommy ought to be home with his family."

Two friends drove Tommy up from Florida in a van. When they parked and helped Tommy to the family's front door, his parents knew the disease had arrived.

"Nobody had to tell us," says Delma Lee. "We just knew he had AIDS."

Tom Wright is even more direct:

"He had the look of death on him."

Gerry Tarr has seen that look too many times. He is a registered nurse. He is director of education and community services for the Tidewater Aids Crisis Task Force. And he is gay.

"That was the whole driving force for me getting involved here," he says, sitting in the task force's stark lounge. "I was losing too many friends."

Tarr had been on the staff three months when Tommy Wright came to the door of the two-story brick building on 41st Street in Norfolk in November of 1986.

"I saw a person who felt like he was doomed," says Tarr. "He'd given up."

Tarr has watched more people die from AIDS than he wants to count — "I don't keep track," he says. But Tommy was special to him. Tommy was one of Tarr's first task force clients. They had both been in the Air Force. In Tarr, Tommy found someone he could talk to.

"We really communicated," says Tarr. "When he had a problem, he'd call me before he'd call his parents."

Tommy was living at home when he first came to the task force. But he was struggling with the same problems he'd always had. He had always rebelled against authority, and now it wasn't just his parents telling him what to do. Now AIDS was giving orders, too.

"So many people who have this disease feel like the rug's been pulled from underneath them," says Tarr. "And controlling his life had always been the most important thing to Tommy."

Tommy had worked through the attack of pneumocystis carinii pneumonia — a parasitic form of pneumonia common in AIDS victims — that had brought him home from Florida. It had left him weak, fragile. But he still wanted to leave home.

"He was unable to get along with his parents," says Tarr. "He felt there were too many rules and regulations. It's difficult for anyone to fit in back at home at that age, and this disease only makes it harder."

So Tommy moved out. For a while, he rented a room from Tarr. He got involved with the task force, attending support group meetings and doing whatever he could to help. He needed something to keep him busy, and the task force gave him those things, from stuffing envelopes to answering phones.

"People with this disease get to a point," says Tarr, "where they're too sick to work but too well to stay at home. That's why we encourage them to come down here."

When Gerry sold his home in June, Tommy made the first of several moves into a string of rented rooms and apartments. He had no car. No job. No money but the Social Security payments to which he was entitled because of his medical condition. Still, he would not come home. And it was tearing his parents apart.

"The places he was living in," says Tom Wright, shaking his head. "It really hurt me. Cold. Dirty. He knew he could get good food and be warm at night here. But it seemed like he was punishing himself."

When Tommy's last roommate, another AIDS patient, moved back to San Diego in August, he had run out of places to turn. He was too weak to live alone, and finding someone to live with him wasn't easy.

"Nobody that's well," says Delma Lee, "wants to live with an AIDS patient."

Nobody, maybe, but his family. When Tommy called in late August, asking to come home, his father picked up the phone.

"Son," he said, "it's about time."

The last two months of Tommy's life were little different from those of other AIDS victims — a steady slide toward death.

At first Tommy could come down from his upstairs bedroom, watch TV in the den, talk with the family. But with time it got harder to climb the stairs. He'd lose his breath and begin coughing — "That hacking cough," says Delma Lee.

So he stayed in bed. Delma Lee did what she could, sitting up with him, waking him every four hours to give him his AZT, changing his sheets when the night sweats soaked them through or the scabs on his face began bleeding. Cheri cooked, taking Tommy meals he didn't eat. Jimmy "spent more time up there than anybody," says Delma Lee. But Tom would only stick his head in for a quick word or two. That was it.

"Tommy's daddy had a hard time going in there and seeing him in that condition," says Delma Lee. "It just tore him up."

It still tears him up.

"To see a healthy, motor-mouthed kid like that," says Tom, shaking his head. "If he could've just stood up and *cussed* at me, it sure would've made me feel good."

But Tommy was too sick to fight with his father anymore. And his father was too proud to reach out to his son. Until, finally, early in September, Tom walked into Tommy's room.

"I said, 'Son, I can handle losing you to AIDS. But I don't want to lose you to a lack of communication.'"

"They made their peace," says Delma Lee.

"That was really something to see," says Gerry Tarr. "To see all that deep-rooted family turmoil that had been eating away at them for years, to see that resolved..."

And just in time. By mid-September the pneumonia had ravaged Tommy. It was all he could do to pull himself into a wheelchair, which he did the afternoon he asked Delma Lee to take him out to Doumar's drive-in restaurant.

"That was the last thing we did together," says Delma Lee. "Ate a Doumar's barbecue."

The next day, Tommy was taken to the hospital.

A week later, he died.

It is hard to say what there is to learn from AIDS.

This is a disease with no happy endings, no clear messages. It is a condition of loose-ends and answerless questions. So many questions.

For the family's friends and relatives, 150 of whom crowded the Wright house for Tommy's memorial service, the questions are about a disease that has not entered their own homes.

Delma Lee says plenty of friends visited her and her family during Tommy's final days: "Nobody was ever afraid to come in this house," she says. "Nobody was ever afraid to go up those stairs." But since Tommy died, friends have called Delma Lee to ask if she and her family now need to be tested for AIDS themselves.

"They really know nothing," she says.

The questions that haunt Delma Lee are the kind that lead her to the Scriptures. She tells herself there was a purpose in the pain of Tommy's life and in the way he died. "Maybe we were meant to go through this so other people could learn from it," she says.

"And I'll tell you this," she says. "It really opened Jimmy's eyes."

For Tom, the questions keep taking him back to Tommy's childhood, to what might have happened if he had been able to spend more time at home while his oldest son was growing up. "She tells me to forget the past," he says, nodding toward his wife. "But I can't. I won't."

For Gerry Tarr, the questions have forced him away from dealing so closely and directly with AIDS victims. He is giving up client services and devoting himself to AIDS education. The pain of this one, he says, was too much. "Tommy's death is the one that hit home the strongest," he says. "I feel like I lost a brother."

And Tommy? He had questions, too. He kept a journal the last year of his life. Among those pages were two passages. One was written last December:

Wow! Having AIDS is such a privilege. Every day is a learning experience. I mean all of a sudden life has taken on a brand new meaning. I'm associating with quality people who aren't afraid to be affectionate or open their hearts. I'm meeting people who are fighters—survivors. It's tearing my family apart from me—maybe this has to be done before we can be stronger.

The other was written in August.

Most of the time I just wish to die, not because I have given up but because it's getting harder and harder to deal with the family and friends. It's not them, it's me. Would you want to die slowly and deal with others as they start your funeral procession? That's what it is. Your funeral has begun. They've started down the path of saying goodbye—letting go. Their process of grief is long and hard, 'cause it's their staying that makes it worst.

November 15, 1987

III. SEARCHERS

The Peace Core

Philip Berrigan has only a half hour to talk. That's all they give him when he receives visitors at the Fredericksburg jail where he awaits sentencing next week for his Easter Sunday blood-and-hammer attack on the battleship Iowa in Norfolk.

A half hour. When you've been talking for 20 years and still no one is listening, how can a half hour possibly be enough? But Berrigan will take what he can get. He is used to working at a disadvantage. He knows how to adjust to circumstances, to adapt.

When his face was thrust into history two decades ago at a place called Catonsville, Berrigan wore the collar of a Roman Catholic priest. When he left prison after more than three years, married the woman he loved and went to Baltimore, where for the past 15 years he has shared an inner-city row house with his family and a rotating cast of young peace activists, his collar was gone and his uniform became a knit cap and baggy paint-spattered slacks.

When he is in jail, as he is on this summer afternoon, the white-haired peace warrior's uniform is a pair of pale blue prison pajamas.

He cringes at being labeled a patriarch. There are no *leaders* in a true community, he insists, and his seminal Baltimore household — an island of white faces among a sea of poor, urban blacks — is the archetype for the few pockets of active organized resistance scattered around the nation.

There are no leaders, he says, but Phil Berrigan can't help but appear as a king of conscience. Even in those pajamas, which he is used to wearing — he guesses he has been arrested 70 times and jailed 30 — Berrigan has what military men call command presence. His eyes shine with passion. He smiles easily, but his laughter is never light. It is irony that amuses him. His is the tolerant, understanding smile of a man who, surrounded by derision and indifference, remains sure of himself.

As Berrigan sits on a stool, speaking through the glass that separates prisoners from visitors in this jail, the two young men standing behind him — Andrew Lawrence and Greg Boertje, both arrested with Berrigan on the Iowa and both residents of that Baltimore house — appear as faithful foot soldiers, flanking their commander. Margaret McKenna, a nun from Philadelphia who was also arrested on the Iowa Easter morning, is in another section of the jail.

At 64, Berrigan looms tall and looks strong. When he is home, he climbs 40-foot ladders to paint wealthy suburbanites' houses, toiling alongside housemates half his age to bring the group what income it needs to survive. Like his housemates, he too digs through garbage dumpsters, collecting discarded food for his neighbors, his family and himself.

"It's a matter of survival," he says of the community he created in 1973, after emerging from prison and witnessing a landscape strewn with the remnants of revolution. While he was behind bars, the resistance had been broken. The streets had emptied. The movement had scattered and gone home.

"We saw very eminently how people had been chewed up by the war when they didn't have community. We found the culture made hamburger out of them. So we realized we had to rely on one another; otherwise, it would be all over for us."

In the time he has, his voice echoing off the tiled floor, Berrigan talks of Gandhi and the Gospel, of the seductiveness of property, of the cleverness of the Navy authorities who have minimized his public stage by charging him with a misdemeanor instead of a felony and by separating the sentencing dates of him and his three friends.

"We've seen the Navy wising up," he says. "They acted very, very quickly down in Norfolk. Very astutely."

He is asked if he imagined 20 years ago that he would be wearing prison pajamas today.

"A few of us foresaw that we'd be in and out of jail for the rest of our lives," he says. "Daniel Ellsburg put it very, very well, way back around the Pentagon Papers. He said, 'If we're *lucky*, we'll be doing this the rest of our lives. If we're *lucky*, we'll survive.'"

Finally he is asked why he stays at it when no one seems to care. Why keep talking if no one is listening? Why be a martyr if no one is watching?

He nods and smiles to questions he answered for himself 15 years ago, when he founded his small tribe of few but like-minded friends.

"The Bible speaks constantly of tiny groups of people, what are called remnants," he says, "that maintain fidelity to God and to other human beings by the strength they give one another".

For these four behind bars in Fredericksburg, that strength is found in a house 100 miles to the north.

The sky is black above Baltimore. Dawn is an hour away, but the windows of the Jonah House are already aglow.

They call this neighborhood Reservoir Hill, a standard slice of inner city — where the faces are dark, where life is lived minute to minute and careers are measured by the hour, where drugs are dealt by the front door and death is just around the corner.

It's not the sort of neighborhood where you'd expect to find a skinny little white man like John Heid — or any white man at all. But there he is, wearing his John Lennon spectacles and ear-to-ear smile, his hair pulled back in a ponytail, a bandanna hanging from the back pocket of his jeans, ushering you into the kitchen and offering you a bowl of cereal with wheat germ or maybe some fruit or at least a cup of coffee.

"Howya *doin'?*" he asks, bouncing around with a gleeful grin. He greets everyone that way. And he always grins.

A "Nuclear Free Zone" sticker in the living room window is the only hint to passersby that the people who live in this row house might be unlike their neighbors.

Inside, there is no doubt.

The walls rising to those high Victorian ceilings are papered with political posters and slogans of non-violence and civil disobedience. There are photo collages of protesters marching at the Pentagon, at the White House, at the applied physics lab of nearby Johns Hopkins University. Nailed above the living room archway is a piece of wood bearing the motto of the people who live here:

Illegitimi non carborundum

The occupants' translation: "Don't let the bastards grind you down."

There are children here. A tiny rocking chair sits by the front window. A My Little Pony puzzle is in the bookcase.

In the upstairs bathroom is a volume of Paramahansa Yogananda's "Metaphysical Meditations" — beside a copy of "Fred Flintstone's 'Double Rubble Trouble.'"

In the library, covered, against the wall, is an aged mimeograph machine, churner of countless leaflets. Across the room, uncovered and ready for action, is a state-of-the-art MacIntosh Plus computer.

There is a television in the living room, and on it sits a Bible. Above the Bible, on the wall, is a rack filled with back issues of Nuclear Times and Progressive magazines. On a shelf sits the household's videotape collection — a copy of "Jane Fonda's Workout Challenge" is mixed in with titles like "Ending the Silence: CD in the Farm Crisis," "Chicago 8 Trial" and "Trial of the Catonsville 9."

That last is a home movie of sorts in the Jonah House. A poster of Philip Berrigan and his brother Daniel, wearing their priest's garb and feeding a flaming pile of draft records outside the Catonsville, Md., Selective Service Office in 1968, hangs in the home's stairway. Printed on the poster are the words: *"Under a government which imprisons unjustly, the true place for a just man is also in prison. "*

If so, the men and women in this house are just.

John Heid, 31, a former Franciscan seminarian who has lived in the Jonah House since 1985, has been arrested nine times, for, among other things, blockading an entrance to the Pentagon, pouring ashes on the steps of the White House, hammering and tossing blood on three Trident II missile tubes in Rhode Island, and allegedly assaulting a federal officer at a grand jury hearing in Washington last month. The Trident attack earned him 10 1/2 months in prison. He is currently on probation in Rhode Island for that sentence. He is also on probation in Baltimore. And he is awaiting a trial date for the assault charge.

Dale Ashera-Davis, 34, a licensed practical nurse for 11 years, has been arrested 10 times, spending 12 days behind bars. Not impressive numbers compared to her housemates, but Ashera-Davis is just getting started — she has been at the Jonah House only a year. Her first arrest was for blocking traffic at the entrance of CIA headquarters in Langley last spring. Her last was for pouring blood in the office of Johns Hopkins University president Steven Muller last Thanksgiving. She has appealed a judge's order to pay for replacing the president's blood-stained carpet. A jury will decide on that appeal next month. She will go to jail rather than pay, she says.

Elizabeth McAlister, 48, a former Roman Catholic nun who was excommunicated along with Philip Berrigan when they married in 1973, has been arrested "between one and two dozen" times, she guesses. She breaks down her jail time into what she calls "overnights" (about 10), "weekends" ("a couple") and "served sentences" (three). The longest of those sentences was 25 months in a West Virginia federal prison for hammering and pouring blood on a B-52 bomber on Thanksgiving Day, 1983. Eleven years before that she faced possible life imprisonment as one of the Harrisburg Seven, charged with plotting to kidnap Henry Kissinger. The jury deadlocked, and a year later, when Berrigan emerged from prison after serving his Catonsville sentence, McAlister married him.

A week after that, the two moved into the Jonah House.

It is still black outside when Ashera-Davis stumbles downstairs. As she pours her coffee, The Pope leaps on her shoulders. The Pope is what the household has named its orange cat.

"We figured," Liz McAlister had explained the day before, "we needed a pope in the house."

Liz is asleep now, as are her daughters, Katy and Frida.

Katy, who knew how to read by age 4 because that was the only way she could understand the letters her mom wrote her from prison, is 6. In a recent issue of the home's quarterly newsletter, Katy wrote an account of police pulling her and other protesters off the roof of the lab at Johns Hopkins.

"We watched the sun rise," Katy wrote of the protest. "It was beautiful."

Frida, who wears floppy Benetton T-shirts, checkered Vans sneakers and braces on her teeth, is 14. She changes clothes four times a day "except when Dad's home." She just finished eighth grade as one of only two white children in her class. She is learning to swim this summer at the YMCA, which is a 10-block bike ride away — "but it's safe as long as you get home by dark." And her best friend lives in a Baltimore suburb called Reisterstown, which may as well be on the moon for all Frida knows about it.

"It's way out there somewhere," says Frida of the friend's house she has never been to.

Then there is 13-year-old Jerry, the only Berrigan boy, whose upstairs bedroom is decorated with photos of racing cars. Jerry is away, helping build a house on the Vermont farm of a former Jonah House member.

That leaves the three in jail: Andrew, Greg and Philip. When that group went on trial in May, the Jonah House joined a crowd of supporters gathered in the Norfolk courtroom to jeer the judge's guilty verdict. Court dates are always marked on the Reagan Countdown Calendar hanging in the Jonah House's dining room.

"It makes all the difference in the world to go into a courtroom with your community there as opposed to going in alone," says Ashera-Davis. "The system is big and scary enough when you go in alone, which is what most people have to do."

Sometimes there are risks. The day after the trial in Norfolk, a photo of John Heid holding a balloon and a poster outside the Norfolk Federal Court building appeared in cities across the country — including Baltimore, where the terms of Heid's probation include strict orders not to leave town.

"I guess," Heid says with a shrug and a grin, "my probation officer didn't see the paper that day."

Not that Heid is afraid of punishment. The whole point of living in this house is resistance, a commitment to non-violence, civil disobedience and total community. Everything here is shared — from the bank account, to the house painting jobs which are the home's sole source of income, to washing the dishes, to doing jail time, to the weekly food run, which Heid and Ashera-Davis are up for so early on this Tuesday morning.

The sun is rising in the rearview mirror as John and Dale and a friend named Lori Lindgren roar west on the interstate in a battered green pickup, headed toward a most unusual harvest.

As John drives, pushing the truck's engine to its cab-rattling limit, Dale opens the morning paper, outraged at a front-page story on Pentagon corruption. John, who wears a Minnesota Twins pin on his cap, is more interested in the sports section.

"I got into the Twins last year," he explains. "If the Twins can win the World Series, then the world can live without nuclear weapons."

John's personal peace odyssey began with the seven teenage years he spent in the seminary before he realized he "wanted to be more on the streets." He talks about going to college in West Virginia, then doing rural social work there, which is where he got into hunting, an odd hobby for a non-violent activitist.

"I know, I know," he says with a grin. "But living up in those mountains, you get this primordial urge to hunt. I loved to get up early in the morning, be in the woods all day long, waiting for animals for hours."

He still draws on those skills to surprise police officers when they arrest him.

"They're always amazed when I start talking with them about ammunition and armaments," he says. "Of course the difference is theirs is the kind of stuff you use on people."

John doesn't hunt anymore. It happened gradually, but there came a time when he could no longer pull the trigger. "My friends said, 'You're not able to kill anymore.' They weren't joking. And they were right."

When he moved to New York in 1983, John joined a study group on Nicaragua, traveled to that nation with a rural farm worker program and returned with a sense of what he calls "sustained outrage."

"I had always been against CD," he says of civil disobedience. "Too much tension, too much havoc. But seeing Nicaragua—the violence, the killing... You talk about turnarounds."

When he came back from that trip, says John, "my relationship with the law had changed. The years of Scripture I had studied suddenly came alive, with a different perspective on what justice is, what the law is, what the faithful person's responsibility is."

In 1984, John joined the Center for Creative Non-Violence in Washington D.C., where he volunteered for the group's food runs — which meant digging in dumpsters for salvageable garbage, a job he relished.

"All the other work there was intense, people-oriented, in shelters, in front of cameras," he explains. "The place was completely crazy. When I was in dumpsters was the only time in my waking hours that I was alone. I found it a perfect time for meditation and prayer."

When he came to the Jonah House in 1985, John found he didn't have to leave dumpstering behind. Because the home is as committed to its poor neighbors as it is to attacking nuclear weapons, its members make a weekly trip to a suburban produce distribution center, filling their truck with discarded vegetables and fruit, two-thirds of which are passed out to their neighbors and a third of which is kept by the house.

"Howya *doin'*?" John shouts at a guard as he wheels the truck onto the grounds of the Maryland Wholesale Food Center, a multi-acre complex of warehouses and loading docks, forklifts and tractor-trailers filled with fresh produce headed for supermarkets throughout the Baltimore area.

But the Jonah House truck is not here for the fresh stuff. You have to pay for that. What's in the dumpsters is free, if you can get it out before the trash trucks arrive. So John wastes no time leaping to it. Before Dale and Lori are out of the truck, John is rummaging along the loading dock, locked into the thrill of a different sort of hunt.

"*Aha!!*" he shouts, sorting through cases of bashed broccoli and bruised tomatoes and pulling out a flat of near perfect strawberries.

"We've got a *gold mine* down here," he shouts from an alleyway, pointing to cases of foul-smelling cabbage and half-molded raspberries.

Dale is a little more reserved.

"It takes some getting used to," she says, picking through a pile of soft, smelly potatoes. "If it was 10 degrees hotter, we'd all be breathing through our mouths.

"But in some respects," she adds with a shrug, "this is every little kid's dream."

John stops to exult over a killdeer on a nearby fence, just the way he was awed by a mockingbird perched on a neighborhood antenna earlier that morning. "I look for the *little* things in the city," he says. "I learned how to look for the little things in jail."

Some of the dock workers cast wary glances at the strange little guy with long hair and the two women picking through the garbage. But most of the workers are used to the people from Jonah House.

"Occasionally we get verbally assaulted," says John.

"They'll say, 'How come you're always taking stuff away,'" says Dale, "'and you never *bring* anything?'"

"I say, 'Listen,'" says John, "'I'm not taking *anything* from you. I'm taking it from a dumpster. *You're* throwing it away.'"

John admits this is a side of the peace movement that is hard for many people to understand. The images on television and in newspapers show men and women led away in handcuffs, preaching to juries and turning their backs on judges, stepping into prison cells with a strength and serenity that puzzles their jailers. Soldiers of peace fighting the good fight. Proud. Devoted. Defiant.

But how to explain the garbage? Where is the pride in digging through a dumpster of dirty vegetables? Where is the honor in crawling on your hands and knees through a pile of spilled, slimy potatoes? Where is the connection between begging for bruised bananas and banning the bomb?

The connection, says John, is waste, excess, misdirected resources. The madness that makes nuclear weapons, he says, is the same madness that throws away a flat of savable strawberries.

"We're beyond the point where we can afford, in any sense of the word, to live any way but communally," he says. "We're communal creatures, but everything in our society militates against that.

"In our society as it is, to even *live* in a community, without any actions at all, is active resistance in itself."

By now the truck is filled.

"This is a *marvelous* haul," says John, climbing into the cab. "The best in months."

Twenty minutes later, the threesome is two blocks from home, where they park and pull out the food they plan to keep for themselves—a box of onions, for instance.

"Frida's been agitating for onion rings," says Dale.

And a basket of red potatoes, which Lori, a 24-year-old nurse at a public health clinic, will bring back to the Lutheran community house in which she lives.

A week's worth of fruit and vegetables for the Jonah House is set aside, then the group heads home, where a crowd of two dozen elderly black men and women collects on the corner, plastic bags tucked under their arms, eager to see what the green truck has brought them this Tuesday morning.

They are patient, orderly. They stand back and chat as John, Dale and Lori — and Frida, who has come out to help — unload the haul and lay it along the sidewalk. Finally John gives the word, and in a matter of minutes the food is gone.

Then so is the crowd, vanishing as quickly and quietly as it arrived.

None of the kids she knows gives Frida any trouble about her family or the way they live. Well, none of them but Willie Hawkins, back in the fifth grade.

"He found out somehow that Mom was in jail," says Frida. "He went around saying she was in for drugs. But that didn't last long."

Frida is in the dining room, helping Dale sort through the morning haul, washing the food they'll keep. The two begin talking about some of the harsher realities beyond the front door. Like the 10-year-old girl who was abducted in February and turned up dead in an alley.

"Right across the street," says Frida, tossing a pepper into a bowl. "It was real cold."

"It was real *hot* in the church," says Dale. "We went to the funeral."

Then there was the night everyone was sitting in the living room, gathered for one of their frequent house meetings, when there was some commotion outside the window.

"This guy fell down the steps over there," says Frida, pointing toward the street. "He got stabbed. Dad went over and helped. I think he died."

Some nights, Dale, whose bedroom overlooks the street, has a hard time staying asleep. Like just the other morning.

"It was 5 o'clock," she says, "and people were already out, going nuts, going crazy, shrieking and hollering over something. And it wasn't even hot yet."

The heat, says Dale, has a way of emptying these row houses.

"Stoop-setting," says Dale. "That's how you get by in the heat, in the city."

Frida says there's plenty to do here. She likes playing Hacky Sack out on the sidewalk with John. Then there's the Y. And sometimes she goes to movies with the adults.

"It's different from the way any of my friends live," she says, "but I kinda like it. I like being different. There are always new and weird and different people coming in.

"I think it would be boring just having Jerry and Katy to play with and Mom and Dad working — if we were a normal five- person family. This way there's always somebody home, somebody who will play or go out to the park or just talk with us."

She tosses another pepper in the bowl.

"I'd like to live in the country," she says.

"But with *everybody*."

It's mid-afternoon, and Liz McAlister is now at the wheel of the truck, depositing a check in the home's saving account, then driving toward the city's food bank. Frida is in the back, the wind blowing through her hair as the pickup weaves through a maze of busy downtown streets.

Liz. She could be anybody's mom, in her jeans and sneakers and pink sweatshirt. Her hair — darker and longer when she was a nun — is now short and as white as her husband's. Her eyes are as strong as his, her voice as sure. Maybe it comes from a quarter century on the ramparts, but Liz is as undeniably a leader of this household as her husband. With Phil in prison, Liz's is the home's voice of seasoned wisdom. Despite their insistence on equality, the others constantly defer to her.

She chain-smokes Winstons, a habit she's tried to kick more times than she can count. But the cigarettes are the only thing in her life for which Liz apologizes.

So much has happened since she moved into this house. She has had three babies. She has been to prison. She has watched 40 housemates come and go. Only a handful stayed as long as five years. Most last no more than three. The ones who leave are often referred to by those who remain as "casualties." But Liz is kinder.

"I think that's jumping to conclusions before the evidence is in," she says. "Many of them are out there, still at it, doing really good work."

As for the others, the ones who have retreated into marriages, families and careers, leaving the resistance behind, Liz understands.

"This culture is insidious and it's seductive," she says. "Trying to stand against it, to sustain, is really tough. We all need a lot of help to do it. Keeping at it is not easy, especially when we don't see much evidence of a turn for the better."

Liz has kept at it, even after her church disowned her, after the college where she taught art history fired her, after her own twin sister, the wife of a career Army officer, forsook her. Marrying Phil and committing to a life of fighting war has had its price.

"It was very rough," says Liz of the transition 20 years ago. "It was full of all kinds of traumas."

Such as her and her husband's excommunication.

"There was a time when I was concerned if Phil was a priest. But I've come to realize we are *all* priests. As Paul said, we are a 'priestly people,' irrespective of age and sex."

The Bible is the foundation of this house. They read from it before dinner each night. They study and discuss it each Wednesday. They have liturgy on Sundays. The church is still the basis of Liz and Phil's life, even if they are not a part of its.

"Those are the roots out of which we've come," says Liz. "That's who we are."

Being shunned by her own family was not easy, but it's a struggle Liz says most people of the peace culture must go through.

"You get over their initial shock," she says of traditional family and friends. "You make a few assays at trying to convince them, then you realize you have to live it out. If anything is going to convince people, that will.

"That's most true with the people who are closest to us—our parents, our siblings. We aren't going to change them by what we say to them. We change them by what we *do*."

Which, says Liz, is why delivering food to the poor is as vital for a person of conscience as marching in a rally.

"I don't think you can keep that up," she says of protests and arrests, "unless you remain in touch with the human dimensions, with the suffering that accrues from a top-sided military preoccupation. You need that touch with reality, otherwise your resistance becomes very cerebral, very divorced— then it stops.

"Where you see the continuity, the pockets of resistance, is where people are keeping in touch with the poor, acting out that reality."

As for the reality of bringing up her children in a place like Reservoir Hill, Liz admits it's not easy.

"It's tough for anyone to raise kids in the city. They need ever so much more watchful attention than in a suburban or rural setting. This is *not* a safe neighborhood for kids."

She says her children are "gifted" by the special people who have come and gone in their lives. But Liz has no idea whether Frida and Jerry and Katy will be better adults for that upbringing.

"There's no way we can know," she says. "My sense, my hope, is they'll be better off. But I don't think anyone anywhere can say with any assurance what will happen with kids. How do they put it in 'The Fantasticks'? *Plant a cabbage, get a cabbage, not a Brussels sprout. When you deal with vegetables, you know what you're about.*

"Kids," says Liz, "aren't vegetables."

Evening, and the jarred, canned and boxed goods from the food bank are put away, some stored for the household, most packed and ready to hand out Thursday morning. Dinner will be an interesting mixture tonight: a spinach souffle, salad and strawberries, all from the dumpsters, and Frusen Gladje ice cream from the food bank. Pints of the ice cream are stacked in the freezer—next to a supply of blood stored in baby bottles, blood that house members draw from their own veins.

Tonight, as so often in this household, there are guests—a group of Catholic Worker volunteers up from Washington to plan protests in that city marking the August anniversaries of the bombings of Hiroshima and Nagasaki. They plan banners and chanting, singing and street theater, and, depending on whose schedule will allow, arrests. Much of this night's discussion will center on which Pentagon entrance would be best to block, and who might be willing to throw blood.

The D.C. group — three men, a woman and a baby — gathers on the stoop out front. The grownups discuss how they will make it down to Norfolk for four different sentencing dates, and they talk about the movement's latest news — the previous Sunday's attack by four members of a New York City peace group on the USS Pennsylvania submarine in Groton, Conn. The foursome had approached the sub by raft, but were stopped and arrested before they reached their target. Among those arrested was a 60-year-old woman named Anne Montgomery, a woman everyone in this group apparently knows.

"I can see Anne getting stopped in that raft," laughs one of the men from D.C.

"So can I," says Liz. "We spent two years together in prison."

The group moves in for dinner, gathering around the living room as Katy sits next to her mother, a Bible on her lap. Shadows fill the room as Katy, in a soft, sure voice, reads from The Acts, Chapter 3:

"... Then Peter said, silver and gold have I none, but such as I have give I thee..."

Outside, a Cadillac crawls past, rap music blaring from its stereo. Shouts echo from down the block. A siren wails in the distance.

Night falls on the city.

July 10, 1988.

The Dead Zone

Noon Sunday and Hampton Coliseum was already awash in a sea of Dead. Waves of tie-dyed T-shirts rippled across the asphalt. The tinkle of tambourines drifted through the air, along with the thick, sweet smell of incense and dope. Everything on wheels — from a schoolbus splashed with Day-Glo rainbows to a unicycle perched beneath a pantalooned cosmic cowboy — was plastered with stickers.

Happiness is Dancing With the Dead, read one. Around it swayed a dozen bodies, moving to unheard melodies, making love to the midday sun.

Nobody Does it Deader, read another. The license plate was from Utah. To the right was a van with Michigan plates. To the left, a Bug from Massachusetts.

Greatfully Deadicated, read another. This was stuck to a tree, lovingly guarded by a bell-jingling, bubble-blowing teenager with a smile on her lips and peace symbols painted on her cheeks.

Yes, spring arrived last weekend, and that means the Grateful Dead have once again hit town, bringing with them about 5,000 of their on-the-road faithful—men, women and babies who have left homes, jobs and families to bounce from city to city, a billowing throng of pilgrims following rock's most timeless act to what they call "never ever land," a long, strange trip that picked up Sunday with a three-night stand in Hampton, traditionally the first stop on the band's spring tour.

Nighttime was when the Dead took the stage. But the show itself began at sunup, when the coliseum parking lot gates were opened. It lasted until past midnight, when the psychedelic twangs of Jerry Garcia's guitar were still resonating in the brains of the Deadheads drifting out into the moonlit night, back to their tents, vans and motel rooms, where they hurried the dawn, praying for clear weather in the morning and hoping they could score another ticket for the next night's show.

These are the flower children who won't go away. They are graybeards who boarded the Grateful Dead bus back in 1965, when the band was entertaining Ken Kesey and his Merry Pranksters in a forest outside San Francisco. And they are children who weren't even born when the Dead took the stage at Woodstock. They are activists who march for peace and hear their universal message in the music of this band. And they are cosmic drifters whose only aim is to cut the anchors, to float as far and as long as they can, riding the currents of energy within the time-warped bubble that surrounds the tribe gathered for each of these tours.

"It's not really a time warp," says Dennis McNally, who became the band's publicist after Garcia read McNally's biography of Beat novelist Jack Kerouac and asked McNally to steer the Dead's ship.

"It's a *reality* warp," McNally continues. "It's like (Dead drummer) Mickey Hart once said: The Grateful Dead aren't in the entertainment business. They're in the *transportation* business — They move minds."

Jason's mind was moved six years ago. That's when the Syracuse University student saw his first Dead concert. He was 12 then. He's 18 now, a veteran of more than 100 Dead shows. He's followed them from coast to coast, putting a crimp in his college career.

"It's kinda hard to say what year I am," says Jason, who drove down from Syracuse Friday night. "Maybe a sophomore or thereabouts. I've seen a lot of Dead shows, and that's cramped my grades a little bit."

Jason was standing on the interstate exit ramp by the Coliseum, one of a dozen scattered hopefuls flagging down traffic, begging for a ticket, knowing all three shows were sold out but counting on the "Miracle" all ticketless Deadheads live for. He wore a scarf tied around his scraggly red hair, a wool parka over his shoulders and tie-dyed pajama pants on his legs — all standard Deadhead garb. And his answer to why his life is geared to the Grateful Dead was also standard.

"It's magic," said Jason. "I mean, you can't describe it in words. You just have to see the light."

The light has been shining for 22 years. That's how long it has been since Jerry Garcia, Bob Weir, Bill Kreutzmann, Phil Lesh and Ron "Pigpen" McKernan became the Grateful Dead. They have recorded "between 15 and 20" albums, says McNally. "It's hard to draw the line," he explains, "between the things they do on their own and the things they do as a group."

But the Dead do not live on vinyl. It is on stage that they set themselves apart, where not only each show, but each *song*, is never played the same way twice. They have performed 1,700 concerts since 1965, playing more than 400 different songs. They have played beneath the Pyramids in Egypt, They have played at Liberace's Aladdin Theater in Las Vegas. Next year they plan to play on the Great Wall of China. The space shuttle, chuckles McNally, is "not out of the question."

It is easier to describe where the Dead play than what they play. In his 1968 book, "The Electric Kool-Aid Acid Test," Tom Wolfe put it this way:

"The Dead's weird sound! agony-in-ecstasis! submarine somehow, turbid half the time, tremendously loud but like sitting under a waterfall, at the same time full of sort of ghoul-show vibrato sounds as if each string on their electric guitars is half a block long and twanging in a room full of natural gas..."

Two years later, David Crosby, of Crosby, Stills, Nash and Young gave it his best shot in a *Rolling Stone* magazine interview:

"I don't know what it is, man. Like, they're magic. Something happens when the Dead gets it on that don't happen when Percy Faith gets it on."

Pigpen is gone now, a 1973 victim of what McNally calls "a bluesman's death" — a body worn down by alcohol. But the rest of the original band, along with Hart and keyboardist Brent Mydland, live on, apparently ageless. Three are in their 40s. All but Weir are married and have children. Jerry Garcia, thick around the middle and gray on top but healthy again after a life- threatening bout with diabetes, has two teenage daughters. Fans his own age slap stickers on their bumpers that read "Jerry's Kids." A national gourmet ice cream chain released a new flavor early this year: Cherry Garcia.

And still he climbs on stage in a plain black T-shirt and jeans, lights flashing off his wire-rims, his head bowed toward his guitar strings as his high-pitched voice brings his listeners the same strange mixture of mellowness and intensity they felt when they crowded the streets of Haight-Ashbury during 1967's Summer of Love to hear the Dead play off the back of a flatbed truck.

"These are not rock'n'roll stars," says McNally. "They don't do tours to flog records. They're not even performers in a conventional sense. They're musicians who like to play. And they still don't decide what to play or how to play it until they get up there. It's honest music, and the audience recognizes it."

But Deadheads are no more an "audience" than the band are per-formers. The line between stage and seats is a thin one, the relationship a curious blend of worship and respect. "It is a communion between equals," suggested a 1981 Melody Maker magazine story, "a true folk relationship in the sense that the band speaks *for* the audience rather than *at* them."

"We have this sort of continuum," Garcia told Rock magazine in 1972, "which is good for us and it's good for the audience, a kind of continuity — from off the street to outer space, so to speak."

Somewhere between those two points is Bill Chengelis. As the sun moved west Sunday afternoon, Chengelis stood outside a van covered with the T-shirts he sells to keep him on the road with the Dead. At 36, the gray-haired veterinarian's assistant has seen "a year" of Grateful Dead concerts — 365 to be exact. It took him and four traveling companions two weeks, with a stop in Arizona, to drive from their San Francisco home to Hampton for the opener of this spring's six-city junket.

"I usually do the summer tour," said Chengelis, who first saw the Dead at Woodstock in 1969 and eventually moved from his Colorado home to the Bay area to be closer to the group.

"This is an extended family," he said, sharing hugs and beers with a steady stream of passersby. "And I wanted to part of it. It's always like a reunion. The audience, the band, you know, *everybody's* the Grateful Dead."

Everybody, that is, except Chengelis's parents.

"They ask me how can I *do* this. I tell them they go on a cruise trip every year, land in a port, everyone gets off, then they climb back on together and move to the next port. For them it's the Bahamas, for me it's the Dead."

Chengelis pointed to the stickers and buttons all around him, most bearing the classic Grateful Dead symbols: skulls and lightning bolts, dancing skeletons and roses. He raised his voice as a Dead tape boomed out of the van behind him.

"Some people think this is all about the devil or something like that. They couldn't be more wrong. The lifestyle, what the music's telling you to do — there are values there. This whole experience is just like the song 'Box of Rain' — this is all a gift from God. If you need it, believe it. If not, fine. Just pass it on."

A couple lying in the grass down the way from Chengelis passed a tightly rolled joint back and forth while a man sitting across the sidewalk looked as anti-drug as a government pamphlet. All three wore feathers in their hair.

"There is no definitive Deadhead," said Toby, a bearded auto parts dealer from Philadelphia. He was strolling the parking lot, hawking handmade jewelry along with his wife Susan, a nursing assistant. Toby, 29, looked like a sandaled, woolly bear. Susan was draped in the peasant garb of an earth mother. Between them, said Toby, they see 35 Dead shows a year.

"She's got a paid vacation," he explained, "and I've got a boss who understands my habit."

For Grant Stewart, the Dead are less a habit than an occasional treat. He works with "troubled" kids in Amherst, Mass. A dozen of them brought him along with them for the Hampton show. They had tickets. He didn't.

"I really don't care," said the 59-year-old, shaking his gray ponytail and clutching a red bedroll as he strolled outside the Coliseum. "It's fun watching people."

Stewart first heard of the Dead in prison, where he spent 11 years, from 1959 to 1970. "Armed robbery," he said. "A bum rap. I was framed. But then I compounded it. I escaped."

"I missed the '60s," he continued. "But I've had a good time for the last 17 years."

Deadheads tend to talk about their first concert in near-mystical terms, and Stewart is no different. His was in 1972, in New York City.

"It was very special. I took about 30 kids. And it *moved* me. I've seen about 30 shows since, and I like 'em. They're the only band that makes we wanna dance."

Stephanie, a 17-year-old with long, brown hair and wide, brown eyes, would have liked to dance. But her 4-week-old daughter Kaya was strapped to her chest, napping as Stephanie and a 23-year-old woman named Kerri walked toward their van. As Stephanie tended to her baby, Kerri explained how she discovered what the initiated call their Deadhead identity.

"I was in college back in Massachusetts," she said. "I was pretty politically active, doing guerilla theater. And I was skeptical of this whole Deadhead scene — the drugs, why somebody would spend their whole life doing this. But I got really burnt out with the politics, and this helped me ease up. It helped me forget my anger. It's so free. The carnival atmosphere, the dancing, the spirituality. It's like therapy."

"There's only so much you can take of the world," agreed Stephanie. "Then it's time to go home to the Dead."

When they reached the van, Stephanie handed Kaya to a man named Sunshine. Sunshine is 23. He met Stephanie two years ago at a Dead concert in Tampa. The two split up for a while, but got back together before their baby was born. Sunshine has "been touring" with the Dead for two years now, working odd jobs back in Massachusetts to support himself. Now he has Stephanie and the baby to take care of, but his only worry about the future seems to be the future of the Dead.

"I don't like what's happening," he said, nodding toward the festooned salesmen hawking everything from beads to balloons. "People have gotten greedy. Look at the guy with the Not Fade Away dye company. He started out just selling Dead T-shirts. Now he's incorporated and doing Motley Crue."

Sunshine handed the baby back to Stephanie, who climbed into the cramped van to change a diaper.

"The hardcoreness is fading," he said. "It's dwindled down to money, to Z-28s and staying at the top of the Hilton. That's who's showing up here now. The mood is changing. It's weird."

It wasn't a Z-28, but it was close. A turbo-charged, fuel-injected Toyota FX-16 GTS, slick and black as oil and sleek as a new bullet.

"Brand new," said the man sitting next to it. His name was Bill. He said he had only been in the parking lot an hour, yet he was parked in a prime spot, next to the Coliseum's front doors.

"Handicapped," he said, pointing at the sticker on his car.

"Wooden," he said, pointing at his left leg.

"'Nam," he said, pulling a soft drink out of a cooler.

Sitting in his metal lawn chair, wearing a sportshirt, Windbreaker and Top Siders, Bill looked more ready for a church picnic than a Dead concert.

"Well, this is a picnic, in a manner of speaking," he said. He had never seen the Dead. But his girlfriend Luzy had, 113 times. He is 39. She is 21. They met at Christopher Newport College. Bill knew nothing about the Dead until Luzy played him her records and told him her stories. Now he was here to find out for himself, and he was already having a hard time believing what he was seeing: the psychedelic swirl of sights, sounds and smells.

"She'd told me about these people," he said. "But I could not believe you could put this many people in this small an area and have it be as laid back as this."

Bill wasn't seated 10 minutes before Luzy had pinned Dead buttons to his shirt and jacket and wrapped a knitted trinket around his neck.

"When in Rome," shrugged Bill. Luzy took a seat, wrapping her peasant dress around her legs and explaining the Deadness she discovered in 1984.

"It blew my mind," she said. "I felt like I'd come home. I've always considered myself in a time warp anyway. The hippies, Haight-Ashbury — I've always felt like a part of that, and that's what this is."

Luzy talked about her father, a Presbyterian minister. She described the peace activist groups she has worked with, the marches she has joined. "A lot of people look at Deadheads as dropouts, as people who don't care about anything," she said. "But we're probably some of the most political people you can find.

"And there are more of us now than ever. What's happening in America lately has brought more people to the Dead. They're being driven away by the missiles and the lies and the limited nuclear war crap."

"That's it," said Bill, stretching his good leg as late afternoon shadows crawled across his chair. "From when I stepped out of the car and looked around, it's been like, wow, 1965, back before the world got ugly."

But the world got ugly Sunday night.

By the time the Coliseum doors opened at 6 p.m., more than 1,000 people in the parking lot had found their tickets were counterfeit. For them there were no miracles. As the 13,800 Deadheads inside went about their pre-concert business, many of them setting up directional microphones to tape the show — the Dead encourage fans to tape their concerts and tape-trading is a major Deadhead pasttime — the cheated mob outside grew restless. A window was smashed. A door was pulled off its hinges. A security man who has worked Dead concerts for four years put his ear to a crackling walkie talkie and shook his head.

"We have never, *never* had this problem with a Grateful Dead crowd before," he said. "I don't know what's gotten into them. I just don't understand it."

After an announcement warning the audience about the bogus tickets and threatening that the band might not return to Hampton if the problem continues, the lights went down and the Dead took the stage, kicking into "Hell In a Bucket" and sending the Deadheads reeling in ecstasy. The people twirling in the hallways outside did not notice the police grab one gatecrasher, then another, struggling to carry them out of the Coliseum. The arrest count finally totaled 20: two for drunk and disorderly conduct, six for trespassing and 12 for possession of drugs.

Outside, the scene was like a war zone. The concrete was littered with broken bottles. An upset throng reluctantly moved backward as police with dogs and a cruiser with a bullhorn pushed them toward the parking lot, which now looked like a refugee camp. The long, strange trip seemed to be taking an unwanted turn.

"I don't believe this," said one of the crowd.

"Dogs, man, *dogs!*" said another, shaking his head and hitting his tambourine with his fist.

Three tired students from Washington, D.C., sat on a curb, rolling a joint and shaking their heads.

"First Georgetown loses," said one, referring to a weekend basketball game. "Then this."

"What a crappy weekend."

March 24, 1987

Timothy Leary Is NOT Dead

This is what the den must have looked like before Daniel stepped in.

Only this time the lions are Christians, a television studio full of them, clutching their Bibles and sharpening their teeth as they await the arrival of none other than that acid-eating avatar of chemical enlightenment, that high head priest of psilocybic searching, that tripping, quipping master of microdots, that pioneering pilot of inner space... can we have something in the way of a sitar, please?... the one, the only, the ever effervescent, never evanescent Dr. Timothy Leary.

But where is he?

It's a half-hour past meal... um, showtime, and the crowd is getting restless. About a hundred of them have huddled here on this hot Tuesday night, eager to become the audience for a two-hour taping of the Christian Broadcasting Network's soon-to-be-nationally-syndicated program "Straight Talk." This is a big show tonight, one they'll be pitching coast-to-coast come November, and they've pulled out the stops, latching on to that hottest, hippest and most happening of topics: The Sixties.

Roger McGuinn will be here, looking back on his 10-year flight with The Byrds. Barry McGuire is on the docket to discuss his personal "Eve of Destruction." And Mark Lindsay, of Paul Revere and the Raiders, is on line too, with the confessions of a re-routed raider.

That's the thing. This whole crew is re-routed. They have, in the born-again vernacular, "come in." They are Christians, each and every one. But Timothy Leary, rest assured, is no Christian, although he was once a Catholic, later a Hindu, and has evangelized with the best of them, spreading his psychedelic gospel throughout the '60s, preaching in the name of his "League for Spiritual Discovery" (that's right—LSD).

That's why these righteous heads are craning, seeking a peek at the unrelenting, unrepenting drug devil come all the way from his home in Beverly Hills to Pat Robertson's Virginia Beach command center with something — but *what*? — to say.

What can Leary possibly say that will make sense of his kaleidoscopic past: of the hundreds of Harvard students whose heads he fed when he was a professor there in the early 1960s, before he was canned for his indiscretions in 1963; of his subsequent meanderings through Mexico and Massachusetts and finally the Catskills, setting up acid wonderlands all along the way, guiding his guests through juiced-up journeys they hoped would bring them face-to-face with God Himself; of his 1970 sentencing for possession of marijuana and his escape later that year, when he hopped the fence of a low-security prison, leaped into a getaway car full of Weathermen and ended up in Algiers living with exiled Black Panther chief Eldridge Cleaver; of the three years he eventually served in Folsom Prison after federal narcotics agents caught up with him in Afghanistan in 1978; and finally, of the fact that the man who has written books with titles like *The Politics of Ecstasy* and *Confessions of a Hope Fiend* is now totally, dare we say *religiously*, sold on — hold your breath and hide your diskettes — computer software?

Turn on. Tune In. Drop Out...

Boot up?

At last, 40 minutes past showtime, the taping is set to begin. The other guests are miked, and there, out of the studio shadows, steps the main course.

But *look* at him! Why, he's nothing but a little old man. He looks so frail in that coffee-colored coat and tie. His short-cropped hair is silver. And isn't that a *hearing aid* in his right ear?

Maybe it's been longer than we thought. Maybe we remember the 1960s Timothy Leary with his caftan robes and ponytail and forget that even then he was nearly three decades out of West Point, where he did his first dropping out as a cadet in 1941. Maybe we forget how the years fly by, until suddenly we're cold-cocked by a fact like this:

On his next birthday, Timothy Leary turns 70.

For just a moment, this crowd of Christians, showing proper respect for an elder, lets down its guard.

For just a moment.

But then Leary climbs — no, *bounces* — up on that set, begins mugging with McGuinn, chatting with the technicians, looking like nobody's grandpa in those sassy white sneakers and socks—the *idea* of wearing sneakers with a suit—and the stage is set once again.

"Will you just *look* at him?" hisses a woman in the third row. "At his age," clucks another.

Yes, look at him. Look into those twin black pools they call the windows of the soul and imagine what's transpired behind them in the past 29 years and easily a thousand acid excursions— a thousand, mind you, and still counting.

The doctor, you see, is still checking out—way out. Or in, if you'd prefer. He's not doing it as often as in his hallucinogenic heyday, but, yes, Timothy Leary still trips.

He talked about that — and much more — in a CBN waiting room before the taping. If his brain has been broiled from all that illicit ingestion — and what more likely candidate for the ravages of LSD than the king of the hallucinogenic hill? — there are no visible signs. Once you get over the obvious marks of age — the liver spots on those active hands, for example — it's hard to believe this man is nearly 70. He fills a room with his energy and compulsive curiosity, quizzing the CBN folks about the biblical artwork on the walls and turning an interview into a tennis match, asking as many questions as he answers.

One of those questions is how many times he's taken LSD.

"That's like asking how many times I've made love," says Leary, whose current wife, his fourth, is 38. "The basic answer, of course, is not enough."

His only bow to time, says Leary, is that his rate of chemical consumption has slowed: "During the early '60s, I was experiencing psychedelic sessions, oh, about once a week. That's always considered to be the maximum. We were told by the biologists that the neurological effects of LSD took about six or seven days to dissipate.

"More recently," he says, "it's been maybe once a month, or sometimes once a quarter."

He understands how the mere thought of taking all that acid all those years might be hard for some to swallow. But Leary says there's no way to compare what he's done with what anyone else out there might think they know about this drug.

"You simply cannot talk about LSD anymore," he says. "Since 1966, when it was made illegal, nobody knows what they've taken. Ninety-nine percent of the people who thought they were taking LSD were taking something some amateur chemist made in a garage someplace. I would say half the black market substances passed around as LSD were not LSD at all — it was just speed or something like that.

"So," he says, catching his breath with a slight, elderly wheeze, "it would be highly irresponsible to say anything about LSD under the impression that it even really exists."

But Leary adds that the real thing continues to exist for him.

"I'm in a very fortunate position," he says. "I'm in touch with the greatest biochemist in the world. I'm not dealing with some kid in a dormitory saying, 'Here, try this.' And I'm *extremely* prudent and conscientious and careful."

Still, the stuff is illegal. But Leary doesn't bat either of his shiny eyes at the possibility of another arrest.

"If they want to do that," he says of the ever-hovering authorities, "what can I do?"

What he does is hit the road 50 or so times a year for appearances like this, where he "performs philosophy," as he puts it. When he's back home, Tim Leary is just another L.A. sports junkie and computer entrepreneur — the latter, thanks to a couple of his four grandchildren.

"I used to like to go to the Dodger games on Saturdays," he explains. "But the kids would drag me down to these dark video arcades. I'm watching them play these things, back about 1980 or so, and I'm bored. So I take a quarter and start to play, and I realize that in Pac-Man or in Space Invaders, you could take away what's on the screen — the spaceship or whatever — and just as well replace it with Einsteinian theory or chemistry or 'Hamlet.' You could play *history* on these things. That was a great conversion for me."

Suddenly, the artist who had spent decades painting with chemicals on the canvas of consciousness had discovered another doorway into — and more importantly, back *out* of — the brain.

"Mind-opening foods, drugs and yogic techniques can help you access sectors of your brain that are not usually accessible," he says.

It was that sort of access he was probing in the early '60s at Harvard, with the blessing of the university, a grant from the state government and free samples of Sardoz Pharmaceuticals LSD air-delivered from the company's Swiss laboratories.

"When we were experimenting with psychedelic or mind-opening drugs at Harvard, the only way we could express our experiences was with the metaphors of the past, from Oriental mysticism on forward. We were having experiences that could not be *expressed* with standard language. We didn't have the digital language of computers, which is the language of the brain."

If they had, says Leary, the history of the '60s — at least *his* history — would have been different.

"If we had had personal computers back then, we would have immediately started hooking our internal experiences to this visible way of expressing them. We would have used the drugs, but we would have expressed the visions through the *computer*. And all those countercul-ture B-movie adventures might never have happened."

Leary nearly leaps out of his seat describing the current frontiering work being done in computer cyber-wear — components that are actually worn by the user, linking physical movements and, conceivably, ultimately, even thoughts directly to the machine. The software company Leary founded three years ago, creating and marking an interactive game called Mind Movies and a self-analysis program called Mind Mirror, now has moved into classroom teaching programs with names like Head Coach. All of it, he says, is aimed at what he calls "controlling the screen," which, in one way or another, has been Leary's goal for the last 30 years.

"My entire life's efforts have been toward empowering the *individual*, to encourage the individual to keep growing and evolving," he says. "It's a matter of control. There's freedom of the press for him who owns the press, for the programmers, and right now that means the tube. He who controls the tube controls society."

That control, says Leary, is lately, literally, at hand.

"With the new software and hardware, any individual can control the screen, can determine what goes on up there. Now *that* is explosive, subversive stuff."

Subversion. Even with the shift from hallucinogens to high-tech, Leary still speaks the language of the radical.

"My role," he says with a chuckle, "has always been the dissident philosopher, to subvert whoever is in power and is controlling the educational system as the evolution increases."

And make no mistake about it, says Leary. The evolution — read *re*volution — that churned through the '60s continues to ripple into the near-'90s.

"The '60s are still happening all over the globe," he says. "Look at China. For a wonderful three weeks there, the kids in China took what they had learned from the Abbie Hoffmans of the world, how to control the screen using headbands and peace signs. And notice what the Chinese communists did to control the screen. They just turned it off.

"I learned so much about America from that. Bill Walton pointed that out to me a month ago."

That's Bill Walton, the basketball star, a New Age aberration on the courts of the NBA and a die-hard Grateful Dead fan who has towed his friend Timothy Leary to many a Dead concert.

"We were talking," says Leary, "and he said, 'All those Chinese students want is to choose their own major." Now *that's* a profound statement.

"I've been running around for 29 years doing this, and Walton comes up with the perfect phrase."

Choosing a major is one thing. Dropping out is another. But Leary says the advice he issued to a generation was misunderstood by most. To him, dropping out has always meant tuning the machinery, not shutting it down.

"You're supposed to drop in and out at least a hundred times a *day*," he says. "You've got to constantly adjust your mental equipment. You know, when you're piloting a plane and you have a map, you have to continually drop out and reboot. You have to continually be adjusting where you are, taking navigational coordinates. You're continually changing your strategy: 'Oh, here's a storm coming up.' 'Hey there's a 707 at 3 o'clock'. 'Oh, my Lord, here comes the blond woman I've been waiting for all my life.'"

Leary is all over the room now, meshing this image of individual flight in the '80s with the group formation that apparently was taking place in the '60s. But the Woodstock Nation, he is quick to point out, was not nearly as united — or active — as history might have us believe.

"Of the 76 million baby-boomers that came of age between 1966 and the next 14 years, maybe 1 percent ever actually lived in a commune. Maybe 3 percent went to mobilization, to a love-in or something like that. The people who actually *did* these things were few and far between.

"There *was* a general sense of exploration. The generation was swept with the notion of a voyage of experience, a journey. But 40 percent of that generation were fully ready to go to Vietnam. *They* were a big part of it, too."

A focus of this evening's CBN taping will be a recent book on the '60s titled "Destructive Generation." The authors, both radical communists 20 years ago, now have leaped the fence, berating Leary and his fellow voyagers as a crowd of anti-American Peter Pans, "the lost boys and girls of the Sixties who never grew up."

The book, and more specifically its authors, strike a nerve in Leary.

"I don't understand what they're talking about," he says, shaking his head. "I never hated America. The people around me never hated America. But these authors, they *were* very anti-American. They came from a very militant left, which I never had anything to do with. They were hard-core Marxists. We were *Groucho* Marxists. They were spoiled East Coast temper tantrum brats, trying to take over a 76 million-soul incoherent demographic movement.

"Now they've jumped the fence, and they're having temper tantrums all over again. They were very American-hating leftists. Now they're flag-waving American rightists...

"Moving with the times, I agree with *that*. Sure. You can't knock that. Get real, grow up. But growing up doesn't mean writing a book where you're doing the same thing you were doing before, wrapping yourself in some pious flag and denouncing everyone else. I don't think that's getting real."

But the drugs. With Timothy Leary, it has to come back to the drugs. And a question that nags is how he resolves the darkness of crack and cocaine with any kind of reality other than horror.

His answer is a distinction between drugs that speaks as well to the differences between this generation and that of 20 years ago.

"Most people would agree that the psychedelic drugs which were popular in the '60s were mind-opening. The very word 'psychedelic' means mind-manifesting. They tend to involve group sharing. The drugs you see today do not. Can you imagine Woodstock, where you had four or five hundred thousand kids, wall-to-wall mud, wall-to-wall drug taking? Can you imagine anyone shooting *heroin* under a bush? Can you imagine smoking *crack* at Woodstock by themselves?

"They're very *selfish* drugs. They close *down* the mind. Those are two basic differences — they're mind-closing, and they're selfish."

Metaphors perhaps for the generations themselves. But Leary is quick to say there's nothing wrong with selfishness itself.

"I believe in intelligent selfishness. Selfishness is *good*, as long as it doesn't exploit or harm other people. I heard some leftists last month attacking the young Chinese kids, saying all they want are Cadillacs. Well, why *not*? I want a Cadillac. You want a Porsche. He wants blue jeans. She wants to go to medical school. That's the whole point."

And what of those same leftists who would accuse the coat-and-tie computer-touting Timothy Leary of being nothing more than a sellout?

"I'm *willing* to sell out," he says, throwing out his hands. "Make me an offer."

But the currency he'll consider, of course, has little to do with dollars. His coins are of the consciousness, his money of the mind.

"Make me an offer," he says again. "What do I have to do, and what are you giving me?"

By the time Tim Leary climbs the "Straight Talk" stage, it's clear the crowd here has nothing to give him but grief. He is assailed by the book authors as a prime and direct cause of the drug and crime problems riddling the nation today. An audience member stands and blames Leary for his own bad trip, the personal hell that finally brought him to the Lord. The few fireworks in the otherwise tepid evening are directed at the doctor, who looks more amused than alarmed by the proceedings.

The session's second hour finds Leary seated in the audience, taking in the show with the rest of the crowd. The patter on stage is shallow, predictable, nothing a man like Leary hasn't heard a thousand times before. But he's polite. He pays attention.

And when it's done, he leaves as he came, stepping into the shadows, navigating his way back to Beverly Hills and tomorrow.

August 13, 1989

Dylan at the Fair

And the princess and the prince discuss
What's real and what is not
It doesn't matter inside The Gates of Eden
Bob Dylan, "Gates of Eden", 1965

The gates were open Saturday night at Kings Dominion, and reality was rolling in. From the Hair Bear lot to the Scooby Doo section, as far as the eye could see, stretched an ocean of empty campers and station wagons, their spilled contents standing six deep at the Waffle Works, clutching their corn dogs, hugging their Huckleberry Hounds, waiting in line for a whirl on the Berserker.

And strolling past posters announcing that the Bob Dylan show was a sellout.

Yes, Bob Dylan — the man, the myth, the king of non-conformity, jeans-clad Jesus for a generation of seekers — was here in the land of Hanna-Barbera, of cotton candy and Quick Draw McGraw. Here with his catalog of 32 albums and more than 600 songs, songs of delusion and desire, of pathos and protest, anthems of an age almost three decades old but still barking at our heels. Here to ascend the same stage Tiffany had trod two weeks earlier and Dolly Parton would climb a week from tonight.

Yes, Dylan had come to Kings Dominion, fresh from a tour of Europe, where he'd shared the mike with U-2's Bono in Dublin, where he sang with Van Morrison in Athens, where George Harrison watched from the wings in Birmingham and a throng of 30,000 roared for an encore in Istanbul.

But he had come back from that trip to play at Bally's Grand Casino on the boardwalk in Atlantic City, bringing cries of betrayal from purists outraged that their priest had deigned to step into the gaudy glitz of the land of slots.

"A scene as surreal as some of his old songs," is how one writer described Dylan's casino foray.

Now he was here, outside Richmond, sharing the Kings Dominion bill with the performing porpoises at Moby's Seaside Revue, with the Yogi's World puppets and with the Yabba Dabba Dino musical revue.

And there were plenty among this night's 7,500 ticketholders curious about the same question a man named Paul Williams used for the title to a 1980 book he wrote about the now-48-year-old troubador:

"Dylan — What Happened?"

He's not selling any alibis
As you stare into the vacuum of his eyes
And say "Do you want to make a deal?"
Bob Dylan, "Like a Rolling Stone," 1965

Two hours before showtime, and Mark Stowell was already rushing for the gates. Camera bag slung on his shoulder, tickets in his pocket, grayish hair hanging down his neck, the 35-year-old Chesterfield County plumber was bracing himself for his fourth Dylan show. The first was in Memphis in 1974. He's been going to a lot of rock concerts lately, he said, "now that some of the older people are gettin' back out and tourin'," but Dylan, he said, remains "somethin' special."

"I've been listening to Dylan since I was 11," said Stowell. "He's a spokesman of a time."

Stowell's buddy Tom Kendall cut him off.

"What Dylan is," said Kendall, a 29-year-old computer programmer from Richmond, "is living proof that anybody can sell out."

Stowell stepped aside, giving his friend center stage.

"I used to take Dylan seriously," continued Kendall, "up to and including 'Blood on the Tracks.' But after that, it's been money, pure and simple. I know he's got a house out in Mailbu slowly walking itself into the ocean. That's going to cost him 3 1/2 million right there.

"He's just filling his market," said Kendall, motioning to the crowd around him. "These are the same people he's always played to. It's just that they have kids and a station wagon now. They're not going to concert halls. They're coming to places like this, so here he is.

"He's in it for the bucks, I've got a buck, so here *I* am."

By the time Kendall was through, Stowell had disappeared in the direction of the show, joining the stream of concert-goers funneling past the Scooby Doo Coaster.

Among that crowd were Greg and Anna Beaty, a couple from Culpeper, where Greg sells curtain rods and Anna is a teacher's aide. They're both in their 40s. Greg's got "a few" Dylan albums, but Anna's not sure if she's ever heard them.

"I don't even know what he sings," she said. "I don't even know if I'll like it."

"Oh, you will if you like folk music," assured Greg.

The blankets Greg carried under one arm were for sitting on the grass of the park's outdoor amphitheater. The ponchos under the other were in case of rain. As an overhead speaker blared the "Flintstones" theme song, Greg admitted he was a bit puzzled by Dylan's appearance here.

"It strikes me as very strange. I see him belonging more in an auditorium. He doesn't strike me as an amusement park type of person."

"No reason to get excited,"
The thief, he kindly spoke,
"There's many here among us
Who feel that life is but a joke."
Bob Dylan, "All Along the Watchtower," 1968

Inside the park's Showplace concert ground, the mood was mellow, sedate. Smells of incense and, yes, marijuana, wafted up from the grassy hillside. The people here had paid $6 apiece for their tickets — plus an obligatory $18.95 for admission to the park.

At the souvenir booth, where eight styles of Dylan T-shirts were selling for $20 apiece, where Dylan buttons were going at $4 a pop and souvenir Dylan booklets cost $11 each, the action was slow. A singer named Steve Earle would be the warmup act this night, but his T-shirts were moving no faster than the headliner's.

Up the hill, Kevin Lipnicki was helping the light crew set up. Lipnicki, a 22-year-old Richmonder, described himself as a "moderate" Dylan fan. This was the first Kings Dominion show he'd worked at, and he was "real interested" to see the star.

"I mean, he *is* regarded as a founder, I guess, of a certain kind of thing, the best at what he does," said Lipnicki. "It's special, kind of like seeing Ray Charles or something."

Seeing Dylan at an amusement park didn't dim the effect for Lipnicki.

It *is* a bit obscure," he said, "but when it comes down to it, it's still a concert. I mean, Yogi Bear's not gonna be up there. Dylan is."

Down below, a crowd of women were pushing their way into the arena. Leading the pack was a redhead wearing a Harley-Davidson T-shirt and hoisting a huge POW-MIA flag. She shrugged at the idea that the banner was an odd thing to bring to a concert.

"Hey," she said, "he's basically an activist singer."

Yes, someone said, that's one way to describe Dylan.

"No," said the woman. "I'm talking about Steve *Earle*."

The woman's name was Jill Spear, a 25-year-old who had driven up from Gloucester, where she and her husband run a home improvement business. She was more excited about Earle's show than Dylan's. But she did say Dylan has been a part of her life since her teens.

"I like him all right," she said. "Matter of fact, we played Dylan at our wedding. You know, *'Everybody must get stoned...'* My mother almost croaked".

Spear's friend Bonnie Butterbaugh, a 29-year-old designer at Newport News Shipbuilding, was more excited. This was her sixth Dylan concert. The first was in Pittsburgh in 1978.

"I'm not really a follower," she said. "I'm a *listener*. And he's someone who doesn't just bang your head with noise. He *says* something."

Saying it to a crowd cradling carnival prizes made sense to Butterbaugh.

"Dylan reaches out to all types of people," she said. "And this is the kind of place where you *find* all types of people. I mean, where else *but* an amusement park?"

George Bourcier felt the same way. A 24-year-old silkscreener from Virginia Beach, Bourcier had come up with a busload of Hampton Roads fans who had won free concert tickets in a radio contest. Dressed in a Grateful Dead T-shirt of his own design—Dead T-shirts outnumbered Dylan shirts 10 to 1 this night—the mop-topped, bespectacled Jerry Garcia lookalike referred to himself and his friends as "Dylanheads."

"There's a magic Dylan brings to what he does," said Bourcier, "and bringing it here makes sense. He's always explored new territory, so why not here?"

Bourcier's buddy Tommy Payne agreed.

"Dylan's always had a carnivalish side to him, and this is a carnival," said the 24-year-old Virginia Beach carpenter. "He's just like one of the rides, and there's nothin' wrong with that."

"Yeah," said Bourcier, nodding at a nearby roller coaster, "and the line's a lot shorter for this ride than the ones out there."

Payne nodded.

"And it lasts a lot longer."

I'm ready to go anywhere
I'm ready for to fade
Into my own parade
Bob Dylan, "Mr. Tambourine Man, 1964

Roger Fleming leaned against a fence as the show was set to start. A Postal Service letter carrier from Alexandria, Fleming was dressed in a sport coat and slacks, cowboy boots and dark shades wrapped around his bearded, balding head. He saw Dylan for the first time in 1974 in Maryland, a late start for a 41-year-old.

"I was in the war, man," explained Fleming.

That was where he first heard Dylan.

"Phu Hip, Vietnam, 1967," he said.

Fleming was a combat communications engineer in the Army. When asked how it felt hearing Dylan at that time in that place, he said nothing. For a full two minutes, he chewed his lip in silence, his eyes hiding behind his sunglasses. Finally, he spoke.

"I'll tell you what Dylan means to me," he said. "My son's name is Dylan. He's 15 now."

Back in the present tense, Fleming relaxed.

"The thing about Dylan is he's much more than an entertainer," he said. "He's a *feeling* man. Dylan talks truth. Dylan *tells* the truth."

And he tells it anytime, said Fleming, anyplace.

"He's a Wilbury, man," he said, referring to the name Dylan and a handful of other rock legends gave themselves when they recorded a recent album together. "A travelin' Wilbury. He's a *minstrel*. And a minstrel plays for the people, for *all* the people."

Including, this night, the Terza family from Altoona, Pa. George, 45, Helen, 40, Craig, 17 and Christy, 12, had driven five hours this morning to spend the day at the park and then catch the concert, the first for both kids. When asked why they'd made Dylan the family's first joint outing, George and Helen nodded toward Christy.

"She's the one who's into Dylan," said George.

Christy couldn't name a Dylan album. She couldn't come up with a song title. But she likes the records she heard at a neighbor's house.

"She's older," Christy said of her neighbor. "She's 13."

Good and bad, I defined those terms
Quite clear, no doubt, somehow
Ah, but I was so much older then,
I'm younger than that now.
Bob Dylan, "My Back Pages," 1964

By the time Dylan took the stage, the sky was dark. The cigerette lighters lifted in tribute among the crowd were matched by the glare from the park's ersatz Eiffel Tower peeking over the pines above. As a monorail slid silently by and purple clouds drifted past a yellow moon, the spotlight fell on a familiar figure, dressed in simple black and white.

No one knew what to expect. Dylan has tossed curveballs his entire career, stunning the acoustic folkies in 1965 when he climbed the Newport Folk Festival stage with a plugged-in guitar, "disowning" his protest songs later that year, disappearing for a year after a motorcycle accident in 1966, avoiding the Woodstock Festival that took place just down the road from his home in 1969, then becoming a chameleon as he waded through the murky '70s, wearing the grotesque white face paint and eyeshadow of his Rolling Thunder Revue tour, donning dangling crucifix earrings during his born-again Christian phase, even slipping into an Arab headdress as he peeked behind this devotional doorway and that.

But now his look was spare. Black and white.

The way it was a quarter century ago. Black and white.

No more groping through the grayness of ambivalence, no more shedding this guise for that, no more fumbling with personas. This was Dylan straight up, no mixers, no chasers, a myth come to terms with itself.

Black and white.

And the crowd loved it.

Sharing the stage with G.E. Smith, the top session guitarist in the business, Dylan took a dozen of his vintage hits, tunes more than two decades old, and kicked them into gears they'd never had. Against a surreal sky show of carnival fireworks, he pulled out diamonds like "All Along the Watchtower" and "Stuck in Mobile With the Memphis Blues Again," "I Shall Be Released" and "Like a Rolling Stone," and sang them as if they were written yesterday. His backlit silhouette was haunting, as if he were once again the 20-year-old kid singing at Gerde's in New York in 1961. But this was no nostalgia show, no retreat to the past.

And it didn't matter that this was an amusement park. Real legends live beyond set and setting. When they take a stage, the time and place become their own.

The man leaning into the microphone Saturday night was a full 48 years old. So were many in the crowd. Some of the songs he sang were fully half that age.

But he wasn't looking back.

He wasn't thinking twice.

And, as far as every man, woman and child leaving the park at 11 that night was telling one another, that's all right.

August 15, 1989

The Silver Bullet

It's out there in the driveway. A huge aluminum egg nesting in the middle of Gorden Hughson's small fleet of cars and trucks. A 31-foot metal blimp on wheels, riveted and welded as tight as a submarine and decked out inside like a garden apartment.

Hughson's three cars and two pickup trucks, his boat in the backyard, his tidy brick ranch backing onto a man-made lake all spell suburban comfort. Life is indeed cushy here at the end of Pillow Court in Virginia Beach.

But the symbol of Hughson's good life — more than the television console sitting in one corner of his den or the cabinet full of hunting rifles standing in the other, more than the business card that describes the parking lot cleaning and striping company Hughson owns — is his 1975 Airstream Sovereign Land Yacht.

With all due respect to their two grown sons — neither of whom has much respect for their parents' passion — the apple of Gorden and Peggy Hughson's eyes is that trailer parked out front, shimmering in the sun.

These days, while they still have a business to tend, the Hughsons only get away in the trailer two, maybe three times a month. But in two years, when Gorden retires at age 62, the couple is going to get down to some serious Airstreaming.

No more little weekend trips to the mountains.

No more watching with envy as their friends hook up their Airstreams and head south for the winter.

No, the Hughsons are talking big-time. Living in their pride and joy for months on end. Crossing the country. Hitting Canada, maybe even

Alaska. Joining caravans of 100 Airstreams or more. Rolling to major rallies where thousands of Airstreams converge on a single destination, swallowing entire communities in a sea of silver.

The Hughsons got a taste of the big-time when theirs was among 3,965 Airstream trailers at last summer's Wally Byam Caravan Club International (WBCCI) Grand Rally in Lake Placid, N.Y. As president of the 88-member Tidewater Unit of the WBCCI, which stretches from Richmond to Chesapeake, Hughson is looking forward to leading his group to this July's edition of the Grand Rally in Boise, Idaho, marking the 50th anniversary of the Airstream.

Yes, this is the year the silver bullet goes gold.

And as far as Airstreaming goes, it may as well still be 1936, the year Wally Byam built the prototype for what would become known as the Cadillac of travel trailers. Airstreams still look the same today, at least on the outside. The owners continue to travel in flocks, following a regimen as precise as any military battalion's. They fly their flags, pull out their curbside patio awnings, parade their pets, unfold their card tables, mix their cocktails, show their slides, recite the pledge of allegiance, share their meals, sightsee, pack it up and move it out, all according to strictly prescribed routine.

Patriotism, organization and can-do rule. It's as if these metallic bubbles are shields against the march of time. The occupants seem untouched by the anarchic turbulence of the '60s, the confused angst of the '70s, the end-of-the-world anxiety of the '80s.

In an Airstream, it's always 1955, and the landscape rolls by. This was Wally Byam's vision of the future: Ozzie and Harriet on the road, an America crisscrossed by lines of carefully spaced Airstream trailers stretching from horizon to horizon like so many strings of silver pearls.

Wally is gone now. He passed away in 1962. But his legacy remains. It's stamped on each of the 1,000 silver trailers Airstream's Ohio plant will turn out this year. And it guides the 36,000 WBCCI members who worship his vacationing codes as scripture and who sport the same style of blue beret that Wally always wore.

"He was a perfectionist," says Gorden Hughson in a reverent tone. "He loved to travel, but he wanted it to be in an orderly way, and he wanted to be proud of *how* he traveled."

Which the Hughsons and the rest of the Airstreamers most definitely are. When they caravan, camp and rally, it is almost always in the exclusive company of fellow Airstreamers. When they can, they stay in Airstream Parks, of which there are 25 in the country, including two in Virginia — one outside Roanoke and one in Temperanceville on the Eastern Shore. At these parks, the gates are closed to the unchosen. No Winnebagos, Prowlers or Shastas allowed.

"We're not snooty," says Gorden Hughson, "but we do want to have the caliber of people who behave themselves properly, have a good time, and don't give a bad name to camping."

Of course there are those who would question whether it's accurate to call this camping. Peggy Hughson notes that her older son Bob, an avid backpacker, refuses to mention an Airstream in the same breath as his own beloved tent. No less an authority than Gerry Letourneau, president of the Airstream Trailer Company, proclaims: "Camping is what Boy Scouts do. An Airstream is a house."

That's what Wally Byam, a Los Angeles advertising copywriter and amateur handyman, developed in his back yard in the 1930s. His original Airstream Clipper was not only aerodynamically sleek, but it featured cedar-lined closets and dry-ice air conditioning. It was a luxury vehicle, selling in the Depression for $1,200. Today, a new top-of-the-line 34-foot Airstream Limited, available at 110 dealerships across the country, including Virginia's only Airstream dealer, in Harrisonburg, sells for $46,000.

But Byam wasn't concerned with cost or cutting corners. He built his Airstreams to last, and they do. It takes 500 man-hours to build an Airstream today, wrapping as many as 700 pounds of aluminum around an interior of hand-rubbed solid hickory and oak cabinets, hardwood floor, refrigerator/freezer, four-burner stove and oven, double kitchen sink, bathroom with shower or tub, double or twin beds, and, of course, central air and heat.

Although the predicted life span of an Airstream is 15 years, most stay on the road much longer. And according to their owners, they appreciate in value. Stepping into the carpeted living room of his trailer, flipping on a portable TV and taking a seat on the sofa, Gorden Hughson won't say exactly what he paid for his 1975 model, which he bought in 1978 from a local campground owner. But he will say it was "a steal," and he plans on selling it for twice the price he paid when he moves up to a 34-footer at retirement.

Believing the only way to test the quality of this product was to take it on the road, Wally Byam began making long-distance excursions during the 1940s. By the 1950s, some of his customers were joining him on his trips. The caravans grew, and by the mid-50s, Wally was leading chains of as many as 500 trailers into Mexico, fanning out into wagon wheel parking formations and puzzling the natives, who, wrote Byam, couldn't figure out "the crazy Norte Americanos who would dare to drive Cadillacs where jeeps feared to tread."

In 1955, Byam formed the club named after himself. Each Airstream owned by a club member — six out of 10 owners are members — is stamped with a number. The Houghtons' is No. 24945. Wally's was, naturally, No. 1.

God, country and the silver bullet — those were the three things that mattered to Wally Byam. And he trumpeted that trinity on the numerous overseas caravans he led. He died in 1962, a year before the club completed its now-fabled Round-the-World Caravan. But Wally's still the leader of the pack in spirit.

And the company continues to thrive, rebounding from a '70s sales slump caused by rising gas prices and America's love affair with automobiles far too small to pull an Airstream. Since 1980, the company's sales have more than doubled, from $22 million to a projected $50 million this year.

The art of Airstreaming itself is apparently bigger than ever. Their dashboards festooned with digital clocks, compasses and altimeters, their glove compartments overflowing with maps, their CB radios tuned to Airstream Channel 14, and their spray paint cans poised to mark each geometrically measured parking spot with a quick shot of silver, Wally Byam's legions will stage 1,500 rallies and caravans this year.

It's that precision, that sense of order, those splashes of silver sprayed on the grass at a rally site that appeal to Gorden Hughson.

"Where that dot is," he says, "that's *exactly* where your jack goes down. The way they line it up, it's like... well... by golly, it's like a parking lot without the lines."

The treasured Airstream "fellowship" is just as precise a business. Everything a rallying Airstreamer enjoys, from bridge to bowling, from parking to pancakes, is organized by committee. And seemingly everyone is officially in charge of something. Besides its 10 elected officers, the Tidewater Unit lists 15 committee chairmen, including a Safety Chairman, a Sunshine Girl Chairman, and a Teen Queen Chairman. Says President Houghson: "It's a democratic deal."

The Houghsons weren't much interested in camping when Peggy Hughson's sister started raving about her own Airstream in the mid-'70s. "My image of camping," says Peggy, "was getting wet when it rains, fighting insects, roughing it. I didn't want any part of it."

"She's a good cook," says Gorden, "but not over a campfire."

One trip in her sister's trailer, however, was enough to make believers out of the Hughsons. Gorden has been tempted since then by some of the more spacious, more luxurious models turned out by other manufacturers. But every time it rains, he's glad he's got his Airstream: "I've seen too many people scrambling around their trailers, trying to caulk 'em up to keep 'em from leaking."

Not even Airstream's own line of self-contained motor homes, which cost as much as $100,000, can lure Hughson from his trailer. "Personally," he says of the self-propelled bullets, "I wouldn't have one. Once you get where you're going, if you want to do a little sightseeing, you've got to take the whole thing with you. With a trailer, you pull in, you level, you hook up, you disconnect and that's it. You're free. Put out your awnings and set up the cocktail table."

From April to November, the Hughsons and the rest of the Tidewater club set up their tables at least once a month at local rallies, usually held in Williamsburg or Virginia Beach. From December to March, they basically hibernate, gathering at monthly dinner meetings and toasting the 40 or so absent members who are down in Florida, "snowbirding."

"We're still working people," laments Peggy Hughson, as are most of those local Airstreamers stuck here for the winter. They range from a William and Mary business professor to active duty military officers, and they include Williamsburg's Robin Kipps, at 29 the youngest unit member, and Virginia Beach's Tom Nance, who they say is the oldest but who will admit only to being "at least 75."

"We're not all 70 and retired," notes Gorden Hughson.

But they are all believers in the Airstream ethic, which, in a literal way, makes them grass-roots Americans.

"The thing about it," says Gorden Hughson, "is we're people who love our country."

"We represent the freedom people have here," says Peggy Hughson. "You can come and go as you please, stop when and where you want, and stay as long as you want. And that's what this country is all about."

Clicking off the TV and stepping out of his trailer and onto a plastic welcome mat laid on the grass of his front lawn, Gorden Hughson surveys with undisguised pride the Mercury Grand Marquis automobile and the Ford four-wheel-drive pickup truck he uses to pull his 31-foot Land Yacht.

"Airstreaming," he sighs, "is a way of life."

March 9, 1986

Tracking the Hobo

The way Bobb Hopkins sees it, this is one helluva great country.

Sure we've pushed it around plenty, bulldozing and building, clearing and carving, stretching and sprawling and hacking out highways wherever we go. But there's still so much that's going untouched, says Hopkins. Rapid rushing rivers. Vast virgin forests. Big-sky prairies where the only sound on a moonlit summer night is the rumbling of a westbound freight headed for the horizon.

Yeah, says Hopkins, look at those rails. Now *that's* the way to see this country — the *only* way, says Hopkins, now that interstates have leveled the rest of the landscape into an ocean of off-ramps and franchises. The tracks, says Hopkins, can still take you places pavement will never reach.

But when Bobb Hopkins talks about riding the rails, he doesn't mean bedding down in a sleeper and taking cocktails in the club car. No, Bobb Hopkins is hoboing, hopping freights just the way Jack London did a hundred years ago. There is nothing, says Hopkins, like the feel of the wind whipping your face as you sit in the open door of an empty boxcar high-balling down the east side of the Continental Divide, the rails singing beneath your feet and nothing less than America whizzing past your eyes.

And what's really neat about it all, what's really, well... downright democratic about this hobo thing, says Bobb Hopkins, is you don't have to be a bum to do it.

Look at Hopkins himself. He lives in a $200,000 house out there in a plush Los Angeles suburb called Westwood Hills—"It's not Beverly Hills," he says, "but it's not the slums." Back when he was in college in New Hampshire, Hopkins was an All-America quarterback, good enough to get a tryout with the New York Jets. He's 38 now, an actor with a page-long resume of appearances on everything from soap operas to "Simon & Simon." He drives a Mercedes. His wife is, yes, an aerobics instructor.

But none of that keeps Hopkins from suiting up in frayed jeans and a flannel shirt, tying a bandanna around that blow- dried blond hair of his and heading out for the nearest railyard, hailing his fellow 'bos, down-and-out old-timers with names like Bones, Stump and Spokane Red. When he's rubbing shoulders with the real thing, Hopkins takes on his own handle — "Sante Fe Bo" — just like he's an honest-to-God hobo. Of course, unlike the other boys in the boxcars, Hopkins carries a credit card in his back pocket, in case he needs to get home in a hurry. There's no telling when his agent might line him up for a guest slot on "Divorce Court."

Yeah, this is a great country. Great that it allows a guy like Bobb Hopkins to get down and dirty every once in a while. And even greater that it has room for Hopkins to turn his hobby into a full-fledged industry.

Check it out. Call directory information for the L.A. area and don't ask for Bobb Hopkins. Ask instead for the National Hobo Association. Hopkins is the founder and director. Dial the number and a guy named "Captain Cook" picks up at the other end. His real name is Garth Bishop, but when you're part of this hobo thing, you've got to play the game.

Bishop, it turns out, is a publisher. Among the things he publishes are a booklet written by Bobb Hopkins titled "The Yuppy Hobo Travel Guide" and a newsletter created by Bobb Hopkins titled Hobo Times. Demands for both have been intense in the last year, what with a slew of newspaper and magazine stories pronouncing "high-rent hoboing" a full-fledged fad. Just last month, Time magazine devoted a full page to Hopkins' exploits. In that story, Hopkins claimed 2,000 people have joined his association. At least a fourth of them, he said, are actually weekend rail riders.

Bishop says he thinks those figures are "pretty accurate." But "Hobo Bobb," as Bishop calls his partner, has the real numbers, and, unfortunately, Bobb is out of town at the moment, up in New England "surveying jungles," as Bishop puts it. One of the features of the newsletter — besides stories with headlines like "Hobo Vacations for Yuppies" and "Hobo Survival Techniques," and advertisements for a 30-minute documentary video titled "The Great American Hobo," starring Bobb Hopkins ($29.95 for members, $39.95 for everyone else) — is a map of the nation's finest hobo jungles, track-side camps where a man can get a nice mug of mulligan stew. Right now, says Bishop, Hopkins is out doing his jungle homework.

"It's kind of like reviewing restaurants," says Bishop. "You've got to keep going back out there because you might find a good spot one year, and the next year, you go back and it's gone, bulldozed."

Anyway, says Bishop, Hopkins should be back in a few days, which, it turns out, he is.

"It's been CRAY-ZEE!" says Santa Fe Bo, speaking by phone from that Westwood Hills house of his.

He hasn't lost the New England accent he grew up with, even though he looks as cookie-cutter Californian as they come in the publicity photos he sends out with his hobo press packet. The packet also includes Hopkins' acting resume. Ask him how things are going, and he covers all bases, hitting his career as well as his hobby.

"I'm working on a John Ritter film right now," he says. "Blake Edwards directing. And I just got back from New England. And I'm getting ready to take off from here next week to head toward Britt for the hobo convention. And..."

That's Britt, Iowa, home of the yearly National Hobo Convention. One summer weekend a year — next weekend, Aug. 12 through 14, will be the 88th annual gathering — Britt is filled with tourists aching for a peek at real live vagabonds and wondering who will be crowned "King of the Hobos." That coronation is always good for a quick feature on the news networks, although some people have questioned the legitimacy of past hobo kings who have arrived at Britt in Winnebagos. One of those skeptics is a man named Ted Conover, who visited Britt while working on "Rolling Nowhere," a book about hobos that was published in 1981. When Conover finally cornered a bona fide hobo at the convention, the man explained what's wrong with the Britt affair.

"There's still hobos," the man told Conover, "but you ain't gonna see any of 'em here. This is fun, but it's fake. Nine out of 10 of these guys have never been on a freight in their lives— they just come to have a little fun, get a little publicity."

Which raises the question of Bobb Hopkins' motives. He says he's not in this for the money, that any profit he makes from the $18 association membership fees, the $9.95 guidebooks and the $3 newsletters he sells goes to hobo missions. He doesn't know how many "official" Hobo Times T-shirts ($10) he's sold, but Hopkins says he has resisted pressure to print membership cards.

"That to me is a little too commercial," he says of the cards. "That serves no purpose."

The question of what purpose Hopkins' actor's resume and photo serve in a packet of hobo information doesn't bother him.

"That's my calling card," Hopkins says of the resume. "That's how I get jobs in Hollywood, that's the way you operate in L.A. That's who

I am. Hey, when I go out there and live on the road or whatever, it's not like I'm a wealthy kid out there trying to play poor. To me it's a lifestyle. People have a right to do anything in this country. It's just a matter of choice."

Unfortunately Hopkins had no real hobo on the line to discuss how it feels to have his life turned into a "lifestyle" to be donned and doffed as easily as a flannel shirt. The question of choice would be a good one to discuss with a real hobo, who is likely riding the rails precisely because he has no choice—as well as no home, no family, no job, no money, no nothing.

When Ted Conover neared the end of his four months riding the rails, whatever glamour had glimmered at the beginning of his trip was gone. "I wanted to get away," he wrote. "I did not want to be a hobo anymore. The life was too horrible."

But there is no hint of the horrible in Hopkins' Hobo Times. Instead there are mulligan stew recipes, hobo puzzles, even a poetry page titled "Vagabond Verses." It's light, it's fun, and Hopkins says the real hobos he knows love it.

"Most of the response I've gotten out there is these guys are happy there's someone like me that's more or less a spokesman for them," he says. "Someone who can educate the rest of the masses on the fact that the hobo is a good person, that there's a lot of tradition there.

"They're very proud of me, and I feel very good when I go out there and these people I've met over the years know me and now they've seen some of this in ink."

After talking with Hopkins, that's all this new-wave hoboing came down to—ink.

A desk covered with press releases and newsletters left unanswered the question of who, besides Hopkins, is actually out there riding the rails — either for fun or out of necessity.

Calls were made to some of the dozen or so Hampton Roads' residents on Hopkins association mailing list, hunting for a hobo hobbyist among them.

No such luck. The people who answered their phones had each ordered the newsletter out of curiosity. None has actually tried the hobo life, not even for a weekend.

"It seems interesting," said John Behnken, 75, a retired sea captain living in Newport News. "But I'm married, and I don't think this is the kind of thing my wife would go for."

"I've never participated in that kind of thing and never plan to," said Theon Outlaw, 66, a retired government worker living in Hampton. "As for the newsletter, I was disappointed. It's kind of skimpy, nothing much to it. If you ask me, it's just another money-making scheme."

"I think Glenn would *like* to do this," said Ruth Goodman of Poquoson, whose husband Glenn, a 61-year-old independent trucker, was on the road. "He's talked about it. But he also talks about teaming up with some old prospector and digging for gold."

The phone is apparently no way to find a hobo. And, judging by a day spent hiking the rail yards of Hampton Roads, neither is walking the tracks.

In Norfolk, where a sea of coal cars converges at Lamberts Point, the only sign of life on a recent Saturday morning was an occasional yard worker trudging across the gravel, stones and cinders. A rickety shack perched at the edge of one set of tracks showed signs that perhaps a hobo or two had been through in the past.

The name WILLIE WHO was scratched on the shack's front. Inside was etched the message STIMY WAS HERE beneath the logo of a shining sun. But Stimy was long gone. Tommy Dalton, a track foreman who's worked these yards for 10 years, explained why.

"Only thing that comes outta here is coal," said Dalton, waving a train past. "Ain't nobody gonna jump on a coal car and ride it outta here. They *may* hop a freight, but I ain't seen that in years."

Dalton said a hobo would more likely be found at the Portlock yard in Portsmouth. But the only person along those tracks Saturday morning was Benjamin Dixon, pushing his trash bag-laden bike through a morning rainstorm. The half dozen bags strapped to his bike were filled with aluminum cans. Dixon was making the familiar trip to a recycling center.

"I know most all the streets around here," said Dixon, a 46- year-old Chesapeake native and "self-employed" sub-contractor who keeps a cluster of pencils tucked under the brim of his baseball cap. Dixon "used to ride the trains myself" 10 or 15 years ago. But those train trips, he said, were "just short hops across town, no more'n a couple of miles.

"You used to see people hopping rides around here," said Dixon, "but that was years and years ago."

Farther down those same Portsmouth tracks were two teens, Chuck and Bill, both 14 and both wary of sharing their last names. The two were on their way to Bill's house. The tracks, they explained, are a short cut they use often. Stepping out of the rain and combing back his wet blond hair, Bill insisted hobos are alive, if not well, in Portsmouth.

"I seen a couple of 'em back here the other day," he said, pointing toward the swampy ground beside the rails. "Two of 'em were layin' in a ditch right over there."

But there is a difference between a bum, a tramp and a hobo, according to Bobb Hopkins. A hobo, he says, is a man who travels and is willing to work. A tramp travels, but refuses to work. And a bum refuses to do either.

Chuck and Bill just shrugged at those definitions.

"I don't know about all that," said Bill. "I ain't seen nobody actually jumpin' on no trains."

"Well," said Chuck, "I seen some little *kids* doin' that. But they get right off, too."

In Newport News, where the Dominion Terminal rail yard is piled with mountains of coal that challenge the city's nearby skyline, the message was the same:

"I've been here more than four years," said equipment operator Glenn Spiggle, "and I haven't seen a hobo in all that time, not around here. There have been some fellas who hang around the tracks, but they may be just homeless people looking for a place to be. I don't think they were hopping a ride."

Security guard Bill Bailey, manning the terminal entrance, wears a 15-year pin on his Port of Hampton Roads uniform. He said the hobos are still at it, "but not here."

"I've never run into one myself," said Bailey, "but it's happening."

"We're more or less the end of the line here," said Spiggle. "Nothing but coal here, and nobody's gonna ride a coal car. But you might check the CSX yard up the tracks. They've got some freight coming through there."

Sure enough, the only boxcars to be seen this day were parked in the CSX yard. One bore the inscriptions of past riders. WICHITA 9-24-80 was scratched on one wall. JACK RABBIT 8-5-83 was etched on another. But these cars were empty, sidetracked, bound for nowhere.

A car inspector with the name TOM sewn on his shirt walked up.

"You can call me Tom," he said, "but that ain't my name."

He refused to identify himself, but the inspector was happy to talk about hobos — or rather about their disappearance.

"We don't have too many of 'em down here, 'cause there's not as much freight going through as there used to be. Once in a while you'll see someone hanging on between the coal cars, but that's it. See, this ain't a switching point, where you get cars goin' north, south, east, west, any direction you want.

"Go to a switching point, like up at the Potomac Yards in Arlington, or even in Richmond, and you might well be seeing some of those people."

Maybe they're out there, the yuppie thrill seekers and the real rail riders. But by the looks of things locally, the hobo is apparently history.

Which means Hampton Roads is one place where Bobb Hopkins will have a hard time hitching a ride — in any sense of the phrase.

August 7, 1988

The Well-Traveled Mind
of Robert Monroe

The Blue Ridge forest shimmers in morning sunlight as Robert Monroe climbs behind the wheel of his black Subaru and points it up the mountain. A hawk swoops low over Lake Miranon, searching for bass. The sounds of saws and hammers echo from the woods as Monroe steers toward a ridge that marks the uppermost boundary of his 800-acre community.

"This is an easy place to fall in love with," he says, ticking off the names of his neighbors as he passes their tree-shrouded homes. Down that drive is mystery novelist Phyllis Whitney. Up that one is Joseph Chilton Pearce, author of "Magical Child." Steve Pauley, a math professor at Purdue University, has a home among these pines, as does Florida social services executive Sharon Alley. There are psychologists living in these woods. And computer programmers. And there's newcomer Eleanor Friede, who edited Richard Bach's "Jonathan Livingston Seagull."

Monroe likes to categorize the world in terms of hemispheres of the brain — the right side being the seat of intuition and creativity, the left being the source of logic and rationale. Here in his own back yard, an eclectic mixture of righties and lefties has come to live, all, he says, with one thing in common.

"All these people," pronounces Monroe, "in their own way are seekers after truth."

When this former radio and television executive talks of truth, he is not referring to anything found through textbooks or prayers or drugs. The truth he has found and toward which he guides others is approached through sleep, through gateways of the mind, through altered states of

162

consciousness. Amid the physical splendor of the Blue Ridge foothills, Monroe and his laboratory entourage spend their days among wires, microphones and EEG monitors, journeying inward, putting their bodies to sleep while their minds wander, literally, across the universe.

For 28 years, Monroe has fiddled with electronically produced soundwaves, using them to trigger a release of the mind from the body, launching what are called out-of-body experiences — excursions of pure consciousness through and beyond time and space. More than 6,000 people have gone through the Monroe Institute's weeklong programs of psychic exploration. Not all have had the pleasure of an OOBE, as they call the cosmic trip. Most, however, come away more attuned to the unused portions of their brains.

For those who cannot make it out the institute, Monroe's brain-tapping methods are available through a catalog of mailorder cassette tapes. No OOBEs are guaranteed, but the 90 tapes on the institute's menu do have their everyday uses. Rhode Island medical students use them to reduce anxiety at test time. Schoolteachers in Tacoma, Wash., use them to soothe, quiet and relax their first-graders. In Oak Ridge, Tenn., the tapes are used to reduce pain for surgery patients.

It is these practical applications of his "hemi-sync" method — short for hemispheric synchronization — that Monroe is quick to emphasize make his work more than just another psychic parlor game to be lumped with fire-walking or bending spoons.

"We think what we're doing here is much more to the point. We want to release all this from pure research to something usable, something valuable. I guess that's my left brain always asking 'How can we use it?'"

Somebody is using it. More than 22,000 of the institute's cassette tapes, which treat everything from insomnia to a shaky golf game, are sold through the mail each year.

But Robert Monroe is ultimately interested in more than ridding the world of bad sleep and bogeys. As his institute's glossy brochure describes it, Monroe wants nothing less than "to change constructively man's direction and destiny."

A cosmic breakthrough is at hand, says Monroe. In a matter of decades, he says, the planet will be peopled by men and women whose control of mind over matter will free them from the bonds of their skin and bones. And they will not need Monroe's labs or his tapes to unleash their mental powers.

"That's the crux of it all,"He says, parking at the top of the ridge and looking down on a hillside of blossoming dogwoods. "Man has a great opportunity in the next 50 years to break out of our boxes, to be something far more than we've ever been."

He is an unlikely-looking new-age frontiersman, this paunchy, 70-year-old, white-haired, white-mustached father of six. Wearing sunglasses, blue sportshirt, khaki slacks and white bucks, he looks more like a gentle grandfather — which he is — than a mind-tripping guru.

But listen to him talk. Even in the most mundane, everyday conversation, Monroe tends to slip into laboratory lingo. A few examples from the morning outing:

After discussing the removal of some old farm machinery from a nearby field, he tells a worker, "Now that I have this information to process, I will let you know."

After haggling with a carpenter over the construction of his new ridge-top home and institute workshop, he sighs: "Carpenters are basically left-brained."

Before turning in for a quick, midday nap, he announces: "I'm going to go ahead upstairs and recycle."

Which is just what Monroe did that night in 1958 when he first spontaneously slipped out of his body and began joyriding the highways of inner and outer space. It was terrifying in the beginning, says Monroe, and it took him a year to convince himself he was not simply going out of his mind. It took him even longer — until the 1971 publication of his first book, "Journeys Out of the Body" — to tell the rest of the world about his experiences. In the meantime, he moved from New York to Virginia, where he established, headed, then sold his interest in the Charlottesville-based Jefferson Cable Corporation, and set up the Monroe Institute in rural Nelson County.

Before the book, he kept his cosmic consciousness in the closet: "In a left-brain world, as president of a major corporation, I didn't quite feel the board of directors or the stockholders would look favorably on a wild guy doing this sort of stuff."

After the book, he found he had plenty of company. More than 350,000 copies were sold, the book was printed in seven languages, and it established Monroe as more than a crackpot among the scientific community. It convinced death-and-dying expert Elisabeth Kubler-Ross to try Monroe's program and to incorporate life-after-death into her own research. Actor Jon Voight has also sampled the Monroe method.

A good number of backpackers still show up at the institute's four-building complex, but most program participants are scientists, psychologists and doctors from clinics and universities around the world — "as against the pure right-brainers and mystics," explains Monroe.

Monroe has lectured at the Smithsonian. Papers on his work have been presented before the American Psychiatric Association. Both Mother Earth News and Omni magazine have analyzed the institute from their own divergent perspectives. Corporations have brought their executives to Monroe's hilltop headquarters for training in tapping the intuitive, creative, right-brain regions of their minds. A helicopter landing site is cleared in the weeds just beyond the institute's outdoor volleyball net.

Credibility is no longer a concern for Monroe. Nor is viability. After more than a decade of pumping his own money into the institute — "I'm not poor; I remember paying in a 90 percent tax bracket when there *was* a 90 percent tax bracket" — the operation paid for itself in 1984 and became a nonprofit organization last year. That freed Monroe to finish his second book, "Far Journeys," which was published last October. He'll be packing soon for a European trip promoting British and French editions of both books.

The institute, the books, the building—lately, Monroe has had a lot on his mind. Too much, in fact, to wander off to that region beyond the body. About 10 years ago, he tired of traveling through the space and time we all know. Leaving the body to sightsee on this or other planets, he says, soon became routine.

"It got old," says Monroe. "There's a certain sameness to it."

Hooking up with other consciousnesses — "I now have a lot of nonphysical friends" — he was guided to a realm beyond the time- and space-limited universe of our comprehension. It is these outer limits that are described in detail in "Far Journeys." After those outings, Monroe had no more interest in cosmic-sailing through the worlds of our comprehension.

"Why bother with local traffic," he asks, "when you can take the interstate?"

But even the "other reality system" he describes, where pure energy forms play God and create planets and solar systems just for kicks, is not enough to draw Monroe out of his body these days.

"I've ceased to do this for my own self," he says. He explains that he's got all the information his mind can "process" in this body. He's got several more books' worth of experiences yet to sort out. So he is leaving it to the institute's volunteer "explorers" to continue bringing back data while he distills it and answers for others the questions he spent 10 years answering for himself.

The question Monroe is most often asked is how he knows these excursions are real and not simply dreams?

"It took me a full year to collect hardcore evidence, to validate that for myself," he says. The evidence ranged from traveling in a nonphysical form to distant friends' homes at preassigned times and later reporting correctly the things he saw, to pinching neighbors in their sleep and seeing the black-and-blue marks the next day.

Which raises another question: Can shimmering forms of pure consciousness have physical properties?

Absolutely, says Monroe, describing two psychiatrists who were lovers but who lived and worked in distant cities. After spending a week at the institute, they asked Monroe to help them rendezvous sexually in their out-of-body state.

"I did," smiles Monroe, "and it worked beautifully. They met halfway between Kansas City and Denver every night."

With all these minds meeting minds and minds meeting bodies, isn't there the danger of misuse? What about governments using the method for brainwashing or spying? What about the threat of cosmic rapists hovering through the bedrooms of the world?

Monroe shakes his head, wearing the patient smile of a man who's heard it all before.

"To be efficient at this," he says, "you have to develop an overview. With that overview, you are no longer interested in the things of this body-ruled world. You lose a sense of the body self, of local customs, of nationality. What we call morality changes radically. What's important and not important changes dramatically."

The zone beyond, which Monroe describes as a realm of deep blackness, bright lights and exquisite joy, sounds much like what some religions might call heaven or nirvana. And Monroe admits it's hard to explain why anyone who has gotten there would ever come back. Why don't all those sleeping bodies lying in the institute's darkened cubicles remain vacant, deserted forever by consciousnesses playing hooky in the hereafter?

"You'd be surprised at the attachment we have to the physical body," says Monroe. "It's addictive. As long as you have that body, the attachment is still strong. You have an urgency to get back."

The call to return to the body, notes Monroe, is not always a deep philosophical or psychological one.

"Ninety percent of the time," he smiles, "it's a full bladder."

Lunchtime, and Monroe drives down the mountain to the nearby town of Nellysford for a cafe lunch and more questions. Over a burger, fries and iced tea, he talks about the past, the future and other lives.

"Never mind religious beliefs, or whether you've been a bad boy or a good boy," he says of life beyond death. "You're going to survive physical death whether you like it or believe it or not. It's a fact."

We have all been in other bodies in the past, says Monroe, and we will all be in other bodies in the future. Each consciousness is eternal, he says, while bodies come and go. The catch, he notes, is that when we're out of the bodies, we can't wait to get back, but while we're in these bodies, we are unaware that there is anything beyond.

"While you're here, you forget you were ever anything but human," says Monroe. "You forget where you came from."

And that, Monroe admits, begs the million-dollar question: Where did we come from? Who or what set up and guides this system, this planet, this universe?

Monroe nods and fingers a fry.

"Just somebody having some fun," he says.

Somebody?

"Some intelligent energy field."

Energy field?

"An energy being. Something the average human would call God, but it wasn't God."

What it was, says Monroe, was one of many consciousnesses permanently unhooked from the cycle of death and life as a human.

"There are graduates from this school of compressed learning we call Earth who are doing this in other places," he says. "It's a lot of fun, creating species, weaving just the right delicate balances for life on a planet."

Monroe knows how much fun it can be, he says, because he has seen it.

"Just a small demonstration," he says of the energy-being who escorted him during one of his OOBEs. The being, says Monroe, created a solar system for Monroe's viewing pleasure.

"It was if someone was making it snow, and creating snowballs, and tossing them out like fiery suns, as it were. Nuclear snowballs. Just having fun."

It was, in fact, just fun and games, says Monroe, that got the whole ball rolling here on Earth. The consciousness that created Earth, says Monroe, began tinkering with its toy, decided to try out its creation first-hand, in human form, and things soon got out of hand.

"To really feel how it is, it had to get down into it. Only it didn't figure on the addiction of life as a human. It thought it was in for a quick shot and out. But things didn't happen that way."

So all this is a result of an accident, of a great cosmic mistake?

"Not a mistake," says Monroe, finishing his tea. "An experiment."

Back at the institute office, Monroe climbs out of his car as another vehicle comes up the drive. A woman hops out, clutching a copy of his latest book. She corners Monroe, gets his autograph and drives away as Monroe heads upstairs to recycle.

Monroe's daughter Nancy, the institute's administrator, is downstairs, doing paperwork to the sound of a faint hum coming from a pair of speakers on her desk. The tape is called "Concentration," one of the institute's better sellers.

"I can concentrate anytime I want," says Nancy. "But I happen to be lazy, so I put a tape on."

Nancy, 33, says she has been having OOBEs since she was 16. But unlike her father's, her control is shaky. During one experiment, she slipped into an out-of-body state, and Monroe asked her to explore the "intervals between lives." Instead she slipped in and out of episodes in what she says were her previous lives — as a man about to be hanged, as a woman about to be executed and as a soldier inside a tank about to be blown up.

Asked why the experiment took her to moments of imminent death instead of post-death limbo, Nancy shrugs and smiles: "I kept missing."

Nancy has worked for her father since 1974 after graduating from college and studying Zen philosophy in Japan. She and her husband, Joseph McMoneagle, a former Army warrant officer who now heads a consulting company called Intuitive Intelligence Applications, live just down the road. Monroe and his wife, Nancy, live upstairs, "over the store," as Monroe puts it.

The office is busy, with several of the 14 staffers handling the correspondence generated by sales of the institute's assorted programs and products. The room also houses the only Xerox machine for miles around, and that's what brings Eleanor Friede through the door.

Friede still has a home and office in Manhattan, where she edits and publishes books, always on the lookout for another "Jonathan Livingston Seagull." But since Christmas, when she moved into her new home on the institute's property, she's been shifting much of her work and time here.

"I was simply curious," she says when asked why she signed up for a week-long institute program in 1982. The week, she says, was worth the $850 price tag.

"I was just more aware. It didn't change my direction, but it made it clearer that I had to get away from the distractions, noise and dirt of New York. Now I've found I can have it both ways."

And now that she's here, Friede says it will be only a matter of time before she moves from relaxation tapes to exploring life beyond the body.

"I have a feeling that's why I'm here," she says. "I want to know how far we can go, to learn more about the universe we live in."

Fully recycled, Monroe spends the afternoon giving a tour of the institute buildings, checking again on the mountaintop construction and explaining why he believes mankind is reaching what he calls "critical mass" in terms of the pressures on our collective consciousnesses. The threat of nuclear war, environmental holocausts and the latest specter of terrorism, says Monroe, are actually pushing people toward the same kinds of discoveries he has been making in his laboratory for years.

"As anxiety levels rise worldwide," he explains, "as the rules and the game change, consciousness evolves to deal with all this.

"The consciousness that can cope," he goes on, "is the developing consciousness. If man does not learn and pass this test and move to a mature consciousness, entropy will set in and man will no longer be the dominant species on this planet."

Which, notes Monroe, would be no great disaster.

"The future of man on earth," he says, "is an interesting, but relative term. If this compressed learning school that is human existence on Earth goes down the tubes, there are others."

Man, however, will not go the way of the dinosaur, says Monroe. And he speaks from more than faith. He says he has seen the future, he has been there, although he will only describe it in sketchy terms.

Nuclear war, for example, will not occur, says Monroe, at least not on a global scale: "There will be contamination, but not from bombs nuking all over the place. The contamination will be astronomical."

People will be able to control their bodies, says Monroe, to the point where a handful of rice will provide sufficient calories for an entire day. In time, a kernel will suffice. Then, no food at all will be needed: "It's just a matter of stages."

Communication, he says, will be nonverbal, requiring neither voices nor ears: "Mind to mind connection in its purest sense."

The aim of all this development, says Monroe, and the object of his work at the moment, is erasing the fear of death.

"When the fear is gone," says Monroe, "the fun begins."

Part of his fun at the moment is conducting death-simulation experiments in his laboratory, and drafting a third book on what he calls "the ultimate frontier, the greatest unknown of all" — death.

Using the same hemi-sync methods that launch his explorers on OOBEs, Monroe and his staff are placing volunteers in a consciousness-free state in which they lower their own blood pressure, body temperature and pulse rate, "synthesizing death in slow motion, as it were," says Monroe.

"We in essence reel them out close to death, pulling away all the mystical, superstitious trappings and trying to cross through the fears to what it's all about."

There is no danger in the experiments, he says: "We can bring them back in instantly." And there is no possibility that death may look attractive after a close look: "It doesn't mean you want to die; you're just not afraid of it."

In all his cosmic excursions, Monroe says he has avoided seeing how he will die at the end of this lifetime: "I don't want to spoil the fun."

All things, he says, come with time. Eventually, we will "achieve escape velocity" and "go home, where we came from."

Now and in the end, says Monroe, we are all in essence God. "But you've forgotten what you are. This heavy physical life experience has blotted it out."

Monroe has been on both sides. The reason he is still here, "hanging around," as he puts it, are the simple pleasures of life, the "addictions" that for him include composing music, eating fresh trout and "occasionally playing a good game of cards."

No out-of-body peeks at someone else's hand, of course. In all games we play, says Monroe, cosmic or otherwise, there is really no way to break the rules. No steps can be skipped. No lives left unlived. Each hand is played out all the way.

And the dealer?

"Something's driving," says Monroe, watching the sun set over his ridge, "but it's not the God of our childhood."

May 18, 1986

IV. THE FAITHFUL

A World Apart

Listen.

The moon is high on this midwinter night. Its light shimmers off the frozen surface of a mountain pond. The trees lining the ridges above the pond are bare, their skeletal limbs thrust against the starry sky, like a picket fence protecting the two tiny cabins huddled in the hollow below.

The door to one of the cabins opens, and two figures emerge, wrapped against the cold. Frozen grass crunches beneath their feet as they drift through the darkness to the other cottage and disappear inside.

In the blackness of the tiny valley, a dog howls. And a goose screams at the night.

White smoke curls from the small lodge's chimney. A soft orange light glows in a window. And suddenly, from within, comes the sound of singing.

Gentle, soothing. Angelic.

The dog falls silent. The goose stops screaming. All that moves through the air are the smoke and the song.

Then the singing stops.

But the silence stays.

And here, deep in the winter, deep in the evening, deep in this mountain hollow, another day begins for Our Lady of the Angels.

They came last spring to these hills west of Charlottesville, six women wearing the simple black-and-white habits of nuns. They came to take what had once been a farm, a factory, a tourist attraction, and turn it into something of their own — something different from anything that had been here before.

The sign on the gate at the bottom of the gravel drive used to say "Landsdale Farm" — 500 acres of fenced rolling pastureland. There was a cheese factory here. And a herd of Holsteins. And horses. And busloads of visitors arriving to tour the factory and taste the cheese.

But the cows are gone. And the tourists. The factory is locked. And the sign on the gate now says "Our Lady of the Angels Monastery."

They are Trappistine nuns, women who have chosen to live a life apart, gathered unto themselves and their God. Their vows of poverty, chastity, obedience, simple labor, stability and— when they are working, reading and communing with their Lord— silence.

"We seek in silence to listen and respond, a listening to which our whole life is geared."

That is how a pamphlet brought by these nuns from their base monastery in Massachusetts describes their approach to their lives and to the Lord.

There are 58 Trappistine monasteries in the world, housing 1,900 women, members of the Order of Cistercians of the Strict Observance. Four of those monasteries are in America: One in Iowa, one in Arizona, one in Massachusetts and, now, one in Virginia. Each is rural, set apart from society, continuing the contemplative life established by the first Trappist monks in France nine centuries ago.

Part of that life includes supporting themselves economically. And so, each monastery produces goods to sell. One bakes bread. Another sells jams. Another sells candy.

Here, sometime next year, these six Sisters will make and sell the same Gouda cheese that once rolled out of that abandoned factory.

Meanwhile, they are moving in.

Dawn, and the eastern sky is streaked pink and turquoise.

Inside the cabin, kneeling on knotted pine floors laid 150 years ago, the six women pray in darkness. The only sounds are the crackling of logs in a wood stove and the whistling of the wind outside, fighting its way through the chinks in the cabin's log walls.

They have eaten their breakfast — rolls and cocoa — and are now deep into their second of seven daily prayer sessions, called Offices. The first, Vigils, is what soothed the geese at 3 a.m. The final, Compline, will usher in the women's 7:30 p.m. bedtime.

As the nuns kneel in the blue light of dawn, a small, balding man with a salt-and-pepper beard sits down to his own breakfast in a brick house down near the farm's gate. At 7:10 he will don a hooded cowl and make the mile hike up into the hollow to perform Mass for the Sisters. But right now he is dressed in a sweatsuit and jogging shoes, eating a plate of scrambled eggs and wheat germ muffins, and listening to the morning news on National Public Radio.

He is Father Dan Kelliher, a Trappist monk, one of 2,900 in the world. He arrived here last August, for the express purpose of performing the Eucharist for the Sisters each morning. This August he will leave, to be replaced by another monk who will perform the same duty.

The number of the world's Trappist monks has shrunk by a third since reaching a high point 30 years ago. The number of Trappistine nuns, on the other hand, has remained almost unchanged during that time. Father Dan, who looks a good 20 years younger than his age of 65, has his own idea why.

"With all due respect fo feminism," he says, "this type of life generally comes easier to the female. They more readily lead the contemplative life than men, who are generally more aggressive and might have a harder time adjusting."

Father Dan himself is having a hard time, even after 40 years wearing the cloth. He is involved with several University of Virginia social issue groups and is not sure he's ready to return to his Colorado abbey when he is replaced in August.

"I do feel a tension," he says. "I tend to get too introspective when I'm alone. So I have to find a way to balance the need to be set apart and the need to be involved."

But while Father Dan has his own struggle, he is not at all apologetic about living a life apart from he world. On his breakfast table sits a copy of Michael Mott's 1984 biography of Thomas Merton, a 20th-century Trappist monk known for his progressive, sometimes radical writings. Sitting next to the book is a pamphlet entitled "Cistercian Life," written by Merton.

"The apparent 'pointlessness' of the monastery in the eyes of the world is exactly what gives it a real reason for existing, " wrote Merton. *"In a world of noise, confusion and conflict it is necessary that there be places of silence, inner discipline and peace; not the peace of mere relaxation but the peace of inner clarity and love based on ascetic renunciation. "*

This is the peace Father Dan is fighting to find.

And it is the peace the six Sisters are bringing to this farm.

It is 7 a.m., and the nuns are gathered in a room off the kitchen, part of the cabin's addition built by the previous owners 10 years ago. The appliances are modern. So is the skylight above. And the phone by a window. But there is no television. Or radio. No need for the noise.

Outside the room's picture window, ducks slide across the pond's icy surface. Inside, Mother Veronica, who helped select this group from among the 57 nuns at the Massachusetts monastery and who leads them now that they are here, reads aloud from the Bible, adding her own comments on the life they have chosen.

She talks of Adam and Eve, of a paradise lost, and of how "the corruption of the best is the worst."

She talks of how man throughout the ages has struggled to get back to God, how "every human being is called to that fulfillment," and how this group of six women is one small step in the right direction.

"In this place and with these people," she says, "we make, as if a single person, our journey back to the Father."

The Sisters sit in a semicircle, hands folded on their laps, listening silently.

"It is when this reverent seeking becomes widespread," continues Mother Veronica, "that we can begin to hope for a return to paradise. And that is what we are trying to do here."

Just then, Father Dan appears over a rise, coming up the gravel drive. Bailey, the Sisters' golden retriever, runs to meet him. The women move back to the old part of the cabin, where their makeshift chapel is arranged. An altar has been placed by the woodstove. Two candles are lit on the mantel, the flames slightly bending in the room's draft.

Father Dan enters. A bell is rung.

It is time for Mass.

Finally, after Mass, the Sisters speak. And laugh, radiating a joy that shatters any image of grimness an outsider might imagine.

Over coffee and cookies, they tell a visitor how each of them came here — not just to this place, but to this life.

There is Sister David, at 57 the oldest of the group. The women here were chosen not just for their spiritual skills, but for their physical ones, and Sister David is the handyman. She is the one who patches the chinking in the cabin walls and floors, repairs the gutters, and occasionally climbs under the hood of the Sisters' Dodge station wagon. A former nurse, she also patches the occasional bump and bruise.

"If the mixer isn't working, the john's overflowing, the lights are out, they call me," laughs Sister David, who has lost none of the thick accent she acquired growing up in Boston. Tall, lean, her light gray hair pulled back beneath her veil, it's easy to picture her in the front row at Boston Garden, cheering on the Celtics.

Neither has Sister David lost the humor it took to endure being raised with six brothers. When Mother Veronica mentions that none of the 10 women who have contacted her since last May expressing interest in becoming nuns has answered her written replies, Sister David chuckles.

"It took me three years to answer mine, Mother," she reminds her friend with a grin. She takes a sip of coffee, then continues.

"I never imagined I'd be a nun," she says. But when she read an article about the Massachusetts monastery, she wrote them a letter. When they sent her back an application, she balked.

"I said no way."

She put the letter in a drawer. She got engaged. Then she broke the engagement. And, three years after she tucked it away, she pulled the application out again.

"Something draws you," she says. "And eventually you start listening."

Sister David listened, and in 1959, at age 29, she became a nun.

"I felt an emptiness in my life," she says. "But this is a life of love. From the moment I've entered I've never had a doubt about staying."

Sister Margaret is 32. Dark-haired, shy. She is the groundskeeper and gardener, hacking honeysuckle from the fences, mowing the lawn surrounding the two cabins and tending the vegetable garden that provides the bulk of the Sisters' meals, supplemented by eggs from their henhouse and an occasional bass from the pond.

Margaret was raised a Catholic in Rochester. Her father worked for Kodak. Her freshman year at college in New York, she joined a group of students for a weekend retreat at a Trappist monastery. She went out of curiosity more than anything else. But it was a weekend that changed her life.

"It was almost like falling in love," she says, "like finding something you're looking for — and I wasn't even aware I was looking for it."

A year later she went on another retreat. At the end of that weekend, she was chatting with one of the monks.

"I told him I really liked it there. I said it's too bad girls can't be monks."

"'Ahhhh,' he said. 'But you can.'"

And that is how Sister Margaret learned of the Trappistines. When she visited the nuns in Massachusetts, she learned more.

"I expected cloistered nuns to look all, I don't know, *cloistered!* But they looked so open and fresh, like the monks I'd seen."

In December, 1977, Margaret graduated from college.

On Valentine's Day, 1978, she entered the monastery.

Sister Mary Beth is the novice of the group. She has yet to take her final vows, and so, while the others' veils are black, hers is white. When the others don cowls, she wears a cape.

Gregarious, bubbly, she looks and acts much younger than her 40 years. But then none of these sisters' faces shows the strains of age. That, they explain matter-of-factly, is one of the more visible rewards of the contemplative life.

It's a life Sister Mary Beth says she imagined even as a little girl growing up in suburban New York City.

"I wanted to be a cowgirl, a police lady, or a nun," she laughs. "And people would tell me, 'Oh, *everybody* wants to be a nun when they're little.'"

Mary Beth followed through, but first she spent 15 years working as a secretary and serving a stint in the Peace Corps in Brazil. She recalls smoking a cigarette at age 13, and she compares her work years to that early puff.

"I really got the taste of what I didn't want," she says of her secretarial and Peace Corps experiences. "Just like the smoking."

When she read a Trappistine booklet, however, Mary Beth wasn't sure this life was what she would want either.

"All it talked about was silence, silence, silence. And I thought, *Me?* Be *silent?* I put the booklet aside and didn't look at it for four years."

Like Sister David, Mary Beth was eventually drawn back to the Trappistines. But twice, after interviews and short stays at the Massachusetts monastery, she was rejected.

"They told me they didn't think this life was right for me," she says. "I was crushed."

But not beaten. She hunted for an alternative: "I went through a catalog of 180 different orders, looking for the right one."

Nothing else, however, would do. So, in 1980, she came back once again to the Trappistines. And her persistence, apparently, was finally as impressive as her piety.

In June of 1981, Mary Beth took her first vows.

Sister Barbara is without doubt the most beatific of the group. At 50 she radiates a serene wisdom ages older.

She is from Southern California, where she lived a "normal life" growing up in Long Beach. "I dated, played sports, was in the student government," she says with a smile that speaks more than her words.

She graduated from high school, worked as a secretary in Los Angeles, but never had a doubt she was going to be a nun. When she read Thomas Merton's 1950 autobiography "The Seven-Story Mountain," she was softly stunned.

"I woke up one morning and just *knew* I was going to be a sister. And I felt so happy. Just simply happy."

Deciding just what sort of nun she would become was another matter. Sister Barbara did her homework. She studied and visited communities of Dominicans ("more intellectual, book- oriented"), Franciscans ("poverty-oriented") and Carmelites ("extremely hermitical") before deciding the Trappistines were for her.

"We're rather an earthy bunch," notes Mother Veronica.

Sister Barbara, who entered the order in 1956, nods.

Mother Veronica is still getting used to her new title, one she took when she was chosen to lead this group on their pilgrimage to Virginia. She is a small woman, but she has the aura of a leader. The others look to her naturally, but she's still getting used to her title.

"I've been a sister 31 years," she says, "so sometimes I forget I'm now a mother."

"A mother of quints," adds Sister David with a gentle wink.

Mother Veronica is 50, a native of Queens. When she was 12 she too read Merton's autobiography, and, she says, "Those thoughts always remained in the back of my mind."

After high school she worked in Manhattan as a secretary, then, at 18, applied to the Trappistines. The day of her interview with the nuns, she arrived with The New York Times under her arm and a cigarette in her mouth.

"I *loved* this world," she says of the life she lived before joining the order. "But I always wanted more. I was the type of person who was never quite satisfied.

"When I got to Wrentham," she says, referring to the Massachusetts monastery she entered in 1956, "I found all the meaning I could ever look for."

Finally Sister Marilyn speaks.

All morning she has seemed the most reserved of the group, a self-consciousness lacing her serenity. When it is her turn to talk of her past, she feints a dash for the door.

The others laugh, and Sister Marilyn sits back down to describe her upbringing — her Jewish upbringing.

"I had absolutely no idea I was going to be a Catholic, much less a nun," she says with a sigh.

Like Mary Beth, Sister Marilyn too is 40, and she too grew up in suburban New York. Her father was an accountant, her mother a teacher. The family observed all the Jewish holidays and rituals, but there was something missing for Marilyn.

"I had a sense I was a Jew," she says. "But once I got to college, I realized it meant nothing to me."

She entered the University of Massachusetts hungry for something beyond the classroom.

"I was searching," she says. "I went through a deep sense of an inner void, which so many know so well. A spiritual hunger."

After leaving school and living in Canada for several years, Marilyn returned to Massachusetts, where, like Margaret, she discovered the Cistercians through a retreat at a monastery of monks.

"I was amazed," she says of that weekend. "I wanted to be a nun."

That was in the fall of 1972. The following spring she was baptized and received into the Catholic church. She then spent a year visiting various orders of nuns. One was in the city — "Not for me." Another had no manual labor — "I needed that." Finally she visited the sisters at Wrentham.

"When I drove up that driveway I knew right away. I said this is it." In 1975 Sister Marilyn entered the order.

And four years ago, on this very morning, she made her solemn vows and received a black veil.

Afternoon, and the February wind blows bitter as Mother Vernoica and Sister David hike toward a hilltop pile of red clay and cinder-blocks. Six workmen move about a small wall, a wall that will become a monastery.

The sisters had hoped to move to the hill last November. Now they are aiming at the end of this year.

They had planned the building to be 6,000 square feet. The architects told them their needs could not be met with less than 11,000.

They had originally expected to pay $510,000. The price tag now stands at more than a million, which they and their sister monasteries are collecting through donations and grants.

"The Lord only knows what price we'll end up with," says Mother Veronica. "I'm just praying certain things will be forthcoming."

But delays continue. Besides the unavoidable snow, wind and rain, there are the sticky details of county codes and compliances.

"They've never built a monastery in Albemarle County before," says Mother Veronica, tugging her collar tight against the wind. "We don't fit into categories very easily."

Why, she is asked, is the monastery rising here on a hilltop when the pondside setting down in the hollow seems so idyllic?

"It is beautiful," she says of the cabins by the pond. "But for a life that is as intense as ours is, where we don't go out and do things, we need a setting that is not so closed in, that is conducive not only to interior focusing but that also has an opening-out quality as well. And look at this setting, this vista."

She is right. Up here, the ridges and valleys of the Shenandoah foothills roll toward the horizon like a bunched, forested carpet. Down the hill, near Father Dan's house, sit the complex of barns and buildings that were once the cheese factory. They are still filled with the plastic tubs, wooden presses and stainless steel tanks used to produce cheese. The cheese-making, however, will wait until the monastery is built, and even then things will be different than before. The nuns, who will ultimately number 24 here, will buy their milk rather than bring cows back to these fields.

"That would be too much," says Sister David. "We can't manage cows, cheese *and* the contemplative life as we live it."

Dusk, and the nuns are gathered back in the cabin for Vespers.

The hollow is still. The geese are sleeping. The woodstove glows as the Sisters sing. Softly. Serenely. A Psalm:

> *"... so we shall not fear though the earth should rock,*
> *Though the mountains fall into the depths of the sea,*
> *even though its waters rage and foam,*
> *even though the mountains be shaken by its waves,*
> *the Lord of the hosts is with us...*
> *Be still and know that I am God."*

The lights go out.
Heads are bowed.
Night falls.
Time stops.
Listen.

February 21, 1988

Okie, the Elder and the Vision

They'll be out there again tomorrow, dozens of them, maybe hundreds, come down from Washington and Philadelphia and Baltimore and New York, down the Colonial Parkway to the banks of the James the way they do every year, to fish and swim, to play ball, eat barbecue, laugh and light fireworks, not a care in the world, hardly a thought about tomorrow or yesterday, about Satan or the Lord, about The Elder or his prophecies.

But Okie Smith knows better.

Okie will be out there, too — out at his barn, tending his cows in the heat and the stink, soothing them with the gospel music on his beat-up transistor, bending beneath the words "Jesus Saves" scrawled on the cinder-block wall behind him, and stealing a glance at the holiday crowd down there by the river.

Okie will watch and he'll wonder.

He'll wonder just how many of those people down there ever actually heard The Elder's voice — that powerful, gravelly voice that rumbled out of radios for three decades, the voice of a black man whose message of happiness and comfort in the Lord and brotherhood among all races rang across the nation's airwaves through a Depression and a World War and the stirrings of The Movement, reaching not just the ears of the poor and the black — the listeners he called "my precious ones" — but touching the White House itself, where men named Roosevelt, Truman and Eisenhower heard The Elder and called him their friend.

Okie heard that voice. He heard it 45 years ago, in Washington D.C., where he was a white family's houseboy from the Eastern Shore. One day he walked past a church, heard preaching so strong, so magnetic that he had to step inside. The voice belonged to The Elder — Lightfoot Solomon Michaux, master of the Gospel Church.

After he heard that voice, Marion O'Connell "Okie" Smith belonged to The Elder, too. Okie became a member of the church. He was proud to watch The Elder come and go in a chauffeured Cadillac. He was awed by the 20,000 people who jammed that city's Griffith Stadium on Sunday nights to watch The Elder lead a gospel choir of hundreds, watch The Elder stage the Second Coming in the center field bleachers, watch him give last rites to the devil down by the pitcher's mound and baptize hundreds of the faithful in a pool set up right there on home plate.

Okie heard that voice then, and he still hears it today, 20 years after The Elder died. Michaux left behind an evangelical empire: churches in eight cities, federally-funded housing projects in Washington, a park on the banks of the James River and a farm across the Colonial Parkway from that park — the farm Okie's been running since 1943, when The Elder himself sent Okie south to fulfill The Vision.

The Vision: That a day will come when this great nation collapses, when people's pockets will be filled with worthless money, when bread and milk will be more precious than gold. That day will come, promised The Elder, and when it does, he vowed his precious ones will have a place to gather, to survive, to wait out the storm. It will be these 1,250 acres on the banks of the James, promised The Elder, that will be his children's Eden.

Okie believed. Before each of Okie's 12 children were born, The Elder told Okie what the sex of that child would be. He was right every time. The man was a prophet. Presidents listened to his advice, thanked him for his prayers.

Okie believed.

But The Elder died and, for all but Okie, The Vision faded. The park, intended as a monument to the dignity of the black man in America, was to have a statue three stories high, with Jesus at the top and proud, strong slaves at the bottom. This spot, two miles upriver from Jamestown, was where The Elder decided the first black men in America had come ashore. That is why he chose this as the place for the park and the farm, a place of dignity and remembrance.

But the statue was never built. Instead there came a Tastee-Freez and a Ferris wheel and a merry-go-round, music and lights and laughter on Saturday night. The park became a place of amusement, a curiosiy to the tourists on their way to Williamsburg. Okie would hear that evening laughter drifting up from the river, and he would clutch his Bible even tighter, gathering his family close to him — his wife, his eight sons and his four daughters — warning them against the sins of temptation. This was not what The Elder had in mind, Okie would say. It is easy to feel abandoned, he would tell them. But this is a test, he would say, a test of faith.

It was a test, too, to watch The Elder's own church, the Gospel Spreading Church, founded in Newport News in 1919 and now head-quartered up there in Washington, allow the weeds to grow around this park, close it down during winters, open it for summers but have only a trickle of visitors except for the handful of holidays that brought church members in throngs: Memorial Day, Fourth of July, Labor Day.

It was a test to watch the farm and its buildings be sold off, little by little, piece by piece, until all that was left was Okie and his family and the cows. Part of the farm became a summer camp for children of the church. It still is, but that camp only lasts two months, hardly the year-round "Bible and Agricultural Training School" The Elder had forseen.

But nothing tested Okie's faith like Michael.

Michael, Okie's oldest son.

Michael, who left home to join the Air Force, who went to Vietnam, and who then came back to the family and the farm, to his wife and three children.

Michael, who on a steamy July afternoon in 1973 grabbed a college girl riding her bicycle past the farm, pulled her into the woods and raped her.

That was hard for Okie to understand. Even harder to understand was why Michael, after spending three years in prison, came back to the farm and did the same thing again, right down there by the park, where he stopped a woman on the beach, helped her pull some thorns from her feet, then raped her, strangled her, drowned her and stabbed her. The woman had two children. It was her birthday that day.

"I don't know of a worse crime," the prosecutor said at Michael's trial. "He killed her three different ways."

Okie hardly heard the lawyer's words. He and his sons, sitting in that courtroom with sackcloths pulled over their clothes, wearing their humility and sorrow for the world to see, had already given up Michael to the Lord. This was not for man to understand, Okie told the reporters. Okie never believed Michael killed that woman — he still does not believe it today. But that wasn't the point. God had his will and God had his reasons.

Okie endured. And he accepted. He could give up his son — after all, he says, Abraham did. Abraham obeyed. And Okie could accept sin among his own family — after all, Okie says, sin is sin. If you commit adultery, if you even covet another man's goods, he says, your soul is damaged as much as if you kill someone.

By the time Michael Marnell Smith was finally executed in 1986, after nine years on death row, Okie was not worried about his son's soul. It was already gone, he says, at home with the Lord. When they flipped the switch on that electric chair, Okie says, all they were burning was an empty shell, the body society needed for its own satisfaction.

Okie talks about Michael fitfully, climbing out from under a broken tractor as late afternoon shadows fill his barn and cover his face. Two of his grandsons are finishing the milking. One of them is Michael's son, who was 6 when his father was put on death row. The boy is 17 now. He and his siblings and his mother still live on the farm. So do two of Okie's sons and their families. The rest of Okie's children have moved away.

But Okie remains, answering his telephone with "God Bless You," running James City County's only working dairy with his leathery 65-year-old hands, teaching the men's Sunday School classes at the Newport News Gospel Spreading Church — the same building out of which The Elder used to lead a weekly parade of white-suited followers dancing down Jefferson Avenue, the same building in which The Elder's wife Mary founded the Young Women's Purity Clubs of America with the slogan "Be a Peach Out of Reach." The Purity Club still meets in that church every Thursday night.

The people there, in the church's offices, act nervous when asked about Okie, about the farm. A minister, Brother Jones, is cheerful when he answers the phone, but when asked about the farm, he puts the caller on hold. A secretary picks up the phone and says Brother Jones has a hearing problem.

A visit to the church's offices brings the same reactions. No, says a woman behind an office desk, there are no figures on the church's congregation. No, there are no files on the church's history or on the life of The Elder. Yes, that drawing on the wall is the monument The Elder hoped would be built at the park, the one with Jesus at the top. Yes, Okie Smith runs the farm, but it's nothing like it used to be when they had vegetables and fruit growing up there. Now, says the woman as if she's talking about a distant place, "all they've got up there are a few cows." Any other questions, says the woman, should be put to the church's headquarters in Washington.

There is only one man in Washington, say the people who answer The Gospel Spreading Church's telephone there, who can talk about the park and the farm. His name is James Stokes, the group's business manager. Messages are left, but Stokes returns no calls.

There is no doubt about The Elder's influence. Old newspaper clippings describe his church, radio and business dealings in Washington and other cities. There are descriptions of him bringing black votes to Truman. There is a photograph of him and his wife visiting Eisenhower in the White House. Time, Newsweek, the Saturday Evening Post and Life magazines all ran stories on Elder Michaux. At his 1968 funeral, held in Newport News and attended by more than 3,000, The Elder was eulogized as "a modern day Moses, a prophet of good will." A telegram of praise from FBI director J. Edgar Hoover was read.

But the park, the farm and The Vision seem as neglected now as those old clippings.

Inside the park itself, where two women tend a soda fountain and a man sits watching television cartoons in a booth beneath a wall-sized photograph of The Elder, no one answers questions about the church or the farm or the brick building out back, a building fronted by bronze statues of The Elder and his wife, a building Okie says is a museum.

There are no windows on the building. The doors are locked. But in one of the doors, there is a hole. Through the hole can be seen walls lined with photographs of black men and women. Mary Michaux's portrait hangs on a wall by itself. In the center of the room, propped on cinder blocks, its wheels removed, sits a black Cadillac with Washington D.C. license plates.

When the women are asked about the museum, one of them leaves. The other is silent for several minutes, then says the museum is "not available right now."

Other questions draw the same response.

"I have nothing to say," says the woman, her eyes drifting toward the farm. "*Some* people get to talkin' too much, their mouths get to flyin' and they don't know *what* they're sayin'."

But Okie knows better.

He knows the members of the church may have forgotten The Vision, just, he says, as the children of Israel forgot their God's plans.

But Okie has not forgotten.

"I'm still here," he says, wiping dust from the oval window of a leather horsedrawn hearse, the same hearse The Elder used to carry the body of the devil into the center of Griffith Stadium. Now the carriage sits in Okie's barn, next to his tractors, its windows pocked with vandals' bulletholes.

"My obligation is to him," Okie says of the man for whom he still keeps the cows.

"I'm still here," he says, gazing down at the park and the haze-shrouded river.

"I've still got my mission."

July 3, 1988

Crisis in the Kingdom

The sky is dark as rain pelts the Billy Graham Parkway this morning before Easter — just another bit of bad news for the masses of faithful flocking to Heritage U.S.A. for a weekend of resurrection.

It's not enough that Jim and Tammy Bakker are gone, exiled from the glittery $172 million Pentecostal playground they built with their on-the-air charisma and tears. It's not enough that their saga of sex, drugs and deceit continues to unfold this very morning, with newspaper headlines announcing that the couple drew nearly $5 million in salaries over the last three years. It's not enough that a civil war has broken out among fundamentalist factions wrestling for control of the theme park, real estate and television empire the Bakkers left behind.

But now it looks like the weather will close the water slide.

"That's all right," says a scrub-faced teen named Joe, eyeing the park's chained-off $10 million water complex and moving toward the Christian rock band tuning up on a windy lakeside stage. "There's other things to do here."

Like take a dip in the Heritage Grand Hotel's lobby pool, where public baptisms are performed every Tuesday.

Or wander the hotel's mock Victorian shopping mall, where believers stroll in perpetual twilight beneath projected clouds rolling across an arched heavenly blue ceiling.

Or sample the fare in the mall's candy-colored shops: the sticky buns in Bakkers Bakkery, the sweets in Heavenly Fudge, the mascara in Tammy Faye Cosmetics.

Or relax in one of the 504 rooms of the Grand Hotel where a morning wake-up call pronounces, "This is the day that the Lord hath made," where Bibles are out on the table, not tucked in a drawer, and portraits of Jesus and Mary hang on the walls.

Or join the studio audience at one of the PTL programs beamed worldwide from the network's Heritage headquarters, where Bakker deputy Richard Dortch carries the torch and keeps the faith—even as his own extravagant salary ($270,000 the first three months of this year) is headlined in the morning paper.

Or walk from the television studio to the nearby Upper Room, where ministers work eight-hour shifts providing around-the-clock hands on healing in a sanctum modeled after the site of the Last Supper — with carpeting and air conditioning added.

For those who want more than just an occasional visit to this "21st Century Christian Retreat," there is the real estate sales office, which offers a menu of condos, duplexes, homes and apartments to believers who, as park spokesperson Linda Ivey says, "want to come not for a day but a lifetime."

More than 2,000 people have made the permanent move to these oak-shaded 2,300 acres in South Carolina. To them it is heaven on earth. Six million visited last year — a figure second only to the two Disney parks. Storms may be raging beyond these grounds, but inside there is little evidence that the kingdom is crumbling.

"Everyone's *UP*!" gushes Gene Feather, one of three hotel doormen decked out in braided white uniforms. Feather turns to hug, hold hands and pray with the pilgrims piling out of a tour bus. "Just *look* around you," he says. "You can *see* God's victorious army. The press, the publicity — it's opened us up to people. They're coming just to see what's here, and once they come, they don't want to leave."

Everywhere on the grounds are signs that the wagons of the faithful have circled. "Enough is Enough" is the title of one of many Tammy Bakker books displayed in the window of the mall's Ye Olde Bookstore. In the last month, the phrase has become a rallying cry, appearing on bumper stickers and buttons, a defiant answer to a mocking world.

The word of the day at Heritage U.S.A. is "Forgiven." It's spelled out in flowers planted at the park entrance. It hangs above the front desk of the hotel, behind which golden gothic letters proclaim "Jesus Christ is Lord." And it is stamped over and over — eight times — on a placard inside the door of the resort's Partner and Information Center, where a portly salesman who identifies himself only as John says business is booming.

"What we've seen in here has been like Ivory Soap — 99 and 44/100 percent positive," says John. "People are coming here now out of curiosity. And they're leaving as monthly partners."

That's $15 a month, which earns membership in the PTL (Praise the Lord, or People That Love) club. A $1,000 donation makes one a Life Partner — which means three free nights a year at the Grand Hotel for the rest of this lifetime. It was on the strength of those $1,000 pledges that Jim Bakker was able to build the $42 million, four-floor Grand — with cash. On any given night, half the rooms in the hotel are occupied by Life Partners reaping the material rewards of their offerings. And John says there is no hint that construction on another 500-room, 21-story hotel will be slowed by the Bakkers' bad news.

"We've got people coming in and saying 'We're here to stand with you'," says John. "People who are already members are coming in and *increasing* their pledges."

And anytime, anywhere on these grounds, they are embracing, praying and praising the Lord as never before. On a balcony overlooking the hotel lobby, Eleanor Beamon and a dozen of her relatives are headed to lunch when they stop to belt out an impromptu rendition of a gospel tune.

"This is kind of a family reunion," says the 58-year-old grandmother from New Jersey. "We're all Christians, so what better place to have it?"

Eugene and Patricia Sorenson feel the same way. They're sitting in the lobby, next to a silver-gowned pianist whose only sheet music is a card that reads "God Bless You." This is the Sorensons' fifth visit this year. They've bought "at least six" memberships, says Eugene, 60, who is a doctor back in Abbottstown, Pa., where Patricia, 57, is his nurse.

"There's no smoking here, no cussing, no drinking," says Sorenson. "But even more than that, you've got something to talk about with every person you meet. You talk about God. Every conversation you hear is someone talking about what Christ means to them."

A woman named Anne — "just Anne" — sits in the sand by the water park, clutches her pocketbook and thinks hard when asked why she's driven here from Charleston W.Va., with her 37 year-old daughter. Finally, she answers.

"I feel safe here," she says.

Christians surrounded by Christians in a holy land. A common-denominator world. Sin-free, trash-free and carefree. That was Jim Bakker's vision when he decided to build an updated version of the Pentecostal campgrounds he summered at as a boy. "My dream was to bring the Christian campground up to the 20th century," he told a national magazine last winter.

Bakker brought that dream with him when he arrived in Charlotte, N.C., in 1974, after he and Tammy cut their televangelical teeth with CBN's "700 Club." In 1978 they broke ground on 900 acres near an old textile town called Fort Mill, just across the South Carolina state line. When critics asked what a water slide has to do with Christianity, Bakker replied, "If you want to be a fisher of men, you better have good bait." When they questioned $90,000 condominiums billed as "the ultimate in Christian living," Bakker answered, "Jesus doesn't teach poverty." And he asked, "Why can't Christians have something first-class?"

As for those who would scoff at the trees trimmed with Christmas lights year round, who would snicker at the religious knick-knacks and curios lining the windows of saccharine "shoppes," who would chuckle at middle Americans whose only vice is overeating and who repent for that sin by buying Jim and Tammy's "How We Lost Weight and Kept It Off" diet book, who would dismiss this entire resort as so much tacky right-wing kitsch, Jim Bakker would point them toward a couple like Edwin and Thela Hacker.

The Hackers made their first trip from Michigan in 1979. Today they are back for the fifth time, celebrating their 50th wedding anniversary, handing out commemorative pens to anyone who happens by and glorying in the monuments rising around them.

"We helped build the Grand," says Hacker, 72, leaning back on a bench overlooking the lake. "And that," he says, pointing toward the water park, "was just a little mound in a field when we first came. Now look at it. Look at all of it."

Hacker turns toward a crane towering over the shell of the new hotel. He nods toward the foundation of a 10-story, sandcastle-shaped Wendy's restaurant, slated to open this summer. More than 200 new condo units will go on the market this year. Blueprints have been made and drawings posted for a 30,000-seat glass-walled ministry center and television studio called the Crystal Palace. The cost of that dream, says PTL Vice President Neil Eskelin, will be $100 million. And he sees no reason, in spite of the Bakker debacle, that it won't become reality in the same way as the hotel and the hamburger high-rise.

"We don't build on speculation," says Eskelin. "We build on actual sales. And we're right on target."

Almost everyone here, through their pledges and donations, has a piece of the Heritage action. And the action keeps coming. Dortch has picked up Bakker's on-the-air gauntlet, continuing to plead for viewers to send even more cash "in these times of testing." A re-creation of Jerusalem as it was in the time of Jesus is on the boards. So is an 18-hole golf course. And there are plans for an amusement park called Bibleland, with rides like "Noah's Ark" and "Jonah and the Whale"— rides that park spokesperson Linda Ivey says "will serve as learning tools, to teach Bible history."

The ultimate ride, says Ivey, will be called "A Trip To Remember"—a journey through biblical descriptions of hell and heaven that Ivey says was Jim Bakker's pet project. "He really believed," says Ivey, "that a lot of young people would make decisions about their eternal future after going on that ride."

But right now the only rides in operation are a kiddie train rolling around the lake and a merry-go-round up in the woods. That's plenty for Jeff Steinke, a 40-year-old contractor from Michigan. Steinke is a Life Partner who visits Heritage "two or three times a year." His two children are with him, and his 15-year-old daughter, he says, is far from bored.

"She goes to a preppy school back home," says Steinke. "The kids are snotty. They take drugs, and she doesn't. So I bring her to a place where she can be around kids like herself."

Beyond his initial $1,000 donation, Steinke has tossed in another $1,000 for a "Silver Membership," giving him free use of the resort's ticketed attractions — including the $10-a-day water park. News of the Bakkers' lavish spending and their staff's exorbitant salaries hasn't made Steinke regret his contributions.

"Yes, I'm hurt about all of it," he says. "But without God's vision, given through Jim, I wouldn't be standing here, and neither would you."

Outside the Upper Room, where the only sound in a stone-walled courtyard is the babbling of a fountain, John Givler sits alone. He is waiting for his wife Sharon, who is still inside. This is John's first visit to Heritage. Sharon has been seven times. His job as an engineer with an Ohio faucet company, explains Givler, 62, makes it hard for him to travel.

"You staying in the Grand Hotel?" he asks. "Yeah, your lavatory faucet and your shower valve came out of one of our two North Carolina plants."

The Givlers planned this visit months ago, and the headlines of the past weeks, says John, did nothing to change their minds.

"In my estimation," he says, "this is all another case of your industry — journalists — doing a large disservice to your fellow man. I certainly don't think this has all been called straight and honest and down the middle."

Sharon emerges from the prayer room. She's 44, and she looks even younger, dressed like the college student she was before she rediscovered her Christianity through "The Jim and Tammy Show."

"I was born again many, many years ago," she says. "Then I went to school, got busy with life, got busy with a career and got back into the world. But one night I started watching PTL, and I learned to love again. I sat up and watched it every night, eating doughnuts and saying, 'Yes! Yes! Yes!'"

Sharon first visited Heritage two years ago, and she was as moved by the park as she was by the Bakkers: "I just cried the whole time I was here. I was so touched by this place, I kept coming back and back and back."

She pauses and purses her lips.

"I guess this is how Catholics feel about the Vatican."

Inside the Upper Room, late-afternoon light filters through stained-glass windows and washes over a semicircle of wooden benches. Scattered among the benches are a dozen men and women. Some gaze at the floor and mutter. Others have their hands raised, palms up, toward the ceiling. At the front of the room, six people stand in line, waiting as a bald, suspended man grips a woman's head in his hands, squeezes his eyes shut and begins a dialogue with the devil and with his Lord.

"Now," says the Rev. Paul McKeel, his voice starting low and rising. "Now! *Now! GO*, you migraine headache!"

The woman's legs wobble as her hands stretch toward the ceiling.

"Hallelujah," he shouts "*Hallelujah!* I *curse* the pain."

The woman's body jolts, her head snaps back.

"Take your hand *off*, devil. This is *God's* property."

He pushes his face into the woman's, whispers, and turns her toward the seated supplicants. Her cheeks are wet with tears, and she leaves the room chanting, over and over, "*Thank* you, Jesus. *Thank* you, Jesus. *Thank* you, Jesus."

McKeel pulls a Kleenex from a box, wipes his glistening forehead and drops the crumpled tissue into a growing pile. Then he turns back, attacking the demons again. A cripple. A stutterer. A man with hypertension. A woman with narcolepsy. McKeel stamps his feet. He giggles with glee. He roars,

"I *curse* the poison in these kidneys, Jesus," he says.

"I *curse* the arthritis in these hands."

"I *heal* this stomach in the wonderful name of Jesus."

"*DEVIL!!* Take thy infirmity and go from this body. In Jesus' name, *go!*"

And one by one they leave, walking back into the daylight, back toward the campgrounds and the water slide.

Among the healed is a 38-year-old woman named Hannah Dalton. She and her two cousins were on their way to shop in Charlotte when they "just decided to come." Hannah sprained her wrist recently and is afraid the injury will cost her an assembly line job at a nearby plastic factory. Now she is rubbing the joint and marveling.

"Look," she says, sobbing and smiling and wiggling her hand. "As you can see, there's a witness in it."

Hannah and her cousins, she says, are all "sisters of the Lord." And they were anything but discouraged by the news about the Bakkers. "It made me feel I wanted to suport them," says Hannah. "I became a member *after* all this."

Hannah's cousin Cora stands by and says she is ready with her own $15-a-month pledge.

"I don't care what nobody says," pronounces Cora. "This is holy ground. And I don't care what they say about Jim and Tammy. They are children of God. If you repent, you're the same as you were with God before. They've repented, and God is gonna bring them back."

"That's right", says Isaac Reynolds, a park janitor who is also a card-carrying evangelist. He points out, however, that the address on his business card is for his trailer, and he moved his trailer last week.

"I just go in the street and pray for people," says Reynolds, bending to minister to Hannah's sore knee. "The Lord has healed, oh, I'd say 7,000 people I've touched."

The tattoos on Reynold's arms and the scar on his throat, he says, came from his 28 years in prison. The Lord, he says, came the day he got out. Reynolds arrived at Heritage two years ago, and he says he's not about to leave.

"God is gonna turn all this confusion for good," he says. "This place is going to be here forever. If it's not Jim up front, God will send somebody else."

Doug Decker agrees. Decker, too, is a do-it-yourself minister who moved to Fort Mill two years ago. Back in Detroit, he says, he was an alcoholic. His wife, he says, had a serious drug problem. "We were two people you'd find in an alley," says Decker.

But after they watched "The Jim and Tammy Show" and brought their two children here with them, they knew they had done the right thing.

"It seemed that this was what heaven would be like," says Decker.

He now runs a small tire business in Fort Mill, his wife sings in the Heritage Valley Church choir and Decker spends what spare time he has in prison ministry — a pet project of Tammy Bakker's. He's never met the Bakkers, but Decker says he was as hurt by the past month's revelations as any member of the PTL's inner circle.

"This thing just ballooned for Jim and Tammy," says Decker. "It mushroomed so fast that they got caught on the top of the mushroom, and when the great amount of money started flowing, they lost sight of who they really were.

"I felt wounded," he says of the bad news. "Not betrayed, but wounded that someone I loved was hurt. Like a divorce, or having a child injured. We all have gone through a period of grieving here, but the consensus is that this thing's still working.

"The water park's nice," he says. "So is all the entertainment. But this place is about *ministering*, about hearing and sharing the word of God. And that's never going to change, whether Jim Bakker is here or not."

Easter morning the weather breaks. Sun splashes the faithful gathered in the park's outdoor amphitheater for a dawn Passion Play complete with trained doves and exploding flashpots. The top draw of the day, however, is the Easter service in the Heritage Village Church. The service is, as always, televised live on the PTL network. But this morning is special. There is hope in the air, prayers that Jim and Tammy might pick this morning to return, to show their faithful that they too can be resurrected — at least for a brief appearance.

"You bet that's on everyone's mind," says an usher as the church's 2,300 seats fill and the television cameras move into position. "I mean, what better day than this?"

The church is filled, and the spillover moves into the 1,600-seat PTL studio where Bakker's deputy, Richard Dortch, delivers the sermon on wide-screen TV. Even the kids in the studio lobby are gathered around a set, hoping maybe the Bakkers will show.

But they don't. And despite all the testaments of faith, a feeling of disappointment and even fear lingers in the air. It's in the voice of Shirley, a 62-year-old retired Floridian who owns a cluster home in one of the resort's quiet, carefully groomed neighborhoods.

"I never did like all the glitter, pushing to make it all bigger and better than anything else," she says. "I moved here to be around people I have an affinity with. I would just as soon all the other things not *be* here."

For David Booker, a 23-year-old PTL youth pastor, there was a more immediate reaction when he was called to a staff meeting last month and, along with 1,500 fellow employees, heard attorney Norman Roy Grutman announce that Jim Bakker had resigned.

"I just bought a house here, and my wife is pregnant," says Booker. "I'm embarrassed to say it, but when they made that announcement, the first thing that popped into my mind was what does this do to the value of my real estate?"

Although critics gibe that PTL now stands for "Plunder the Loot," the operation's $179 million in annual income and $200 million in real estate assets seem to be intact for the time being. There are more clouds on the horizon, however, including a report in the Charlotte newspaper that although PTL's revenues exceeded expenses by $19.8 million last May, new PTL leader Jerry Falwell has noted that the "previous PTL management" had applied for a $50 million loan from an unspecified party in England. The report also quoted Art Borden, head of the Evangelical Council for Financial Accountability, as saying PTL has "substantial debt on all its building programs."

Still, the picture this Easter Sunday is rosy. The Grand Hotel is booked, as are the Heritage Inn motel and the time-share apartments. The line at Susie's Ice Cream Parlor stretches out into the mall. The water park is open, and determined teens brave a chill April breeze to take a dive. Richard Dortch is preparing for a Monday PTL telecast from the Upper Room itself, where he will announce the construction of a "Wall of Faith," commemorating the viewers who "stand by us in this darkest hour." For a $100 donation, says Dortch, "your name will be printed on this wall."

And Gene Feather is all smiles.

"God spoke to me before all this happened," he says. "He told me he was going to do something, something big. He said he was going to turn over the tables, just like he did in Jerusalem. And he has.

"Everything's been exposed that needs to be exposed. God is putting the fire to all of us, and it's the fire of purification."

A bus pulls up, more new arrivals spill out and Gene gives them a wave and a greeting.

"Praise the Lord!"

April 26, 1987

One Cool Commie

This would not seem the best of times to be a Bolshevik. The wall has fallen, the curtain is crumbling, the party is in a panic. Marx's minions are on the run, with nothing left but to count the losses.

So why is Maurice Jackson smiling?

Strange enough to find him still in business. Yet there he is, the 39-year-old chairman of the Communist Party of Virginia and the District of Columbia, manning his tiny third-floor office, across the street from the National Geographic Building in the downtown heart of the nation's capital.

There is no red flag outside, no hammer and sickle on the door, nothing but Jackson's name listed in the directory by the elevator. One step inside his cramped headquarters, however, and there is no doubt this must be the place.

Busts of Lenin and Marx are perched on a bookshelf. A framed photo of Gorbachev is mounted on one wall. Beside it hangs a collage—cutouts of Castro, Stalin and Ho Chi Minh peering down on their point man in these parts.

One look at Jackson, as well as a glance at the other items decorating his office — photos of jazz musicians Charlie Parker and Ornette Coleman, of dancer Maurice Hines, of pool pro Willie Mosconi — indicates more than a mere dialectical materialist at work.

This is one cool commie.

He's got a quick answer for the Washington Redskins button pinned beneath a poster supporting striking shipyard workers: "Sure," he says, nodding at the football souvenir, "I'm an all-American guy."

He grins at a framed placard for a Soviet jazz concert, its script written in Russian: "No, I can't read it," he says. "Actually, I bought it at a bourgeois bookstore in New York."

He hoists a small chunk of cement from atop his desk—a piece of the Berlin Wall. "The wall," he muses, holding the rock up to the late afternoon light. "It should have come down. No doubt about it."

As for everything else that's been coming down lately — Romania, Hungary, Czechoslovakia, Lithuania — Jackson sighs. And he smiles.

"Nothing I can do about it," he says.

"Of course, not all of us feel the way I do. We have some comrades who are having a hard time accepting recent events in Europe. They think the party wasn't staunch enough, that it couldn't clamp the wheels on its own people. They're the ones who have the most trouble with Gorbachev.

"Personally, I think his party chose the right man for the right job.

"Personally, I think this is, in many ways, the second Bolshevik Revolution."

He shrugs, tossing the chunk of cement in the air.

"Personally, I'm not crying the blues about it."

Comrade. Bourgeois. Bolshevik.

Not exactly everyday lingo in the land of the free, especially in 1990. But according to its national headquarters in New York, the Communist Party of the United States of America has 20,000 card-carrying members. A 1989 State Department report puts the number at no more than 5,000. Experts who study the American left say it is closer to 10,000.

In any case, Maurice Jackson is one of them. Has been for 20 years. He spent the first half of his communist career working his way through the ranks, traveling to the Soviet Union for congresses, going to Cuba with a work brigade, immersing himself in the mechanics of the party. In 1979, he was elected chairman of the D.C./Virginia district, inheriting a membership he hesitates to describe in detail. Most own the party's red membership card, stamped with a hammer and sickle for each month they pay dues. But few carry it, says Jackson.

"They have fears," he says.

And, he says, they have reason. The rout may be on in the East, but the F.B.I. remains tense in the West. At least according to Jackson.

"They follow you," he says. "Sometimes they stop you. I've been stopped. They just want you to know they know what you're doing."

The telephone on his desk, Jackson says, is tapped.

"I assume it is. But I don't say anything on the phone that's of such a nature that I'm concerned. I'm not doing anything illegal."

What he is doing is manning the battlements he helped build two decades ago.

"When I joined in 1971, there was nothing here," he says. "We pretty much started from scratch. Most of us were young — I was barely out of my teens. I've seen a lot of people come and go since then."

Precisely how many remain is something Jackson can't — or won't — say. He allows there are "maybe a couple hundred" active members in Virginia and D.C. And he will say they have expanded beyond the classic constituency of union laborers and left-wing academics.

"Many are professional," Jackson says. "Bureaucrats, government workers, lawyers, writers, artists. They're people who have a hatred for oppression. They don't believe capitalism and greed are going to solve our problems.

"They aren't people who are necessarily struggling for themselves. We've got a lot of communists making $40,000 a year. I know many people giving money to the party making more than that."

They don't, however, give a lot. Jackson has no staff. He answers his own phone, types his own letters, even builds his own bookcases. Volunteers occasionally drop by to lend a hand.

"The party," he says, almost proudly, "is not rich."

Its money comes from donations and from monthly membership dues, which range from a maximum of $5 for people with annual salaries of $20,000 or more to a minimum of 50 cents for the unemployed "and those making minimum wage," Jackson says.

The income goes mostly to pumping out the office's paperwork, which ranges from newsletters and leaflets written by Jackson to stacks of the People's Daily World, published at the party's New York headquarters and distributed to anyone who's interested.

"We get strangers dropping in now and then," Jackson says. "Some are just curious. Others like our position on particular issues, like rent control in D.C. or right-to-work in Virginia. Some join simply because they see us out on the street struggling, and they respect that."

But there are nowhere near as many Leninists out there as Jackson once hoped. There was a time, he says, when he believed Communism would be the party of choice in America by the year 2000.

"When I first joined, I thought, 'Jesus Christ, man, people gonna rise up,' you know?

"But I was a young guy."

He's a 50-cent-a-month man now. He buys his clothes at thrift stores. Most days he walks two miles to work from the three-bedroom home he shares with his wife and two children.

"What would you want me to do?" he says of owning a house. "Live in a commune somewhere?"

He has collected "a couple thousand" jazz albums and teaches a jazz history class through the D.C. Public Schools. He runs marathons. Photos of his family cover an office cabinet. Dolls collected from his travels spill off his shelves. A box of toys is stored beneath his desk.

"My kids," Jackson says. "They're the joy of my life."

Their names don't matter, he says. Nor does his wife's.

"She's a worker, like you and me," he says. "Just refer to her as the love of my life."

He won't say if she is a communist.

"I wouldn't tell you if *anyone* was a member of the party," he says. "So I certainly wouldn't tell you if she is. I can tell you this: Most of my friends are not members of the Communist Party."

But they know he is. And that doesn't keep them away.

"I have friends over, I go out to shoot pool, I work out at the gym. I'm in a group of black men who discuss jazz. They aren't communists, but they respect me for fighting for my beliefs, even if they don't agree with everything I believe."

He is on the nine-person board of advisors of The Afro-American, a national newspaper. He is on the 22-member national Communist Party central committee. In 1981, he drew 25,000 votes as a delegate to the D.C. Statehood Convention, and he now chairs the Statehood Party. He has run twice for D.C. City Council, and he intends to run soon for the D.C. School Baord. He regularly writes letters to the Washington Post. And he occasionally visits New York, where aging U.S. Communist Party chairman Gus Hall continues to present the party line from his Manhattan headquarters.

Jackson, however, says he is free to interpret that line in any way he wants.

"I don't look to the preacher to get the word about God," he says. "I can get the word myself."

He first got the word in Alabama, in a rural black schoolroom, in the 7th grade. He had lived in Alabama since he was 4, when his parents had separated and sent him from Newport News to stay with his grandmother.

"Pearl Dickinson was her name," he says. "She washed clothes for rich white people."

He worked odd jobs with his older brother: "Picking pecans in the winter, cutting rich people's yards in the summer, throwing papers in the morning, cleaning up the rich white man's store in the evening."

His grandmother saw that he studied hard in school, "so I wouldn't have to scrub filthy floors with somebody on my back calling me names."

He read Martin Luther King's "Stride Toward Freedom" when he was 12. But a year later he read something that impressed him even more.

"We had this teacher who set up dialogues," he says. "One person had to read about and defend Nazi Germany; another had to read and defend the Communist Manifesto. And we were supposed to hate both of them."

Jackson knew no more about communism than any other boy in Alabama in 1963. "All I knew was Walter Cronkite's voice on the TV. All I knew was there was gonna be this war and we should be prepared to crawl up under our beds."

But the manifesto struck a chord.

"The notion of from each according to his ability and to each according to his need, that made a great impression on me. That made a lot of sense."

Still, it wasn't until he had returned to Newport News, graduated third in his class at that city's Carver High and earned a scholarship to study political science at Nashville's Fisk University that Jackson really began reading. And it wasn't until he spent a winter working as a rigger at the Newport News Shipyard that he felt he fully understood Marx's message.

"I developed there a great appreciation for workers," he says. "You see a crew of black men making $2.60 an hour and this white man, he's the boss. The initial, simplistic notion would be that this is totally racist. But I saw enough poor whites in Alabama and in Virginia to know it's not that simple.

"There's a lot of racism in this country, but I've been lucky enough to be able to look beyond that to the class problems behind it."

Although he was "half Black Panther" when he arrived in Washington in 1971 as an intern in the office of California Congressman Augustus Hawkins, Jackson was ripe for a different sort of revolution than racial supremacy.

By the end of that summer, he was a communist.

In the past 20 years, Jackson's jobs with the party have taken him to almost every country in Europe, five times to the Soviet Union, four to Cuba and once to Vietnam, where he addressed the 6th Congress of the Communist Party of Vietnam in 1986. His speech included an assurance about America:

"Comrades, we do not despair," he told his audience. "Our people have shown a new and increased willingness to fight for what is just and right."

But that fight, says Jackson, is no longer the sort he once envisioned.

"I don't have the belief I once had, that one day somebody would go to the barricades and seize the power."

The image of a Red Menace radical with a gun in one hand and a grenade in the other is off the mark, he says.

"I suppose if I lived in a country where I thought the gun and grenade would be helpful, I would have them."

Still, he remains a revolutionary.

"In every society there are people who have visions, who want their society to be equal and just. I think I'm fortunate to be one of those people."

The question arises — he's faced it often — why, instead of trying to reshape this country, he doesn't simply move to a Marxist one.

"I've often been asked that," he says. "But I was born in this country. I've put a lot into it. I've raised my family here, and I have a right to be here.

"I've made my choice to make this country better because I love it. What I do is I think for its salvation."

He smiles when asked whose side he is ultimately on.

"I'm on the side of the American people."

And if it came down to a choice between the Soviets and America, if he had to choose one to stand and the other to fall?

"I can't think in those terms," he says. "That's like asking me if I had to lose one of my children, which would I choose. I just can't think in those terms."

What he does think is that communism remains the hope for America's future, even as he admits a red flag will never be hoisted over the White House.

"My vision is that eventually the communists will play a role with other progressive forces to one day create a government whose main interests are the health and well being of the majority of people, black and white.

"I doubt that government will be communist, but there will always be a communist force here that people can believe will fight for and with them."

So even with the winds of change howling through the socialist world, even with upheavals cracking the face of communism around the globe, this is one comrade who insists the Party is not over. Three months ago, Jackson was among a group of local liberal leaders in Washington who held an emergency meeting the day after D.C. Mayor Marion Barry was arrested in a drug raid.

"Just about everybody in that room was in shock," he says. "Their heads were hung so low. So I said to them, 'Look, this past year I've seen so many changes in socialist countries, in many ways my whole belief system has collapsed. So seeing this cat fall is just another setback. I'm bothered, but we have to move on from here. It's not the end of the world.'"

Ho and Joe and Fidel stare silently behind him.

"It's not the end of the world."

May 6, 1990

A Simple Mission

Midday in the Shenandoah Mountains. Puffs of morning fog still hover over the greenness of Shifflets Hollow. Blossoming dogwoods splash white across the hollow's gentle slopes. In these hills, beyond the moneyed paddocks of Charlottesville's horse- breeding estates, only the chirping of bluebirds and the swishing of a soft spring breeze disturb the silence.

That, and the clatter of silverware echoing from within a tree-shaded stone lodge.

With the single ping of a bell, the clatter stops. Then a swell of guttural groans, grunts and wails rises from within the building. At first, the sound is indecipherable. But as it floats down the narrow valley, the noise becomes recognizable.

Jesus loves the little children.
All the children of the world,
Be they yellow, black or white,
They are precious in his sight.
Jesus loves the little children of the world.

It is the sound of singing. And lunchtime at Faith Mission Home.

The placard at the bottom of the steep drive reads "Faith Mission Home: A Residential Training Center for Handicapped Children." But the phrase comes nowhere near capturing the essence of this isolated, nine-acre community.

To the parents who have sent their children here to live, it is more than a "home"; it is a small slice of Eden.

Many of the "children" who live here are in their 20s.

The volunteer staff of 33 Mennonite men and women who watch over them night and day refer to the residents not as "handicapped," but as "brain damaged."

Mennonites do not mince words. If their philosophy can be described in a phrase, it's "Keep it simple." These bearded men and prayer-capped women do not want the network of rules, regulations and terminology that frames and binds the institutions of the outside world. They feel the Lord gives them all the instruction they need.

But recently, the state of Virginia has been forced to disagree.

Faith Mission made headlines two years ago when the General Assembly debated the home's practice of mild corporal punishment. Since then, the spanking has stopped, but the sticky issues of staff qualifications, dormitory housing and educational licensing continue to cloud the home's technical legitimacy and its very future.

For 20 years, the Faith Mission Home has taken children with wounded, damaged brains and worked what the children's parents call miracles. If a child is 12 or younger, has an IQ below 70 and can walk, the home will accept him if there's an opening and will keep him indefinitely. Without credentials or formal training, the staff of volunteers runs a live-in program of physical therapy, vocational training and classroom education based on what the home's administrator, Nathan Yoder, calls "love, control and bite-sized goals."

The setting is unabashedly religious. Scriptural verses and biblical drawings are hung on the home's walls. The drone of recorded a cappella hymns (Mennonites frown on the use of musical instruments) spills out of speakers throughout the day. There are no Mennonites among the 40 residents — 20 boys and 20 girls — who live in the home; there's just one among the 18 former residents who have "graduated" to adjacent cottages and tend to the home's farm and bakery. But while Yoder denies that the home seeks to create Mennonites, he also makes it clear that religion is the foundation of the home's success.

"We don't indoctrinate, per se, but they are exposed to scripture," he says. "We have nothing to hide. The parents know what's happening here. It's a transparent situation."

And it is one based on strict routine. Schedules of each staff member's duties and each child's tasks for the day are posted on billboards. Meals are marked by four rings of a bell — one for gathering, one for saying grace, one for collecting plates, cups and silverware and one for the post-meal song.

"I guess our philosophy is that without order, it won't work," explains Nathan's older brother Reuben, a tall, balding rail of a man who is the home's director.

"What we're trying to teach the children here," he says, "is to make every move count."

From the moment they are roused from under their quilted blankets at 6 a.m. until bedtime, the children of Faith Mission Home are like children anywhere: a whirl of motion.

But theirs are movments that are guided, deliberate and, most of all, regimented. Not quite every move counts, but most of them do.

"Our entire day is a training program," explains Nathan Yoder. "Stacking dishes, mopping the floor, toothbrushing. It's all a repetitive type of training. The key is to do these things over and over and over again.

In the girls dormitory room, a horizontal ladder is bolted to the ceiling. As a staff member looks on, a child swings easily from bar to bar, an excited smile on her face. The routine is part of what the staff calls "cycling." A series of physical exercises aimed at increasing muscular coordination and stimulating the brain.

In the hallway outside, a tiny girl shoots past on roller skates, her braided hair flying behind her. She stops on a dime in front of a chart listing the rewards given the children in exchange for tokens earned for effort and good behavior. Twenty tokens are worth a half day off. Two tokens entitle the owner to butter the group's toast for breakfast.

"Oh, they love buttering the toast," notes staff member Rosemary Miller, tying the sash on the skater's dress.

In a small room off the girls' dormitory, seated at a compact, well-lit cubicle, a large girl with pigtails picks through a jumble of plastic letters, arranging and reciting them in alphabetical sequence. Next to the letters is a colorful woorkbook, one of a series of math and reading booklets called Accelerated Christian Education. The book is filled with scripture verses marked with vowel sounds and missing letters. If a student fills in the proper letters, or turns to another page and connects the dots that outline figures of lambs and Jesus Christ, the reward is a star pasted on a chart next to the student's name.

Since few of the children here can read beyond the third-grade level, says the home's classroom teacher, Sharon Mast, stars are given as much for effort as for achievement. Only the top-level students can read at all. The middle-level children struggle with colors, numbers and the alphabet. The lowest-level classes concentrate on simple exercises to develop hand-eye coordination. There is an Apple computer in the room — an oddity in a place devoid of radios or televisions — but few of the children are able to use it.

"It has a few games on it," says Mast, "but they are more fun for the staff than they are for the students."

Outside the classroom, four girls shuffle behind a young black Mennonite woman. Each girl's hand is on another's shoulder, and the cluster moves as one into a closet. As the group huddles in darkness, the woman periodicaly flips the light switch on and off. The staff calls the exercise "eye-flashing." It is supposed to stimulate the brain.

In the cafeteria/living room, two girls sit mutely on a worn couch, leaning against each other and gazing at the morning light filtering through the windows. One girl's dark braids dangle from beneath a snug-fitting protective hockey helmet.

In the boys' dormitory, another type of "cycling" is taking place. Two boys are scrambling up and down the length of the room's waxed wooden floors on their hands and knees. At the end of each trip, they sit at the feet of Ruby Eicher and stare silently as she rapidly flashes a set of cards before their eyes, quickly reciting the words on each card. The cards are grouped by topics like "Weather Descriptions," "Things to Handle Money" and "Miscellaneous Vehicles." At the moment, Eicher rushes through a set of cards titled "Outside the Group."

"Banished, dejected, unwanted, rejected, lonely, sad, gloomy, exiled, excommunicated." Eicher rattles off the terms in staccato bursts, flashing the cards as quickly as she can pronounce the words. Then she gives a signal, and the boys fall back to their hands and knees and scurry toward the other end of the room. Every fifth trip, Eicher reaches into a bowl of dried apples and pops one into each boy's mouth.

"We don't really know how many of these words they're actually learning," she says, as the boys crawl toward her and she readies another set of cards, "but the more you feed into the brain, the more it's stimulated."

There is a crafts room at the boys' end of the building, where the children string beads, fashioning them into small ornaments. There is a woodworking shop in the basement, where the boys sand and connect pieces of wood into picture frames and small benches. There is a playground outside, with swing sets and a trampoline. There is a small outdoor track for running.

And there are trees.

And there are mountains.

And there is peace.

"Most of these children have come from settings different from this," says Nathan Yoder. "They've known disruption at home, problems at school, social non-acceptance in the neighborhood and at school. Here, they're accepted both by the staff and by each other.

"Here, there's nothing odd about them."

"This is a place where the children can get what they need," says Iva Miller, a beaming 24-year-old who has been working at the home for 11 months. "And what they need is just a lot of love and care."

Miller will be leaving her group of four girls — three have speech defects and one has periodic seizures — in two months to return home to Michigan. The average stay for Faith Mission volunteers is 16 months, but Miller says the turnover rate has more to do with "God's will" than burnout. She does, however, admit that spending 12 hours a day with four brain-damaged children can be draining.

"Every morning you get up with an extra bag of patience," she says, smiling and clipping a barrette in one of her girls' hair.

"Being able to give someone a cup of cold water and not get a lot back in return teaches self-sacrifice," says Reuben Yoder, explaining the Mennonite belief in volunteer services.

When the members of the Faith Mission staff talk about their qualifications to work with handicapped children, they use terms like patience, love and respect. They are unfamiliar with the professional language of clinical psychology. They have no degrees in counseling or physical therapy. But Nathan Yoder maintains that his staff doesn't need the credentials that come with formal training.

"I don't want to imply that the staffs at state institutions do not love their residents," he says. "But our staff are volunteers. They are not paid. They are here because they love God, so God's love radiates through them. And God loves all humanity, both the lovely and the unlovely."

Although he speaks with the sophisticated manner and vocabulary of a college graduate, 28-year-old Nathan Yoder did not go beyond the ninth grade in school. Like his 34-year-old brother Reuben, who dropped out in the same grade, Nathan left school to work on the family's Minnesota farm. But the lack of formal education among the staff and administrators of the home, notes Nathan, does not mean they have no training. The staff members, he says, teach themselves through books and through visits to organizations like The Institutes for the Achievement of Human Potential, a Philadelphia group that teaches specific therapeutic methods for working with brain-damaged children.

"We're not proud of any kind of ignorance," says Yoder. "We want to do a quality job."

Bill Wald knows something about the value of a formal education. Ten years ago, he was a sophomore in Penn State University's architectural engineering program when he met a Mennonite family headed to a church meeting and tagged along out of curiosity.

"The service lasted four hours," laughs Wald, a red-bearded, burly 32-year-old with the glee of a leprechaun. "I didn't understand a word they said. It was all in German."

Within a year, Wald had left college behind, as well as almost everything else in his life. "Movies, mixed swimming, stuff like that," he says. "I had never been taught that those things are wrong."

He became a Mennonite. Last year, when Faith Mission's church pastor, Roman Mullet, made a trip to Lancaster to recruit volunteers for the home, Wald was interested and visited soon after.

"I was touched," he says. "I come from a broken home, and seeing these children who really need help, well, I just fell in love with them. When I left, I was crying. And I wanted to come back."

Wald came back seven months ago, and now has his own group of five boys to work with.

"I don't know," he says, watching one of his boys fill some cups with ice and helping another dish cole slaw onto each of five plates. "It just seems to make my life more fulfilling."

Down the hall, Thomas Miller, a 21-year-old from Ohio, is giving fellow staffer Dave Kuhns a haircut. Perched around the pair is a small cluster of the home's children, watching the process with a mixture of awe and delight.

"It takes some adjusting to teach someone how to do the little things you and I do every day without thinking," says Kuhns, a 21-year-old from Illinois. "Things like tying your shoes, bathing, blowing your nose."

His job, says Kuhns, is so all-absorbing it can even erase the surrounding forests and mountains themselves.

"Day to day, every day, it's from here to the staff house and back," he says. "You don't really notice anything else. But on your day off, you get out and take a look around. You notice the trees are greener. The air's warmer. Yeah, you realize where you are."

Kuhns, too, will be leaving in two months, and he has mixed feelings about returning to his family's farm.

"It's one big family here is what it is," he says. "The staff are all like your brothers and sisters. And my group is like my children.

"I'm gonna miss 'em," he says, reaching out and mussing the hair of one of the boys at his feet. "I'm gonna miss 'em a lot."

Faith Mission Home does not advertise, yet children come here not only from across the country, but also from foreign nations like Germany, Egypt and Paraguay.

A third of the residents are referred by social service agencies; the rest are brought by their parents.

The $525 monthly fee charged for each child is supplemented by the support of Mennonite organizations around the country.

Beyond crediting God and faith, Nathan Yoder has trouble explaining how the home operates.

"The state wonders that too," he chuckles. "I've had visits from state people who say, 'It's obvious that it's ticking, but what *makes* it tick?'"

The state's questions became more than rhetorical in 1981, when a detailed set of guidelines were published. For the first time since it opened in 1965, the home was scheduled for careful scrutiny by several state agencies involved with licensing residential training facilities for handicapped children.

"That's when we winced," says Yoder.

"We felt we'd gotten along this long, and the state was satisfied," he explains. "It was more an issue on paper than anything else."

The arrangement Yoder and his staff have worked out with various state agencies is just that — an arrangement. The home now keeps more thorough written records. It has done away with spanking. But the state has in essence looked the other way in terms of issues such as the home's dormitory setup (state regulation prohibits more than four children in a room), staff training requirements, the absence of an in-house psychologist and classroom educational standards.

Joseph Avellar, director of the Office of Quality Assurance with the state's Department of Mental Health and Mental Retardation, describes the Faith Mission Home as a "unique, complex" institution.

"I think all of us who have had contact with the program there have been impressed with their honest, straightforward, direct approach," he says.

"This is not a summer camp, it's not a monastery," he continues. "With any institution like this, we look to see that some active treatment or care is actually being provided. In this case, it is. They wouldn't have a license if it were not."

Barry Craig, the state's coordinator of interdepartmental licensure and certification, describes Faith Mission Home as "a particularly interesting, and potentially controversial subject."

"We're dealing with a group of people who have strict ideas about what they're doing," he says. "It's difficult to fit their complex situation into the letter of the law."

The most sensitive issue, says Craig, is the school's educational standards.

"There's some kind of, quote, education going on there, but the staff doesn't meet requirements," he says. "That being the case, we have a problem."

The state has yet to make a ruling on the home's classroom standards. If the home failed to meet those standards, it would have to bring a certified teacher into its classroom, bus its dozen school-aged children to nearby public schools or send those children away from the home. The first choice is out of the question, says Nathan Yoder. The second choice was vetoed by the local public school system, which does not accept students who are not local residents. The third choice, says Yoder, is a possibility.

"If the state did decide to come take the school-aged children away," he says, "we would not stand in the way."

When Philadelphia's Institutes for the Achievement of Human Potential was contacted and asked for a description of its program, upon which Nathan Yoder says Faith Mission's "cycling" methods are based, that organization refused to provide any information, sending a letter that said "... some of the personnel from the institution you are writing about did at one stage visit these Institutes, but they were not trained as staff by us, and their knowledge of what we were doing then, and certainly of what we are doing now, is very limited."

Lee Pattinson, an Institutes' spokesman, elaborated in a telephone coversation that her organization stresses physical therapy by the family in the family's home.

"We just about go spastic if we are associated with any kind of an institution," she said. "That's totally opposed to all our principles."

Most of the parents who bring their children to Faith Mission Home, says Nathan Yoder, are beyond caring about governmental principles. They are desperate, he says, and the home seems like the answer to their prayers.

"Most of them are at their wits' end," he says. "For many of them, it's become so much of a stress on the family, they can hardly cope anymore. When they come here, it's kind of a light-at-the-end-of-the-tunnel effect. And it's also the rational sense that this *is* the best place for their child."

The parents themselves are overwhelming in their praise of the home.

"These folks have a true love and concern for these little ones that most institutions cannot fathom," says one parent.

"Russell is an entirely different person now from what he was when he was admitted," says the mother of a 29-year-old who has lived at the home since it opened in 1965. "If it had not been for Faith Mission Home, Russell might very well be little more than a vegetable in a state institution."

Adele and Kurt Lehnert of Portsmouth brought their daughter Nancy to Faith Mission Home 13 years ago. Nancy was 12 then; multiply handicapped with epilepsy and cerebral palsy.

"Being home was not right for Nancy," says Adele Lehnert. "We'd love to have her with us, but at home she would not be among her peers."

The Lehnerts visit their daughter once a month. Nancy's progress, says her mother, is remarkable. Adele Lehnert describes Nancy's ability to pull some of her clothes from the home's laundry — "even if it's only a pair of socks" — and put them away in her dresser. She collects her utensils at the end of a meal. Her goal is to add five new words a month to her vocabulary.

"These are things that she has *learned*," says Lehnert.

Another sign of progress is that Nancy has fewer convulsions.

"When she's at home, she'll have a dozen seizures in a week," says Lehnert. "Up there, she'll have one a month."

The mountain setting and the Mennonite attitude, says Lehnert, are the keys to Faith Mission's success. And, she notes, these are things not easily captured by governmental, administrative, institutional guidelines.

"I think it's the best place in the world for children, normal or not," she says. "The children there play the way children played 20 or 30 years ago — naturally, not with all the props we've put into our society. A bird singing is something they pay attention to up there."

Nathan Yoder is as vague about the home's goals as he is about its guidelines. The current residents range in age from 10 to 29. Some are eventually able to move into one of the "cottages," to work in the bakery or on the farm, to attain a certain level of independence. Three young women, who were among the home's original group, recently left the home, moving to Lancaster, where they now live on their own in an apartment. But Yoder hesitates to guess how many current residents would be able to do the same thing.

"Our goal is not to simply *keep* them," he says.

"We keep them as long as this is the least restrictive environment for the child," he adds.

"They *can* be here indefinitely."

Dusk soaks the trees in a fine mist as the sun sinks into West Virginia. Dinner ends with the ping of a bell and three verses of "I've Taken My Harp Down From the Willow Tree." Then the children are released for an hour of play before they will return to the cafeteria for the evening's snack and religious devotion.

As the children gather in the cafeteria for the close of the day, listening to a Bible reading, chewing on popcorn and singing a hymn, the sky outside turns dark purple. Floating up from Roman Mullet's chapel down the hill comes the sound of other voices, clearer, more in tune than those of the children. Mullet's evening congregation of local Mennonites and friends fills the chilly mountain air with the strains of "We Gather Together."

It is bedtime at Faith Mission Home.

Some of the boys sit on their beds, rocking to unheard rhythms. Others lie on their sides, watching those walking in and out of the bathroom. One boy stands in a corner, facing the wall, repeatedly calling himself by name and telling himself to "calm down, calm down, calm down."

And one boy sits against a wall, opening a dog-eared Bible to one page, then another, each time holding the book up to a bystander, pointing to a word on the page and asking the stranger to pronounce it.

Each time, the word is the same.

Children.

Over and over and over.

April 26, 1985

The Painting Preacher Man

When he's alone in his asbestos-shingled, two-story home, fixing meals in his grimy windowless kitchen or sleeping in his cramped, paint-peeling bedroom, Anderson Johnson is a 70-year-old black man in the grip of poverty.

When he takes his weekly walk to the corner grocery, leaning on a cane and dragging his limp left leg behind him, he is a solitary cripple.

When a half-dozen or so of his downtown Newport News neighbors file through his front door two days a week, sitting among the six pews crammed into his living room and joining in as he chants scripture and belts out gospel hymns on his slide guitar, he becomes "Elder" or "Bishop" Johnson.

But when he sits on his upstairs porch, where portraits and paintings are tacked to the wall and a breeze rattles the mobiles and contraptions hanging from the roof and banister, he is called other things by the people passing on the street below.

They call him a lunatic.

A madman.

A witch doctor.

They wouldn't think of calling him an artist. But then, neither would Johnson.

He's not sure he knows the meaning of the word.

He can't explain the balance and composition of the scenes he paints on wooden boards, tablecloths, pieces of glass and metal, on the very walls and ceilings of his house.

He can't diagnose the reasons behind his choice of watercolors for one painting and roofing tar for another, or of bleach bottles for one sculpture and oatmeal boxes for another.

He can't analyze why one of his paintings is gripping in its dark, stark loneliness and another washes the emotions in a pastoral bath of vivid color.

He has been sketching, painting and putting things together since he was 8 years old, and in all that time, he says, not once has he stopped to consider whether what he was doing was "art."

"Noooooo," he says, smiling and scratching the gray-bristly hair on the sides of his bald head. "I just draws pictures for my own pleasure."

And, he adds, for the pleasure of God.

"That's where they comes from," says Johnson. "I come out here and says to the Lord, 'Let me draw,' and I sit and stare and something begins to form."

The forms, renderings of people and vistas he has seen and others he imagines, fill his house, making it not only a home and a church, but an art gallery, featuring a perpetual one-man show, unseen by anyone but him, his God and his tiny congregation.

If Johnson has trouble clarifying what he is, and if the neighbors dismiss him as an eccentric crank who fills his home with bizarre visions, there are others who might know just what to call him. Consider the following definitions from a 1982 art book:

There are few visual conventions, the incongruities are rampant, and the rules of art history do not help us understand what we are looking at...

Their art graced their homes and yards and work spaces, almost never traveling beyond its place of creation...

Virtually every artist... claims to have been commanded by an inner voice or by God to make art...

It is an esthetic which seems to understand the beauty which inheres in intentional crudeness or indecorum; at times it assertively denies "the beautiful." It is in great measure an esthetic of compassionate ugliness and honesty...

The title of the book is "Black Folk Art in America."

And the words come tantalizingly close to describing the things that fill Anderson Johnson's house.

Crude. Undisciplined. Naive. Raw. Self-taught. Isolated. Original.

Folk art is the childlike innocence of Grandma Moses' paintings. It is the rustic robustness of Miles Carpenter's wood carvings. It is hubcaps and soda-pop bottles, tin cans and costume jewelry, crayons and colored pencils, all wielded as artistic tools by people with no formal training or contact with the world of "fine" arts. And yet their primitive work is as evocative, in its own way, as that of schooled masters.

"A sense of intelligible gesture is uncannily *right* in so much of this work," writes Jane Livingston in her introduction to "Black Folk Art in America." "We instantly know what is intended."

Anderson Johnson is more comfortable speaking with a brush and a sheet of paper than with words and explanations of intentions. When the spirit moves him, when he is up and leaping on his one good leg in the middle of his Sunday morning service, the words flow in song and praises to the Lord. But when he's sitting alone on a weekday morning, answering questions about the artwork hanging on the walls all around him, he is reticent, shy, awkward.

"Yes, I pretty much make something out of everything," he says, running his leathery hands over a brightly-painted sculpture made from an egg carton and feathery shreds of paper. Dozens of other sculptures splashed with the same stippled array of colors as the egg carton, dangle from the ceiling of the small stage at the back of the living room.

"Anything people gonna throw away," he says, "sometimes they bring it over to me and I make something out of it."

Sometimes neighbors bring him more than their trash. Occasionally, says Johnson, they bring him paints and paper. It's hard to buy brushes and canvases on a monthly Social Security Check of $151, but when friends bring him the materials, the rest, he says, is easy.

"I can take a blank paper and look at it," explains Johnson, "and the picture will form. Then I just paint it."

The scenes he paints, with oils, watercolors, crayons, chalk or whatever he can get his hands on, range from Monetlike vistas of wood farms, streams, ducks and horses to rough-stroked, grotesque images of faces he has seen or imagined. One portrait, painted in slashing strokes on a plastic fast-food tray, stares out with haunting eyes from his upstairs bedroom wall.

"That's from my imagination," says Johnson. "It's of a woman that got raped in Hampton."

Most of Johnson's work is not so topical. The bulk of his paintings are of scenes from his rural childhood in Lunenberg County. He was the youngest of six children — "all of 'em dead now, but me." His father farmed corn and tobacco, and so did the children. Johnson's schooling totals four months. "That was the time they brought a hired teacher in," he says.

He began preaching at 8, he says, after a vision came to him one night, and his next several years were spent riding a mule door to door and delivering the word of God to anyone who invited him in.

Not everyone was so kind.

"Some people thought I was crazy," he says. "Others thought I just didn't want to work."

In the same way he was able to preach from a Bible he could not read, Johnson also learned to play the guitar without the help of a teacher: "Didn't know one note from the other, but I got to playin' pretty good. And it helped, cause the music drawed 'em in more than the preachin'."

His father died when he was 12, and he moved to New Jersey to live with an uncle. Then it was on to Newport News, where an older brother lived. Then he hit the road, spending the next four decades traveling up and down the East Coast, "doin' nothin' but singin' and preachin' on the street." He slept at churches and got jobs washing dishes or cleaning floors — "Didn't have no trade."

He eventually returned to Newport News to tend to his ailing mother, and when she died 10 years ago, he moved into her house with his brother. When the brother died, Johnson was left alone to turn the house into the live-in temple it is today.

"'Course it ain't no real church," says Johnson. "It's just a house. But some preachers got it worse than me. They ain't got nothin'."

Johnson hardly has more. When his left leg became infected five years ago, doctors told him he'd be in a wheelchair the rest of his life. Since his kitchen and living room are up a flight of steps and the only running water in the house is downstairs, Johnson says his only choice was to work himself into shape, which he did with exercise (hopping for minutes at a time on his good leg) and a careful diet — "I don't eat no pork, don't use no sugar, no coffee, no fried food, no flour bread." Now he is able to limp up the stairs, carrying a bucket of water in each hand, and he only needs his canes or crutches when he goes out in public.

"If nobody looks at me," he explains, "I can walk good. But if somebody looks at me, I don't know what it is... it cuts somethin' off in my head and I gets to limpin' real bad."

So Johnson spends most of his time alone in his house, filling his hours with the artwork he says has always been his companion.

"I drawed a lot from the beginning," he says, "'cause I couldn't read."

During his years on the road, he would draw with chalk on wallpaper, leaving his pieces at the churches where he slept. Occasionally he would sell them to someone who came across his work.

"I was drawin' just to draw," he says. "And I'd be surprised when somebody'd want to buy one."

People would give him a dime or a quarter for a drawing, says Johnson. "But remember," he adds, "in those days, a dime was a dime.

I could buy a hamburger sandwich for a dime. And a glass of orange juice."

Now his art hangs in his house, seen and bought by no one. But for him the pieces are more than decoration. When he paints a scene of trees, flowers and winding roads on a wall and hangs curtains over it, he is literally creating a window to another, brighter world.

"When I want to fill in a place," he says, "I just go to work and put in some kind of picture."

Like most folk artists, whose inspiration is primarily religious, Johnson refers to many of his pieces in terms of scripture. An oil painting of a turquoise river bounded by a white fence, patches of colored flowers, floating swans and puffy clouds against a blue sky is a literal rendering of one of Johnson's favorite biblical phrases: "Straight is the gate," he says, "and narrow is the way that leads to the light."

Another oil is of a house in the evening, its eerie reflection mirrored in the surface of a dark stream. "The Bible talks about 'the shadow of evil,'" says Johnson, "so I put the shadow of the house in the stream."

But not all of Johnson's creations are religious. Some of his work is purely ornamental, like the black spirals swirled on the pink ceiling of his bedroom: "Just took a candle and held it close up there and moved it around," he says.

And some of his work, like a blue-and-white propeller plane made from pieces of wood and a bleach bottle and mounted on the upstairs porch, has a practical purpose: "That's so's I can tell which way the wind is blowing," says Johnson. "A lot of things out here move," he adds. "Keeps the birds away."

The porch collection also tends to keep the neighbors away. "A lot of people come by and pass to the other side of the street," says Johnson. "Some of the children throw rocks."

But when Tony Shiver began passing by early this summer, he saw more than the debris of a crazy old man. Shiver, 30, is the son of former Norfolk Redevelopment and Housing Authority director Jack Shiver. He is also an artist, with undergraduate and graduate fine arts degrees from Jacksonville and Ohio State universities. He was a visiting artist at the University of Mississippi, and he has taught art at Thomas Nelson Community College. His own art, which has been exhibited at Richmond's Virginia Museum and Anderson Gallery, is influenced by the folk art he studied in Mississippi while working on his master's thesis. Johnson's home, just around the corner from Newport News Shipbuilding, is an out-of-place jewel in an urban setting, says Shiver.

"It was just amazing to me to see that stuff on a porch down here," he says. "I'm used to seeing folk art in rural areas."

Once he knocked on Johnson's door and saw the pieces inside the house, says Shiver, he was convinced this was the real thing.

"I saw a real high level of originality," he says. "Educated artists study art, and they're familiar with other artists' work. Eventually that all finds itself in their individual works as well. That's influence. Mister Johnson doesn't have any of that. He's never been exposed to, quote, unquote, art."

If Shiver was excited to find an artistic diamond in the rough, Johnson was just as glad to find someone who looked at his work with more than a snicker.

"I was glad to see him," says Johnson. "I'd been sitting down here all these years, and all I got was disencouragement. It was like I'd met a friend."

Shiver says he would like to see what experts think of Johnson's work. Johnson says he wouldn't mind being "discovered": "That'd be fine with me," he says. "I could produce more then. I could really paint. The only time I get worried is when I'm ready to paint and I don't have anything to paint with or on."

But there is a paradox for the folk artist who is suddenly exposed to the mainstream art world. Dr. Regenia Perry is professor of African and Afro-American art history at Virginia Commonwealth University and author of a forward to "Black Folk Art in America." She says many of the 20 artists profiled in that book were forced to move from their homes to find privacy after they were invaded by folk art speculators. Some, she says, are no longer making art.

"It's hard for people who have lived 50 or 60 years making their art alone to be suddenly inundated by phone calls and people driving on their lawns and pounding on their doors," says Perry. "Folk art collectors are relentless speculators."

For the folk artist who isn't shocked by a sudden onslaught of attention, there are other dangers, notes Perry.

"They very often lose a lot of strength of style when people begin buying their art," she says. "They turn commercial, looking to make things to sell. Their work loses the strength of purity of design, of being art for art's sake."

Right now, Anderson Johnson continues to paint not even for art's sake, but for himself and his Lord. As far as he comprehends what it might mean, success is fine with him because it will allow him to paint even more. But he can't see his art ever being anything more or less than what it is right now.

"I just do it to be doin' it," he says. "And every picture, it becomes a part of you."

August 22, 1985

V. AT LARGE

A Reporter At Large

It was raining in Princeton, N.J., a misty afternoon drizzle that cloaked the hunched students and teachers strolling across the campus courtyard. Any minute now, somewhere among those figures, John McPhee would appear. But I had no idea where.

McPhee had called a week earlier, inviting me to meet him at his Princeton office. He was a bit halting over the phone, almost awkward. And his invitation was a reluctant one.

"I don't really like to do much of this sort of thing," he had said.

But since he was going to receive an honorary degree at the College of William and Mary's commencement (this afternoon in Williamsburg), since he would be inducted three days after that into the American Academy and Institute of Arts and Letters (joining the likes of past members Mark Twain and Robert Frost and current members John Updike and Arthur Miller), and since the writing class he teaches at Princeton was through for the semester and he had yet to dive into his next book, the week was shot anyway. So McPhee told me to come on up.

"Meet me by the sculpture in front of the library," he said. "I've got a beard."

I knew that. I'd seen a photo of McPhee somewhere, maybe on the jacket of one of his books, although I couldn't say which one. After all, there have been 22 of them, all written in the last 25 years and all containing glimpses of the author as he immersed himself in a dizzying array of subjects: breeder reactors; the history of the bark canoe; oranges; basketball; the Alaskan wilderness; firewood; the Sierra Club;

tennis; the geology of North America; rural doctors in Maine; the Metropolitan Museum of Art; Scottish lairds.

Not only is McPhee's range of topics more widely spread than any nonfiction author writing today, but he is also more widely *read* than any of his colleagues — nine of his books have made the bestseller list. And each of them appeared first in the pages of The New Yorker magazine, for which McPhee is a staff writer.

There is no question of McPhee's status in both the realms of journalism and literature — two worlds that are not often mentioned in the same breath. McPhee, however, transcends such distinctions, and reviewers have recognized his gifts from the beginning.

Time magazine: "McPhee consistently works like a reverse pickpocket, slipping facts deftly and painlessly into the folds of his narrative."

The New Republic: "Sometimes it seems that McPhee deliberately chooses unpromising subjects just to show what he can do with them."

The Wall Street Journal: "He has a boundlessly diversified range of curiosity, a gift for portraiture which enables him to capture real people as memorably as any novelist does his imaginary ones, honesty and accuracy beyond what is common in journalism, and a Balzacian zest for the details of what things are and how they work."

In an anthology titled "The Literary Journalists," containing works of figures such as Tom Wolfe and Joan Didion, it is John McPhee who is hailed in the book's introduction as "a writer's writer."

Indeed, when Tracy Kidder, who won a Pulitzer Prize in 1982 for "The Soul of a New Machine," was asked what writer influenced him most, he ticked off a list that included George Orwell, Truman Capote and Norman Mailer before proclaiming, "McPhee has been my model. He's the most elegant of all the journalists writing today."

All of which told me little about McPhee himself. I knew how he works, spending months at a time latched to the side of some expert or another, then returning to his lair of an office, where he turns his expeditions into magazine articles and, inevitably, books. I'd seen his name pop up now and then in stories about other people — a recent Esquire magazine profile of Princeton basketball coach Pete Carill, for example, mentioned McPhee as Carill's tennis patner and occasional drinking buddy. I knew McPhee used to be seen playing pickup basketball in the Princeton gym; I also knew he is 57 now, too old to play that game anymore.

But mostly what I knew of McPhee is that he lies low. In a town accustomed to importing its live-in celebrities — Albert Einstein, Brooke Shields — McPhee is home-grown. He was born, raised and schooled in Princeton. For the last quarter-century he has worked here.

When he works, he *works*, and he is always working—quietly, far from spotlights, chatter and gossip.

So there I stood, in the rain, searching for a slightly eccentric recluse with a beard.

Which is just what he looked like when he suddenly appeared across the courtyard, waving somewhat shyly in my direction. Small, owlish, bespectacled, wearing a down vest and jeans, he looked as if he could have just returned from one of his trademark back-country journeys.

So did his car, a beat-up 1973 Volvo station wagon with 170,000 miles on its odometer. We climbed in and headed for a legal parking space. He apologized for being sick — "Something I ate. Fish, I think."

As we circled the library's new wing, he pointed out the stones it was being built with. "Schist," he said. "*Pennsylvania* schist." I remembered I was riding with a man who spent a year driving just like this from one coast to the other, eyeballing rocks every inch of the way. That journey has already yielded three books on geology (each a bestseller), with a fourth on the way.

A van towing a rowing shell passed us, heading toward the river.

"How long do you think that shell is?" McPhee suddenly asked.

Was this a quiz or a riddle? I studied the shell.

"Sixty feet, maybe?"

"Hmm," said McPhee. "I've heard they're 90."

Maybe, I thought, McPhee is in the first stages of a book on rowing. Or maybe, I thought again, he is just simply, truly, innately... curious. A man with an eye for details and an ear for the words that can make those details spring to life on the printed page.

A reporter.

I had expected eccentricity. A reader, pondering a list of McPhee's topics — a whole *book* about *oranges*? — would expect the same. But I realized, as we walked, that McPhee had me as interested in the stones that made up that library wall and in the length of that rowing shell as he was.

That is what I had come to talk to him about — the something that sets his work apart from science and above mere journalism, the something that propels it into the realm of compelling literature. The man is a born storyteller, with the added ingredient that his stories are all grounded securely in fact.

Indeed, the title of the course McPhee teaches to Princeton undergrads is "The Literature of Fact." He's quick to point out that the title is not his doing. "It's a little grand, I think," he said, squirming just a bit as he slipped a key into the door of his office, high inside one of the campus' older buildings.

McPhee doesn't mind talking about writing — he's just finished his 13th year of teaching college students how to do it. In fact, in his low-key, matter-of-fact manner, there is hardly anything McPhee minds talking about. Except himself.

But now, on this rainy afternoon, when he wasn't due at his doctor's office for another two hours, this man who is so much like the single-minded experts he studies, was ready to be studied himself.

One of the earliest collections of McPhee's works is titled "Pieces of the Frame." The phrase could just as well describe the cluttered contents of his garret office.

A plate of rocks — no doubt remnants of one of his geologic journeys — roosts by the room's only window.

A platter of cacti and lava, retrieved from a recent volcano-watching trip to Hawaii, sits between an old Underwood typewriter and a new IBM computer.

A sign nailed near the ceiling issues a warning:

Danger
Bear Trap
Do Not Approach

A photo of McPhee with Bill Bradley, the current U.S. senator, former Princeton basketball player and subject of McPhee's first book, "A Sense of Where You Are," hangs by the door. A quarter century after that book was published, the two remain close friends. McPhee is the godfather of Bradley's daughter.

A squash racket juts from a box in the corner. It has been there since January, when McPhee tore an achilles tendon playing that game. Now, he says, the racket is good for one thing: "Killing flies."

The refrigerator behind his desk is as far as McPhee usually goes for lunch. "Cold cans of anything," he says, are his standard fare. That, or a quick swim, are all that interrupt him when he's into his 12-hour-a-day writing rhythm.

"There's a momentum," he says of the writing. "You've got to keep it going."

But two out of every three spring semesters, McPhee stops writing to teach. This is the end of one such semester, and one of his students is at the door. A young blonde, she turns out to be the daughter of William Greider, the reporter who wrote the David Stockman story for The Atlantic magazine and who later left the Washington Post to become an editor and columnist for Rolling Stone magazine.

"She's... skillful," says McPhee, after Greider's daughter has left. He pauses to pull on a heavy sweater and to take some juice from the refrigerator. There is the sense he could say more about the girl, but he holds back. Many of his former students are now accomplished journalists themselves. More than a few have sent him manuscripts of their own books. McPhee is proud, but he won't let himself gush about any of them.

"When somebody's that age," he explains of his undergrads, "you shouldn't tell them they're too good, because it only takes another, oh, 50,000 years or so to get yourself together.

"That's a matter of paramount importance in dealing with young writers," he continues. "You don't want to under- *or* over-encourage them."

With all that he does both as a magazine staff writer and an author (his publisher is Farrar, Straus and Giroux), it is surprising that McPhee teaches at all. But his answer is quick when the question is asked.

"I teach because it takes me out of myself," he says. "It's kind of a balance wheel, a sea anchor, a complementary activity to the principal activity that I do."

That activity, of course, is writing — 12 hours a day, six days a week. For McPhee, the process is one of total immersion, from preliminary research, to the field work of reporting, to the final act of putting all he has seen, felt and learned into words — the right words. While standard journalists typically turn their stories around in a matter of hours, days, or — occasionally — weeks, McPhee spends months and even years reporting and writing his. He is famous for literally moving in with his subjects, spending so much time with them that his presence eventually goes unnoticed, and *that* is when he is able to plunge beyond the superficiality of the typical journalist's hit-and-run reporting. There is a tenacity to this approach, a persistence McPhee notes is not to be confused with aggression.

"I have a sort of basic shyness about getting in touch with somebody the first time around," he says. "If I have to go to, say, somebody's factory and interview him, and I've made this appointment, I have to drag myself there. I don't look forward to it. I don't know what I'm going to say to him.

"But once I've been around the person a while, and this person is showing me his or her work and how they do it and so on, I get absorbed."

Absorption is the hallmark of McPhee's work, which is hardly begun once he returns from his road trips and digs in for the task of writing. As much time as he spends in the fields, he guesses he spends 10 times as long actually writing. The notes for each of his books are bound and shelved along one wall of his office. Each volume is far thicker than the book it produced — clarity and condensation are also McPhee's trademarks. His writing reads easily, but it doesn't come that way.

"See that bed over there?" he asks, nodding toward a spartan cot pushed against a wall. "That's a very important writing tool.

"I do my first sort of blurting out on a machine," he explains, pointing toward his computer. "But after that it's all by hand. That's really where the writing comes in. I lie down in that bed with a green clipboard and a single sheet of my rough draft and I work on it. That's how I write. That's how the thing evolves."

Evolves. It seems an apt term for a drawn-out writing process that, as McPhee describes it, sounds almost as tortuously and expansively geologic as the continental drifts he ponders in his books.

"I waste a lot of time getting myself together," he says of his standard morning, which begins about 8. "I have a real fear that I'll go home with nothing written. I panic with the need to get something done, and I guess it's a concatenation of these psychological forces that gets me together. By about 4 or 5 o'clock I really get going, and then I work through steadily until about 8."

McPhee has gone as long as 15 months between published magazine pieces — longer, of course, between books. He acknowledges that having all the time he wants is a luxury: "That's the essential difference between what standard journalists are doing and what I'm doing." But he shakes his head at those who think he's living a journalist's dream.

"Yes, I have lots of time and space," he says. "I also have *no* salary. I'm paid by the piece. I get 1099s for my taxes, not W-2s.

"Yeah," he says, "I have all the time in the world—as long as I can afford it."

His books of course bring him an income beyond his magazine paychecks. But even after nearly two dozen of them, he continues to consider himself no more than a staff writer for his magazine.

"I see myself as a person who writes for The New Yorker," he says. "That's where I am now, and that's where I started."

That's the only place he ever wanted to be. To hear McPhee describe it, it was inevitable from the beginning that he would become a writer, and specifically what kind of writer he would become.

"Ideas for pieces of writing go by every day," he says. "They just flow past. So what makes you grab onto one, to something that's going to cause you a lot of anguish, that you're gonna stick with for a year or whatever? Why do you rivet onto that? Well, I think it's the fact that you've been interested in the subject for a long time.

"If you look at all the pieces I've ever written," he says, "and put a little tick mark beside the ones that relate to childhood interests, you'd have over 90 percent."

For McPhee, those interests included a love of the outdoors born of summers spent at a Vermont camp and a love of sports born of his father, a doctor who not only treated Princeton University athletes but was also head physician of the U.S. Olympic team for two decades. McPhee played basketball in high school and actually made the Princeton freshman team before he faced the fact that a 5-foot-7 guard, even in 1949, had no future on the court. His last fling with organized ball was during his year of graduate school in Cambridge, when he toured England with that college's team. He later chronicled that experience in a piece titled "Basketball and Beefeaters," the first McPhee article ever published in The New Yorker.

That piece, however, was years away when McPhee was a 20-year-old dreaming of writing for that magazine.

"I *always* wanted to write for The New Yorker," he says. "I liked the stuff that I read there, these long fact pieces... I remember thinking I would like to do that, and also that I *could* do it."

The New Yorker, apparently, felt otherwise. It took 13 years of "lobbing things to them and having them sent back" before he got his break. Meanwhile he forged a career most writers might dream of, but that for him was merely "what I did while I was still hoping to get connected with The New Yorker."

His first job after graduate school was writing plays for a live NBC television program called "Robert Montgomery Presents." Then came six years as a staff writer for Time magazine, covering show business.

"Book reviews, off-Broadway, profiles of actors and actresses and all that," McPhee shrugs, explaining his Time beat, which included cover pieces on Richard Burton, Sophia Loren and a young Barbra Streisand.

He published free-lance stories as well, in places like The Saturday Evening Post, the Transatlantic Review and the New York Times Magazine. He even dabbled in fiction — a McPhee piece was included in "Best American Short Stories of 1962."

But all that was mere prelude to the break that finally came McPhee's way in 1963, when he was commissioned by Esquire magazine to do a piece on his Cambridge basketball days. "They rejected it," he says. "In my depression, I sent it to The New Yorker."

They bought it. But that didn't mean McPhee had a job. That didn't come until he brought the magazine a profile of a prolific Princeton undergrad named Bill Bradley. Bradley's story became a book, and, in 1965, McPhee became part of The New Yorker team.

"Bradley changed my whole existence, in every conceivable kind of way. I mean, I no longer was a commuter, I was working at home. Once that was published, I was working for The New Yorker and nobody else."

That photo of Bill Bradley hanging by his office door means a lot to McPhee. So do the ones surrounding it, shots of his four daughters. One is a college photography professor, another is a graduate student in art history at Columbia, a third works with a publisher in Milan and the youngest, who graduated from Princeton last year, is traveling in Sri Lanka. McPhee laughs when asked about grandchildren.

"Not yet," he says. "Not with this crowd."

Another photo of his second wife, Yolanda, and her four children hangs above his cot, next to a massive wall map of the United States. Stretched across the map is a length of green nylon cord, tracing the cross-country geologic trip McPhee is still not finished chronicling, a journey that began 10 years ago. This June, he'll return to that map, meeting one of his geologist friends in Arizona "for a piece I'm gonna write a couple of years from now."

"I joke with him," says McPhee, "saying we're getting old together."

Maybe so. But in the pages of his writing, John McPhee never gets old. Twenty-five years ago he was a writer whose name appeared under The New Yorker's "A Reporter At Large" heading. That's still what he is today. As for *who* he is, McPhee says there's no need to look further than his writing.

"If I'd ever write an autobiography," he says, "it's in bits and snatches in all of my work.

"A writer," he says, "can't help but be a figure in his own carpet."

May 15, 1988

Bustin' Loose

It wasn't easy tracking down Hacksaw Jones.

The last man to interview him, a Miami reporter who got to The Saw two years ago, is now on long-term assignment in Peking.

The Tallahassee Federal Corrections Institute, where Hacksaw staged not one but *two* of his fabled escapes, claims it's got no record of an Edward R. Jones Jr.

Neither does that name flash on the computer screens at the United States Bureau of Prisons Inmate Locater Center in Washington. According to records there, Jones does not exist.

I knew Hacksaw was good, but it was hard to believe he could vanish into thin air, although there are jailers from Seattle to Atlanta who will swear it's possible. Hacksaw, you see, is simply the best there's ever been at getting out from behind bars. He's done it 14 times in the past 23 years, shedding leg irons and handcuffs like loose pairs of pajamas, dodging manhunts like a phantom and smooth-talking his way in and out of jobs, wives, friendships and identities only to find himself back in the slammer again.

The word was that Hacksaw had decided to play ball with the feds this time around, to go straight, to sit tight and sweat out the years till a parole date. Five years ago, when he was arrested, he'd made a promise to his mother that he was through running, and he'd kept that promise. His mother was dying in Richmond, where Hacksaw was raised, and it seemed there was a good chance he might come back to Virginia once he was a free man. Virginia is, after all, the last place The Saw was free and the first place he was put behind bars, 24 years ago.

He was 17 then, and he's been either an inmate or a fugitive ever since. He's currently serving concurrent sentences of 55 years for a jewelry heist and 29 for escape and interstate transportation of stolen property. But now he has people like Senator Paul S. Trible Jr. sending letters in his behalf, not to mention a folder full of character references from district attorneys, prison wardens and federal lawyers attesting to his value to society, to the fact that he is one exceptional convict and that he should be granted parole when his eligibility rolls around next June.

Modest, polite and articulate, Hacksaw tells his life story, which sounds like the scripts to *Cool Hand Luke, Papillon* and *The Fugitive* rolled into one. Indeed, he has sold the option rights for his personal saga to an independent motion picture company. (He rejected the producer's first draft of a screenplay as "too sensationalistic," he says, but a new script is in the works.) He also has gotten offers from two publishers for the hardback rights to his autobiography, he says, but is holding on to the 600-page manuscript "until the book is finished."

It's still far from finished, but the story line to date is irresistible: Legendary escape artist, always a loner, reforms behind bars, is cornered by violent mobster types who need his help to bust out; not only does he turn them down, but he turns them in, fingering the criminals in a couple of cop killings; he testifies, ends up a marked man and is secretly shuttled by the authorities from prison to prison, becoming a consultant to the federal government, exposing corrupt guards in one jail, helping beef up security in another, developing a patent on a bank robber-snaring revolving door and offering behind-the-scenes rescue advice to the government during the Iranian hostage crisis.

The Federal Bureau of Prisons is hush-hush about Jones's whereabouts, because, until he's free, his life is in danger from cons who don't take kindly to turncoats. "He's marked," says Daral Kennedy, a California criminal investigator who worked with Jones on one of the mobster cases. "These people want to kill him."

Hacksaw is the first to admit he's no angel himself. He's lied, stolen and sneaked his way through more than half his life, but he also maintains that he always acted with honor, that he never hurt anyone, that he always operated alone, that at worst he's been bad at petty thievery and good at slipping handcuffs, and that his only goal has been freedom.

"I've been a big fool, and I've only got myself to blame," he admits during a call over a prison phone from an undisclosed location. All he wants now is peace. He promised his momma he's quit escaping, and he'll keep that promise, even though she died in April. Prison authorities wouldn't allow him to attend her funeral for fear he'd be too easy a target and because he'd slipped their grip once too often. But The Saw says he's tired of running, of looking over his shoulder. He just wants to settle back and try on the shoes of a free man. "If I'm going to come back to Virginia, I want Virginians to know everything about me," he states.

There's a lot to know.

Imagine the film. Title and credits roll. The opening scene comes up: Richmond, 1948. Little Eddie Jones is already in Dutch with his aunt, who is babysitting while his mother works. The 5-year-old is locked in a utility room, punishment for slipping away earlier. But the kid won't stand for it. He pushes an old highchair to the door, stacks a couple of soft drink crates on it and climbs out through the transom. Edward Hacksaw Jones has staged his first escape. He gets a block before he's caught. Next time he's tied to a washing machine, but he slips the ropes and takes to the streets again.

By age 8, he's a street-savvy truant, hanging out with teen-agers. One day they hand him a paper sack filled with rings and tell him to hawk them on the street. Fifty cents apiece, and he gets to keep a dime for every sale. So he wanders up Broad Street, tugging at coattails. The first coat belongs to a juvenile officer. Authorities discover the rings are stolen, and a social worker learns that the boy's father deserted the family soon after Eddie was born, and that the mother works long hours packing pharmaceuticals at a factory. The boy needs "strict male supervision," the social worker tells the court, and the judge sends him to the Beaumont School for Boys, a juvenile training school in Powhatan County.

It will be four years before he comes home again.

"That place was an abomination," remembers Jones.

Of the 400 boys at Beaumont when Jones arrived, the youngest next to him was 11. Some of them were in for violent crimes— stabbings, robberies. They lived in groups run by "cottage fathers." Jones's group spent its days marching down to the James River in chain gang fashion, attacking briar patches and clearing foliage with grubbing hoes from morning to dusk.

"Some things happened there that I could never talk about," Jones explains. "I had a couple of experiences that took a while for me to shake off.

"There wasn't a day that went by that I wasn't told, 'You're no damn good. That's why you're here. Nobody wants you.' When you're that age, it doesn't take long to start believing it."

A few years ago, Jones traced four names he remembered from his Beaumont stay: Three had died violently, and one was on death row in California.

"That tells you quite a bit about the Beaumont form of indoctrination," says The Saw.

Back in Richmond, Jones is now a hardened 18-year-old in a 12-year-old body. His mother has remarried, and Jones hangs out at his stepfather's garage, living under the hoods of the older man's small fleet of trucks and trying to grow up fast. At 17, he drives to South Carolina with a girlfriend and comes back a married man. Problem is, the diamond on her finger is hot and he knows it. So does the pawnshop dealer where his new wife takes the ring to get it appraised.

"They appraised it all right," says Jones. "They appraised me, too."

Tried as an adult, he gets 10 years for possession of stolen goods, has two years suspended and is sent to work on a chain gang at a prison camp in Stafford County. He's not there two months when he gets some good news and some bad news. The good news is that his wife is pregnant. The bad news is that she has had their marriage annulled. His daughter will be 15 before she knows who her father is.

He gets more bad news when he comes up for parole after a year at the camp. His request is denied. "So I decided to make my own parole," says Jones.

It's a hot day. The prison work crew is digging the foundation of what will be a highway department building. Jones is in a ditch running a pneumatic dirt tamper. The guard is lazing in the shade. The steady pounding of the tamper almost puts the man to sleep. But Jones is nowhere near the tool. He's wired down the trigger and is long gone, tearing through the underbrush and heading back toward Richmond.

In Richmond he gets rid of the baggy shirt and pants he's been wearing since he yanked them off a backyard clothesline, hitches a ride to Philadelphia in a circus truck with Happy the Baboon and signs on as a security guard for a detective agency. "The best cover there is," grins Jones. "Who's going to suspect a security officer?"

The Philadelphia police department did, after the company registered fingerprints of all gun-carrying employees.

Jones is soon on his way back to a work camp in Chatham, Va. Three weeks later he's shackled, handcuffed and loaded in the back of a prison truck headed for Richmond, to be tried for his Stafford escape. The truck is barely picking up speed outside the Chatham city limits when Jones slips his cuffs and chains and leaps out the rear door, leaving two fellow prisoners bouncing down the highway in the back of the truck with their mouths hanging open.

Jones had picked up more than simply a few paychecks in Philadelphia. Being around handcuffs day and night, he had toyed with the locks until he could pick them with his eyes closed. He found that a metal ball point pen cartridge, broken and bent at just the right angle, was the perfect picking tool. Before the Richmond ride, he fashioned a key and slipped the inch-and-a-half piece of metal up his nose. "They never check your nostrils, even during a strip search," notes The Saw.

So Jones hits the road running, grabs another change of clothes off another handy clothesline and waves down a cab for the 50-mile trip to Richmond, Jones's mother pays the cabbie, mother and son have dinner, and Jones hustles downtown to catch the next bus out.

The police are waiting at the terminal. He gets two more years slapped on his sentence, one for each escape, and is packed off to a prison farm in Goochland County. "The worst place I've ever been in," says Jones. "Guys have broken their own legs and cut their hamstrings to get back in the [state] pen from there."

Jones busies himself collecting scrap pieces of cardboard and wire, even hair from the prison barber shop. Then one night, when the guard makes the rounds, Hacksaw is counted as he sits on a latrine reading a newspaper. By the time the guards find out "Hacksaw" is a dummy, Jones has already scaled the camp's hurricane fence and is gone.

"That one tickled me a little bit," laughs Jones. "It dominated my thoughts wondering how long it took those guys before they asked themselves how I could read a newspaper in the dark."

The Saw makes his way to Miami Beach, where he works as a hotel cabana boy, passing out beach umbrellas and rubbing suntan oil on women. Women have always taken to Jones. "I've been with women," he admits, downplaying his Casanova reputation. "But never more than one at a time." One woman he couldn't get out of his mind was his mother.

A year after arriving in Florida, he's homesick, so he makes a quick trip to Richmond. He only stays a day, and early on a rainy Sunday morning, he slips away. Coasting through the wet empty streets of Chesterfield County, he glides through a red light and ends up trying to outrun a siren, hitting a curve at 65 m.p.h., ramming into a ditch and staring down the barrel of a sheriff's .38-caliber revolver.

Before the police have time to process his fingerprints and discover they have the now infamous Hacksaw Jones in their jail, he pulls the steel arch support out of one of his shoes — "I always wear well-made shoes," notes Jones — chips the concrete away from around an air vent grill and climbs out of the building.

This time he's headed West.

Ask The Saw why it is that he can carry out the most elaborate escapes, yet end up back behind bars because of sheer carelessness, and he gropes a bit.

"I've had it suggested to me that subconsciously I *wanted* to be caught," he says. "Maybe to escape again. But I don't think so."

"The basic fact is that it's difficult to stay in society when you're being hunted.... That's where the pressure really comes in. The escapes were nothing. A couple were difficult and made me feel kind of good, I admit, but that wore off quickly.

"You've got that shadow hanging over you, the fear that any moment the doorbell's going to ring. It's a constant state of tension, and it takes its toll.

"You've got to remember, the authorities can make a thousand mistakes a day, every day, and they usually do in their quest to capture you. But they're still going to get another chance tomorrow morning. On the other hand, you cannot afford to make one mistake. And no one's that good."

The traveler's checks are a big mistake.

They're just sitting there, $3,000 worth, begging to be pocketed. It's been four years since the Chesterfield County escape. Jones has crisscrossed the country, tending bar, drifting, picking up a secondhand Marine Corps uniform to make hitchhiking easier.

But tonight Jones is no soldier. He's a drummer in a rock- and-roll band. He's fooled with drums in a prison recreation room, has a passable voice and so here he is, performing at a penthouse party in a Honolulu hotel, mingling with Don Ho and Robert Conrad.

Then he sees the traveler's checks. "They were tempting, and I gave in," confesses Jones.

He gets as far as Seattle, cashes one too many of the checks and is nabbed. He's thrown in a holding tank in Seattle's King County Jail, sharing the cell with a drunk who's sleeping off a charge of disturbing the peace. Jones begins chatting with the man, memorizes his name, address, birth date, even his social security number. By the time the drunk's name is called and the cell door is activated by a guard sitting at the end of the hallway, the drunk is bound and gagged with sheets and Jones comes strolling down to the front desk, wearing the other man's identification wristband and giving all the right answers to the smiling desk sergeant. By the time the jailers discover the switch, Jones is gathering his things at a nearby motel.

Once again he's not quick enough. He's collared in the parking lot, and this time no one's smiling. He gets 10 years for the escape and is sent to Washington's Walla Walla state penitentiary. After 14 months, he is shipped to Richmond on a detainer for the Goochland break, is put in the state pen and is given a court-appointed lawyer, who discovers Jones was never given a juvenile hearing before being tried as an adult for the diamond ring conviction. He wins an unconditional release from prison. Chesterfield County, which also has an escape charge waiting for him, never gets word The Saw has been returned to Virginia, and by the time they find out, he's left town a free man.

Another year in Florida, and once again Jones comes back to visit his mother. Only this time his stepfather bars the door, tells him he's nothing but trouble. Tempers flare. Jones leaves in a fury, has a few too many drinks at a nearby bar and ends up in the Henrico County Jail. Before his 30 days are up, Chesterfield County picks him up on its escape charge and the ball is rolling again.

He isn't in his new jail cell 10 minutes before he pulls out a hacksaw blade he's hidden in the sole of his shoe, slices through the barred window and heads West again. It's his fifth and final escape from a Virginia cell, it's 1970 and it's the last time Jones will set foot in the state.

"I had high hopes for Eddie. I really believed he was sincere about his future plans."

The words are Richard Repp's. Repp was Jones's court- appointed attorney when The Saw was brought back to Richmond from Washington. Repp got Jones out of prison, sat with him over a three-hour breakfast the morning he was released, listened to The Saw's plans, wished him luck, received an occasional post card from Jones over the next year, then heard Jones was not only back in Richmond but that he was back in jail.

The second time around there was little Repp could do. "The Chesterfield authorities were bound and determined to get him for everything they could," the Richmond attorney recalls.

"There are none so vindictive as those with wounded pride," is how The Saw explains it.

Things go right for Jones after his last Virginia escape. He wanders into Las Vegas, fools around at the baccarat tables, hits a hot streak and walks out with $14,000. He buys a new Trans Am, a demo model right off the showroom floor, and airs it out with a cross-country drive. He knows he's really on a roll when he hits Louisiana on a rainy night, sees a car pulled off the roadside, stops to help and meets a pretty girl named Susan Black. He follows her to Shreveport, courts her for three months and marries her.

His money holds out for a while and so does his story to Susan of an import-export business in California. But after a while he has to work. He takes a job at a Dodge dealership and feels the rows of cars begin closing in. "Taking people's hard-earned money for a car they'll end up using as a boat anchor is not easy. I don't know what I am or was, but it wasn't a used-car dealer," says The Saw.

He tells Susan he needs a break and takes a quick trip back to Vegas. Only this time he loses all he has. Sitting at the bar, nursing a drink, he watches two Japanese men stuff wads of hundred-dollar bills into their travel bags. He follows them in the elevator, notes their room and goes back down to poolside, waiting for their lights to go out. At 4 a.m., he scales the motel's balconies, slips into the room, grabs the bags and climbs back out. As he hits the ground, he feels something smash his head.

When he awakens, Jones is in an intensive care unit. A hotel night watchman had clubbed him, and now he is under armed guard in a Las Vegas hospital. His skull is fractured, IVs are hooked in his arms, a tube has been run up his nose, a catheter is inserted in his penis, both legs are shackled to the bedposts and two policemen are stationed outside his door.

"I heard them saying they were going to move me as soon as they could," recalls Jones, "so I knew I had to make my move."

He pulls an IV needle out of his arm, bends it and picks three of the leg iron locks. He doesn't waste time on the fourth, wrapping the remaining chain around his leg. He takes a deep breath, pulls out the catheter, creeps to the door, sees the two guards flirting with a couple of nurses at the end of the hall and sprints in the other direction, out of the hospital and down the crowded city streets, a turban of bandages on his head and his hospital gown flapping in the breeze. Jones hardly draws a stare from passing tourists. "People are used to anything in Vegas," he explains.

A day and a half later, wearing pilfered clothes and a hat over his bandages, Jones is on his way out of town. He passes a newsstand and sees his face on the front page of the local paper. "Escape Artist Must be Singin' 'It's Magic,'" blares the headline. It's not the last headline Jones will make, and it's not the last time he'll have to tell someone that he's not the person they think he is. That's what he has to tell Susan when he calls her collect for a plane ticket back to Shreveport.

After a reunion of tears, soul-searching and confession, Jones convinces Susan to stay with him, and the pair leave Shreveport for California. There, with a typewriter, some fancy stationery, the Sunday *Los Angeles Times* and a little local research, Jones creates an impressive resume that lands him a job as a property manager of an apartment complex.

"I've never had a problem getting a job," he notes, and this one's not bad. He gets a free apartment, a decent salary, even the private pleasure of hiring off-duty police officers as security guards. He takes a better offer from another company, then another, and ends up in Sacramento running a 16-story downtown high-rise filled with businessmen, state senators and bureaucrats.

Then the walls start crumbling. No sooner does Susan give birth to a son than Jones gets word that the owners haven't made mortgage payments in two years, that foreclosure proceedings have started, and he's out of a job. He writes himself a check to cover a month's salary and moving expenses and takes his little family to Houston, where he's given the management of a 980-unit apartment complex. He hires two moonlighting sheriff's deputies, changes the locks and ends up on a local television news program where he's hailed for his model security campaign. The safety of the complex is so well advertised that it draws tenants from far beyond the city.

Too far. One morning, a station wagon with Virginia tags drives up and out steps a face Jones recognizes, an old chain gang guard from the Chatham prison farm. "You don't forget shotgun guards," says Jones. "I slid into my office and flopped behind my desk in a state of shock."

Time to move on, but this time Susan's not coming along. She's had enough. She takes the baby back to Shreveport, leaving Jones with an open suitcase and a fifth of Chivas.

Now in Atlanta, Jones is "feeling downer and downer," and chasing the ghosts with liquor. One morning he climbs into his used Fairlane and points it toward Shreveport. All he wants is a day visit, but he's pulled in Ruston, La., for speeding. He's ushered to the small town's police station and begins peeling bills to pay his fine, when he feels a gun barrel in his back.

"Hold it right there, mister," says the voice behind him. "Don't blink. Don't move."

The desk sergeant leaps up, jumps back and hollers, "Hot damn! What we got, Carl?"

"I'll never forget those words," chuckles Jones. "Right out of a movie. That really tickled me."

Jones had been ushered into the computer age. Ruston had just gotten its brand-new police computer, and they'd decided to try it out on The Saw. The McCombs name on Jones's driver's license latched onto several other aliases, and the printout went crazy. The Ruston police had hit the jackpot, and Hacksaw was behind bars again.

Nobody worried about the nice Cross pen clipped in his front pocket when they put him in a holding tank. And the deputy who let him make a call thought he was being real clever handcuffing Jones to a hot radiator near the phone — "That'll keep your call short," the deputy cackled. But when the deputy ended up shoved into Jones's cell and could only curse at the bars as Jones dashed out the front door, he wasn't laughing anymore.

Neither was Susan when Jones called her for a plane ticket back to Atlanta. But she bought it for him, while her mother snickered in the background. The only time anything happens in Shreveport," the old woman hooted, "is when Ed comes to town."

Not long after the Ruston breakout, Jones is sitting in an Atlanta lounge nursing a Scotch when he sees a familiar face. It's an old friend of his stepfather's who is now into robbing banks. Jones isn't interested in something that serious, but he's open to a proposition that might set him up once and for all: a jewelry scam.

The way Jones tells it, a Fort Lauderdale jeweler named Joseph Sirgany was looking for someone to stage a robbery of his gallery, make off with a set amount of gems, deliver them to a friend of Sirgany's in another city and collect a healthy payment for the job while Sirgany raked in the insurance money as well as eventually getting the jewels back. It sounded good to Jones.

"I had decided if I could come up with a big score, I could get Susie and Derek and get out of the country for good," he explains. "Up until the Sirgany job, I was just bush league, a petty criminal, more of a nuisance than anything else."

Now things get serious. Jones meets the old jeweler, who promises him $20,000 cash and six pieces of jewelry. Details are worked out, Jones buys a pistol, rents a car, and a couple of afternoons later he strolls into Sirgany's gallery, puts the gun to the man's head and roars away with three trays of gems.

On the way to Los Angeles, where Sirgany wanted the jewels delivered, Jones stops in Shreveport to pick up Susan and Derek, explaining that this is their chance. She says she'll come. But at 5 a.m., the door breaks down and the F.B.I. and the Shreveport police pour in.

From now on, The Saw will be dealing with the feds.

The time Hacksaw is serving today is primarily for the jewelry caper. The court didn't buy Jones's claim that Sirgany was in on the heist, nor did it believe Jones when he insisted that he'd only taken three trays of jewelry. Sirgany testified that six trays had been stolen.

In June of 1981, six years after the robbery and two years after Hacksaw was last put behind bars to stay, Sirgany confessed to faking a $5 million robbery. Fort Lauderdale police records revealed that the jeweler had reported five large thefts in the previous six year. For this confession, Sirgany was given five years probation. Jones says officials have told him Sirgany's old age and clout accounted for the light sentence.

"He [Jones] thought it was a little unfair, with Mister Sirgany getting probation and him getting fifty-five years," admitted Broward County Circuit Judge Paul Marko III at the time of Sirgany's arrest. It was Marko who sentenced Jones in the Sirgany case. "I must say Jones's story has always been consistent. Another thing that leads one to suspect he may be telling the truth is the fact that, when the dust cleared, the police only found fifty percent of the stolen jewels."

"If I'd stashed some jewels," Hacksaw says, his resentment simmering. "I certainly had ample opportunity to get at them when I escaped for a year and a half.

Hacksaw still had a few escapes left in him when the feds picked him up in Shreveport.

First there was the Tallahassee Federal Corrections Institute, where United States marshals stored Jones to await his trial in Fort Lauderdale. Jones had slipped through a Tallahassee strip search with two hacksaw blades taped to his right forearm. Twice he cut his way out of the same cell only to be caught and returned.

Then came the trip to Fort Lauderdale, where he was held in the Broward County Jail under 24-hour surveillance in solitary confinement. John Ferdinand, then a local public defender and now a private attorney, handled Jones's case.

"I believed he was the ultimate con man," says Ferdinand, "but I didn't believe he was conning me. I did know, however, that he'd do anything to escape. He even tried to walk out of jail as me."

He almost made it, too. Carrying a briefcase and wearing a suit he was allowed to bring with him to jail, Jones impersonated Ferdinand and got as far as the jail's lawyer-inmate interviewing room, where he actually began questioning an unknowing con, before he was discovered.

"He was the most unique client I ever represented," says Ferdinand.

Smelling a stiff Federal sentence in Fort Lauderdale, Jones became desperate and told the F.B.I. he did indeed know where the three missing trays of jewelry were, that they were buried in a rural lot on the outskirts of Atlanta and that he would lead the authorities to the loot.

Flanked by three Federal marshals, Jones flew to Atlanta, where the party was joined by three F.B.I. agents for the drive into the countryside. Two cars pulled up to a junk-strewn lot, the group stepped out, and Jones pointed to the base of a tree. As the lawmen began digging, Jones, handcuffed to a marshal, bent over to stub out his cigarette, reached under a rag on the ground and came up with a pistol.

"I had to tell them twice to hit the ground before they realized what was happening," remembers Jones.

This time he got as far as the Georgia border before he was caught at midnight lounging beside a motel pool.

A guest who had seen Jones's mug shot on the evening news recognized him and called the police.

"Ed Jones," snorts Don Forsht. "What a guy. He put some embarrassment on quite a few people around here."

Forsht was chief marshal for South Florida when Jones was making the state's prison system look like a joke. Back when Forsht got word that the F.B.I. was taking Jones out of his hands to go to Atlanta and hunt for buried treasure, he barred the door.

"I said, 'No way! You take this guy out of here, and you've got an escape on your hands," recalls Forsht, who is now a private investigator in Miami. He was overruled, and when he heard Jones had indeed escaped, Forsht went nuts. "I flipped. I actually flipped. I walked right around to the judge's chambers and said, 'Reality has kicked us right in the ass.'"

But Forsht held no grudge against Jones. "He was actually a very likable fellow. And with handcuffs, he was almost a Houdini. It was almost like a game with him. He'd carry his little escapades right to a point, and then he'd give up.

"But he certainly hoodwinked the Bureau, and they don't like that."

Jones finally got his Fort Lauderdale trial, where he was found guilty of armed robbery as well as escape. Then he was shipped to Shreveport to face a charge of transporting the gun he had used in the Sirgany heist across state lines. There he was put in a maximum security cell watched by a closed circuit video camera. The cell was the pride and joy of the Shreveport police, and no one had ever tried breaking out of it—until The Saw. He did it, but didn't get very far.

He got three years for the gun charge, three more for the escape and a ticket to the Atlanta Federal Penitentiary, one of the tightest institutions in the Federal prison system. Only one inmate had ever escaped from the Atlanta pen, a fact its warden crowed about in a 1977 *National Enquirer* story written after Jones was sent there. That was all it took to set the stage for the escape The Saw is proudest of.

"I knew I could escape from Atlanta but I was determined to do it in as confusing a manner as possible," says Jones.

He planned the break for months, fashioning a dummy out of wax collected from the prison dentist's office, tape-recording 30 minutes of snoring and collecting materials to cover his trail with false clues. When he made his break, he stuffed the dummy in bed, hid the tape recorder, replaced the sawed bars of his cell window, taped and painted them, had a line thrown over the north wall of the prison to make it appear as if he had climbed out and then hid in a railroad boxcar used to carry goods manufactured in the prison.

Through the night and into the next day he huddled in the boxcar until it finally rolled out of the freight yard. When it reached a warehouse outside the prison walls, Jones took off, pausing just long enough to mail the warden a copy of the *National Enquirer* story and his best wishes.

His Atlanta breakout earned Hacksaw a spot on the F.B.I.'s 10 Most Wanted list, but Jones was no longer a risk to anyone. He was beat, wandering from job to job over the course of a year, ending up in San Diego, where he was caught passing counterfeit currency. "I didn't even care about finding legal work by then," he says. "I was ready to be caught."

A halfhearted escape attempt from a San Diego jail — "Just force of habit," explains Jones — got him a transfer to a nearby Federal prison. There he met Lieut. Frank Moe, the prison's investigation supervisor and a semi-Messiah to Jones. "He was the first person I ever talked to in the prison system who really seemed to care about me," says The Saw.

Moe has been in the business 17 years, but he says he never met anyone quite like Jones. "He was a cut above the average convict. Well-spoken, not running one game after another on you. A friendly person. You couldn't help but like him. And he was far and away in a class by himself as far as his ability to break custody. He seemed like the type of person who would've been a success in anything if he'd put his mind to it."

That's what Moe talked to Jones about: "We talked about his age, about the wasted years, about the time he'd spent in prison and running and the fact that he'd caused a lot of grief to his mother and his family," says Moe.

The upshot of those talks was Jones's word to Moe that he was through running. "I've never broken my word to anyone who's taken the time to ask for it," says Jones.

"He's always kept it with me," says Moe.

More than anything else, Hacksaw's commitment to the straight and narrow can be traced directly to a letter he got from his mother after he arrived in the Marion Federal Penitentiary outside Chicago, where he was transferred from San Diego. He hadn't heard from her in years, and the letter opened up the past. "Eighteen pages, and pain on every one of them," recalls Jones. His stepfather was dead, both his mother's parents had died, and he was all she had left. A phone call home sealed it. Jones was going straight.

His mother's death hasn't changed things. "Too many people are just waiting for me to prove them right by escaping," he says. "I'm not going to give them the pleasure."

Jones's word was tested almost immediately. Some of the most dangerous criminals in the Federal prison system were at Marion, and they'd all heard about Jones. "I didn't want to be a hero," he says, "but suddenly these people were coming at me left and right."

Jones turned down pleas to help with several elaborately planned breakout attempts involving extensive conspiracies and transfers to other less secure prisons. But saying no wasn't easy. "With people like these, you're either with them or against them," explains Jones. "There's no middle ground. You have to choose sides."

So Jones made the most important phone call of his life. He tipped investigator Kennedy in California to an escape attempt planned there and ended up testifying to details a convict had shared with him about an unsolved California murder. The con was tried for the killing and convicted. "His [Jones's] testimony made the case," says Kennedy.

In several other cases, the details of which authorities have kept secret to protect Jones's life, his information and testimony have uncovered corruption among prisoners and among prison guards. In pursuing his parole, Jones has collected an impressive list of letters praising his actions behind bars. An Atlanta assistant district attorney, an Illinois Federal prison warden and an assistant United States attorney working with the Senate Permanent Subcommittee on Investigations are among those who have written character references for Jones.

Jones's reputation apparently stretched even farther than the confines of America's prison system. During the Iranian hostage crisis, says Jones, who is reluctant to share any but the sketchiest details of this episode in his life, he corresponded with the Iranian desk of the State Department, receiving blueprints and diagrams of the embassy compound where the American hostages were being held. Scanning the layout and noting the extensive sewer system running beneath the compound, Jones says he mailed back a detailed rescue plan, but that he heard nothing more until the news broke of the aborted helicopter rescue attempt.

A State Department Spokesman says its Iranian desk had nothing to do with rescue planning, that the military handled all hostage dealings. A Defense Department spokesman says he never heard of Jones's advice but doesn't rule out the possibility that it was received. "The Joint Chiefs of Staff have never commented on details of the rescue mission," says the spokesman.

Jones insists his story is true, and he claims his plan would have worked. "I guess President Carter had the Entebbe syndrome," shrugs The Saw.

Now Hacksaw spends his days pushing for parole and juggling several projects, not the least of which is the planned movie of his life. Mike Petryni, a Los Angeles producer-screenwriter who bought the motion picture rights to Jones's story, has no doubt the film will be a success.

"This story strikes a chord," says Petryni. "It's got a considerable amount of escape drama, of course, but more than that, this is a man who never was violent in his life, who, when he was on the breaks, tried to have an ordinary life but wasn't able to. That adds poignancy. There's a potential hero there."

All his deals and schemes, however, are nothing more than hobbies compared to Jones's passion to be freed and to start a new life. He's read Adler and Freud and claims he now sees clearly what he's been doing the past 20 years: "It's a consensus among most psychologists that a person who has not had a childhood matures very slowly later on in life. They tend to want to make up for that lost childhood."

Jones's current attorney, David Rudolf of Durham, N.C., agrees. "Ed is an intelligent, capable person who got started on the wrong track early on and was never quite able to get off it," maintains Rudolf. "Most of the time he's spent in prison has been for escaping, and it's all traced back to an original conviction that never should have taken place. It's almost Kafkaesque."

Virginia long ago dropped its detainers on Jones. As far as the State Department of Corrections is concerned, he's a free man. Kennedy, who still keeps in touch with Jones, has no doubt Jones is ready for freedom. "In eighteen years, I've only gone to bat for two guys with a criminal background, to say they could be redeemable products for society," says Kennedy, "and Mister Jones is one of them.

"When Jones offered to help us," he continues, "he asked for nothing in return. I've dealt with narcotics kingpins turned born-again Christians, criminals looking for protection, people with all kinds of reasons to come forward, and they're almost always looking for something in return, but I've never seen anything like Jones. His apparent lack of motive was a mind- boggler. But what it comes down to is his mother. It takes time to believe someone, to cross a line of trust, but I can say now that it wouldn't bother me to have him as a neighbor."

Jones himself says he'd like nothing better than a quiet neighborhood. He has already begun healing the wounds of the past, corresponding with his daughter and also with his son, Derek, who only recently learned that Jones is his father. His wife, Susan, divorced Jones after his Atlanta escape.

"I'm tired," says Jones, who turned 41 this past January. "I just want peace, and I want to make whatever positive contribution to society I can."

Then he'll only have the tattoos on his arms, remnants of his teen-age chain gang days, to remind him of the past. Those, and the nickname. "I guess," deadpans The Saw, "that's one thing I'll never be able to escape."

September, 1983

Sheltered Lives

Dawn in Guinea.

The water of Mundy's Creek, ashen and choppy in the morning grayness, laps a shoreline littered with oyster shells and tattered nets. On the eastern horizon, beyond the distant pines of Big Island, streaks of orange split the darkness. But here, where a cratered dirt driveway marks the end of Jenkins Neck, it's still more night than day.

This is where John West lives, somewhere among the tiny, weather-beaten old houses and lonely trailers clustered along the waterfront. West is a waterman of almost legendary renown in a community where men have worked the water for centuries. When he was at his peak, oystering, crabbing, fishing his pound nets, West was unquestionably a "highliner," the man who consistently returns with a larger catch than his comrades.

But West is off the water now, in his 70s and retired. At 6 in the morning, a working waterman is two hours into his day. If smoke is still curling from the chimney of one of these houses, as it is from the white-frame, green-shingled one at the end of this drive, chances are whoever's home might know where John West can be found.

A knock on the rickety screen door brings a smallish man with slicked-back, jet-black hair, thick glasses and an unquestioning welcome in his smile. Before you have time to say who you are, he ushers you into the overwhelming warmth of his tiny, spartan home. When you finally ask if he knows John West, he settles into a worn sofa and answers, "You're lookin' at 'im."

As he talks, curling his green-stockinged toes in front of the blazing, tinny wood stove that fills his home with near-stifling heat, West nods

243

toward a shadowy presence lurking in the darkened hallway. It's his nephew, Roger Maris West, son of his brother, James.

Although he's half a century younger than his uncle, Roger Maris West has earned his own admirable reputation in Guinea. Barely past 20, he makes his living crabbing part of the year and hunting the rest of the time. People say he's been known to sneak up and catch a rabbit barehanded, just for the fun of it.

But you won't hear Roger Maris West talk about his fabled hunting prowess. You won't hear much of anything from Roger Maris. He lurks in the shadows. And when there are no shadows to hide in, he creates his own, pulling down the bill of his camouflage hat so it throws darkness over half his face. You can't see them, but somewhere in that darkness are his eyes, wide-open, taking in everything.

In a way, these two men stand as symbols of all that is Guinea. John West — affable, generous, honest. Roger Maris West—cryptic, impenetrable, vaguely threatening.

Like many of their neighbors and most of their families, these men's lives are defined by the lowlands, marshes, bays and creeks that bound Guinea, a southeastern neck of Gloucester County a mere 30 miles from Norfolk.

But Guinea is separated from the urban or suburban lifestyles that surround it by distances that can't be measured with an odometer.

All watermen live distinctive lives, close to the forces of nature with which they form a partnership — the winds, the tides, the rain. But Guineamen have been marked as a category unto themselves, their reputation, bordering on the mythical and soaked in apocryphal legend.

Mention Guinea and even the most distant outsider will likely have a nugget of lore to share. Images of clannish violence and shootings, grotesque knifings, belligerence to strangers, inbreeding, ignorance and isolation conjure visions of a coastal "Deliverance."

The truth, however, is more complex than lurid fables sprouted from scattered seeds of fact. There is an undeniable mystique to Guinea, an aura the Guineaman has earned through more than three centuries of living at necessarily close quarters with the water and with his brethren. His qualities are a puzzling blend of charm and menace, and they become more undefinable each year, as his community is infiltrated by outsiders and thinned by its own emigrating youth.

Some Guineamen say the area is no different from the way it was decades ago. Others say it's changing every day, that soon there will be no Guinea. Captain Rosser Blake, a Guineaman who lives across the road from the house in which he was born in 1893, ponders the question, then carefully phrases his own answer.

"I tell you, this Guinea thing is a far-reaching thing," says the captain, chewing thoughtfully on a toothpick and running a hand through the shock of snow-white hair leaping up from his head.

"It involves so much," he nods, "it's hard to tell where anything starts and where it stops."

Determining where Guinea itself starts and stops is impossible. You'll find an area labeled "Guinea Marsh" or "Guinea Neck" on maps, but there are no official boundaries. No Guinea government. No downtown Guinea.

Most folks agree that Guinea is bounded on the north by the Severn River, on the east by Mobjack Bay and on the south by the York. It's the western border that gets confusing. If you accept the notions of newcomers and merchants eager to draw visitors to the recently established "Guinea Jubilee," held in a shopping center parking lot on U.S. 17, Guinea takes in everything east of Hayes, where 17 intersects Guinea Road (Virginia 216).

But old-timers are reluctant to say Guinea stretches that far. They say it more likely begins when you drive Guinea Road about two and a half miles and hit Buck Rowe's general store in Bena. Purists go even further and say your're not in "true Guinea" until you've hit Maryus, where the homes back up to marshes and a drive on the roads at high tide means wet tires.

The Gloucester County government is no more precise about Guinea's population. Earle Dunklee, who works in the county's Office of Community Development, hesitates to say exactly where Guinea starts but estimates that of Gloucester County's recently mushrooming population, counted at about 20,000 in the 1980 census but reportedly pushing 30,000 now, Guinea numbers "about 3,000 people."

Many of those residents are newcomers who have never worked on the water, and even among the born and bred Guineamen, more and more are turning from the water, traveling instead to jobs at nearby military bases, with Newport News Shipbuilding or with any number of inland Gloucester County businesses.

Sitting at the counter inside Charlie's General Store in Severn, 80-year-old Irving West talks about his two sons and his daughter, all grown and moved from Guinea. One son is a contractor in Florida, the other drives a tractor-trailer and his daughter manages a Williamsburg motel.

"I would have liked them to stay here in Guinea," says West, who spent most of his life farming, fishing, firefighting and packing seafood. "But there wasn't nothing to do but go on the water, and that's a rough life. It ages you."

As nebulous as its geography or population is Guinea's history. Without documentation, folklore abounds — ranging from tales of Spanish castaways or Hessian soldiers to refugees from Europe's Thirty Years' War or remnants of Cornwallis' British army.

The last seems most plausible.

The names dotting Guinea's mailboxes are indeed distinctly Anglo-Saxon: West, Smith, Haywood, Shackleford, Blake. And the unique patois of some of the more entrenched Guineamen, a rapid-fire, hard-to-grasp dialect smattered with Elizabethan cockney provincialisms, is more than simply another brick in the wall that has traditionally distanced Guineamen from the society around them. The dialect is also evidence of British roots, although no one seems able to pinpoint those beginnings.

While the edges are fuzzy, however, the physical heart of Guinea is unmistakable. It is a distinct network of communities marked by simple signs — Bena, Perrin, Achilles, Maryus, Severn — and roads lined with houses ranging from ramshackle huts to brick ranches. Tiny general stores and post offices dot the landscape, many of them decayed and abandoned. The death of the old stores, once the social heart of each community, is a signal of one sort of change.

"The people used to put back into this community what they got out of it," says Betty Brown, 42, a Maryus native and postmistress for the 35 boxholders and 40 general delivery customers at the closet-sized, sea-green cinderblock Maryus Post Office. She inherited her position from her father, who hung the American flag out front for 28 years and who ran the family's now-defunct general store in the attached building.

"The Guinea people used to shop at the country stores," says Brown, "They built up credit if they needed it, and they paid it back when the crops or fish came in. But now things are changing."

Supermarkets and fast-food joints are sprouting along U.S. 17 as Gloucester County's population booms, notes Brown. A new Hardee's marks the main highway turnoff to Guinea, and its tables are filled from morning to night.

Another sign of the times was in evidence at the sixth annual Guinea Jubilee, a two-day festival in October, organized by Gloucester County merchants. Where in years past the surrounding communities spat out the Guinea name like a mouthful of bad fish, now the entire county embraces the festival as its own.

Take Frances M. Burruss, retired educator, psychiatrist and co-author of a sentimental pamphlet on the area entitled "Is This Guinea?" She admits she has lived a relatively short time in the house at the western edge of Guinea where she and her husband retired after he left the military. But she was busy at the Jubilee, showing her pamphlet and sharing her theories on Guinea-ness. "I claim to be a Guineaman, just for the heck of it," she winked.

As Burruss spoke, a young woman dressed in the preppy threads of a University of Virginia alumna walked by wearing one of the hottest selling items at the festival — a button that read, "Kiss Me, I'm a Guineaman."

Betty Brown just cracks a smile of ironic proportions.

"When I went to school, nobody wanted to be a Guineaman," she says. "It certain seems to have become fashionable lately."

You won't see anyone wearing buttons around Buck Rowe's store.

The men who walk out of the night's blackness into the warmth of Rowe's 110-year-old establishment at 4 in the morning are there with the same habits and for the same reasons their fathers had when they stopped in every working day at the same time. They're grabbing a bite to eat, a cup of coffee and a little bit of conversation before the day begins.

No sooner has Rowe put the brew on and unlocked the front door than Clyde Green ambles in. A tall, lanky 74-year-old, his dark face creased with wrinkles, his eyes yellow but twinkling and his mouth perpetually pursed in an amused smile, Green heads straight for the back of the store, an apple pastry in one hand and a cup of hot coffee in the other. An hour from now he'll be on the line at a nearby shucking house, splitting oysters the same way he's been doing for he can't rightly say how long.

"I'm too old to remember now," Green says with a smile, adjusting the orange leather cap on his head and rubbing his calves through the knee-high rubber boots that are the mark of a man who works around the water. "But I still keep up."

Down the back counter from Green, Doris Rowe, Buck's 62-year-old wife, is preparing breakfast for herself, her husband and her 51-year-old brother, a waterman himself. In this back corner of the store, behind the aisles crammed with work gloves and diapers, thermal underwear and brooms, kegs of nails and coolers of soda, a table is carefully set for three and the aroma of sizzling bacon fills the air.

Doris was raised a couple of miles down the road, in Severn. Her father was a waterman — "He fished six or seven deepwater pounds" — and though she's spent her 35 married years inside this store, she's far from out of touch with the watery pulse of the population. So many of the locals spend their spare time in or around Buck Rowe's store that he's known as the unofficial mayor of Guinea. When Doris comments on the area, she speaks with the authority of the men crowded around the counter up front.

"The people here in Guinea are some of the finest people you'll ever hope to meet," she says. Yes, she says, the store has been robbed. "Three times," she nods, "but not by people from Guinea. Nobody from Guinea's ever bothered anything that belonged to us."

Up front, Buck is sweeping a wooden floor that has all the pitches and rolls of the York itself. His white hair bristles like short combs on a brush, a pair of wire rims rests comfortably on his nose and he does his talking through an easy toothy grin.

For 31 years, Buck ran a post office in the front of the store, but seven years ago it was closed. "We just don't have as much traffic as we used to," he says. But he quickly adds that business is just fine, with the early-hour watermen, then the shipyard workers waiting to catch the 5:20 shuttle bus to Newport News and finally the local laborers who stop in at the store before heading to their jobs.

It's a little past 5, Clyde Green is long gone, and 18-year-old Bill Smith is leaning against the counter, a duffel bag in his hand and a Gloucester High School baseball cap on his head. His father is a boat builder, and he's a student at the shipyard's Apprentice School. He plans to get a job at the yard and settle "somewhere in Gloucester." He hears his friends talk about leaving, about their big plans, but he's skeptical.

"They *say* they want to leave," he says, handing Buck a few coins for a soda and some chips, "but then they try it and they end up coming back."

By 6, Smith and the other shipyard workers are gone, replaced by a circle of other Guinea residents. One is a retired engineer from NASA-Langley who moved to Guinea from Arlington 17 years ago. Another is a carpenter, born and raised in Bena. Another works at the Yorktown Naval Weapons Station. He came to Guinea 25 years ago from Maine. But 25 years is not long enough, he says, to claim the name of a Guineaman. He was reminded of that when he bought a barbecue sandwich from a Guinea native's booth at the recent Jubilee.

"Where you from?" asked the woman in the booth.

"Bena."

"No, where you from?" repeated the woman.

"Bena, just down the road here in Gloucester."

"No, I mean where you *from*?" insisted the woman.

His story finished, the Maine transplant looked down at his coffee and chuckled. "That's how it is around here."

One way to recognize a true Guinea native is to ask about the Oyster War. If he knows about it, chances are he's been around awhile. If he has first-hand memories of the 1928 conflict, it's a safe bet he's a Guineaman.

George Ashe was a local boy of 13 the year a Hampton businessman named Frank Darling staked a claim to some seed oyster beds off of Jenkins Neck near Perrin. When Darling's claim was backed by the state, the outraged Guineamen who had worked the beds all their lives took matters into their own hands, blockading the approach of Darling's boats and forcing Gov. Harry Byrd to send state troops into Guinea.

"It was a joke," says Ashe, who runs his own ancient general store in Achilles, just down the road from Buck Rowe's. As the morning sun filters into his empty store through dusty windows, Ashe tells his version of the Oyster War.

"Yes, the Guinea boats met Darling's boats and cussed and ranted and sent them back. A state patrol boat claimed it had been fired on.

"But the local sheriff called the governor, he phoned him from right there in that room," pointing to the back of the store, "and he told him *not* to send troops, that everything was under control. The governor sent troops anyway."

The result, to hear Ashe tell it, was the biggest party Guinea has ever seen.

"The locals went and met the soldier boys down at Gloucester Point and took them down to Severn Wharf. Most of the folks was treating them like out-of-town guests.

"I went down to see it. We all did, just like you'd go to see a carnival. They had oysters roasting, bootleg whiskey, everything.

"They couldn't have kept order if they had to. if we had been hostile, my father said, we could have laid around in the marsh and picked them all off without them knowing what happened."

The troops were eventually recalled, Darling's claim was nulified and the Guineamen were given the oyster beds. Some locals recall the incident with pride. Others, like Captain Blake, think the episode gave Guinea a bad reputation. "It's a sad story," says Captain Blake, "something that never should have happened."

George Ashe knows all about Guinea's reputation for violence, clannishness and illiteracy. He argues with all three but is most fierce about the charges of ignorance. Ashe himself says he studied physics and chemistry at the College of William and Mary after graduating from old Achilles High School.

"I'll tell you something," he says, pushing aside the Wall Street Journal laid open on his counter. "People here know more about ratios and proportions and combining numbers and counting clams than any academic mathematician could ever teach you. They know what they need to know."

Other locals point out the Guineaman's native canniness, his ability to navigate miles of foggy waters without a compass. They applaud the way many native families survive in less than adequate housing, in homes with little heat, the barest of appliances and, in some cases, no plumbing. They point to the residents of Big Island, off the tip of Jenkins Neck, as prime examples of Guinea fortitude. Now just a handful, the Big Islanders' numbers were at one time much larger, living on a waterlocked piece of marshy land with no plumbing or electricity, their children taking boats across Mundy's Creek in order to meet the buses that shuttled them to school. More often than not, the school trips faded out as the children got big enough to work on the water.

"You walk six miles through pouring-down rain and sleet and cold, it's not easy," says John West, who was raised on the Island before moving into his Jenkins Neck home 30 years ago. He didn't stay in school "more than a couple of years." There were more important things to do.

"The only reading you need is to read the Bible," notes West. "What else do you need on the water?"

Although the lure of the water has weakened with a depressed local fishing industry, and Guinea children are on the whole staying in school longer, formal education is still a problem, says John D. Briggs. Briggs is the principal of Achilles Elementary School, grades kindergarten through fourth.

"When these kids get to the sixth or seventh grades," says Briggs, "they are big enough to out on the water in the summer and they have the opportunity to make big bucks. That can be habit-forming. Then they come back to school and they're bored.

"By the time we've had 'em five years, we can tell whether they're going to make it or not, and there's still a high number of children here who aren't."

Some of those children must not only struggle with family traditions that do not place a high priority on schooling, but they must also cope with the judgments of classmates and teachers who have trouble understanding their unique dialect. If they do leave school, they take with them a language rich with Guinea expressions their classmates will never be taught at a desk: A baby who is "quiet as a clam"; a shingled roof so steep "its top did split a drop of rain"; a boat builder so skilled "he could caulk a picket fence to keep the tide out"; a rainstorm so violent, "it filled a wire basket."

"Whatever's true of these people," says George Kissinger, who was pastor of Guinea's Union Baptist Church for 11 years and who is currently researching the area's history, "they have a native wit and sharpness that's very undervalued."

Calvin Haywood didn't finish high school, but he's done well enough for himself. His business, Haywood Seafoods Inc., is the largest of Guinea's dozen seafood processing houses. In 1947, Haywood began his company with two six-wheel trucks and a waterfront setup in Maryus. Today he runs two 18-wheelers, 14 six-wheelers and eight pickups in and out of the shell-strewn parking lot of his fenced compound, shipping oysters, crabs, clams, shrimp and fish across eight states. He has 115 employees, and although he usually arrives at his cubbyhole office wearing slacks and a rumpled sweater, he's not averse to occasionally climbing out of his silver Lincoln Continental sporting a three-piece suit.

"I'm not ashamed of my education," says the 62-year-old native, born and bred in Maryus, who now lives in Gloucester Point. "It all depends on how you use it. It's not hard to find an educated fool."

His employees are deep-bred Guineamen, "all from within five miles of here," says Haywood, cracking open a fresh box of Roi-Tans. Many of them, he says, are Big Islanders, at most one or two generations removed to the mainland. "Most of them are related somehow," he says, adding, "They're some of the finest people you'll find anywhere."

The Rev. Kissinger notes that the reputation worn by Guinea today was earned by the generations of families isolated from the Peninsula and Tidewater areas by the York River, which was bridgeless between Yorktown and Gloucester until 1950. By necessity, they developed their own subculture, with its own norms. Occasional shootings were part of that development.

"There was a type of order and law about the violence," explains Kissinger. "They had their own code, not without its guidelines. It was a complete, self-enclosed society.

"The old system is breaking up, but there is still a standard and a way of life they have to maintain because they've traditionally been left to their own. For many years, the county didn't seem to feel it was responsible for Guinea."

Gloucester County Sheriff William E. Gatling agrees that until recently, some Guineamen deserved their untouchable reputation.

"Ten years ago, almost all the people living down there were from just a few families," he says. "It was a clan. Outsiders just didn't go in there. They tended to take care of their own problems."

But with the growth of the entire county and the influx of newcomers to Guinea, says Gatling, patterns are changing. Of the more than 100 incidents his deputies responded to in the Guinea area last month, says Gatling, most were the same sort of daily crimes reported anywhere.

"Larcenies, domestic fights, speeders," says the sheriff. "And you have to keep in mind that while these complaints come from Guinea, the people involved are not necessarily from there.

"I'm sure there are still some serious incidents that go on that are not reported," he admits. "But you're going back to the old days with that. People are reporting things now."

Jeri Baker wishes they reported more. Baker is a senior social worker with the Gloucester Department of Social Services. She defends the Guineamen's character, noting, "Their values are the same as other people's. Clean houses, very religious, a very close-knit community."

But the very closeness of the community sometimes keeps it from getting help when it needs it. Health problems, says Baker, end up much worse than they should be because the people are often reluctant to seek treatment until the condition reaches emergency level. Diet and nutrition are sorely neglected, she adds, noting a case of rickets recently reported.

Her office provides financial help, fuel, food stamps, child and adult protective services, employment aid. But most cases reach the office through referrals, says Baker, and there are few referrals made in Guinea.

"We don't get as many as we probably should," she says, "because they tend to protect one another. They see outward services as being intrusive, as interfering in their lives in some way."

The Guineaman is hard to know, agrees Baker, but for anyone who cares to try, she has her own advice on where to begin: Big Island.

"If you really want to see what's happening with these people, you have to go and trace it back to there and take it forward."

In the winter of 1977, the water around Big Island was frozen solid. Alarmed by the plight of the 20 or so people then living on the island, the Coast Guard launched a well-publicized airlift, helicoptering in food and supplies.

Some locals still chuckle about the delivery.

"Hell," laughs one. "They were better off than we were. They know how to take care of themsevles out there. They was sittin' there laughin'."

To hear Harry Truman Smith and his wife, Edna Marie, talk, that's probably right. Smith lords over Big Island now, providing for his wife and his three children. Willie Jesse West, his wife, Peggy Sue, and their children are the only other permanent residents of the Island, although a host of extended family members come and go.

On a recent chilly morning, Smith was wading in the water off the mainland below John West's house, emptying three barrels of freshly caught crabs — pulled from 400 pots — into the back of a truck. His wife was standing on shore, having just taken her oldest daughter, 7-year-old Anne Marie, to the school bus stop. Noting that it's just about the end of crab season — "Gettin' too cold" — she hollers over at Jesse James West, who has just come back from emptying one of his gill nets.

"How much you got there?" asks Edna Marie, a stocky, pleasant woman.

Jesse James, a young, dark-haired man clad in oilskin overalls, tips his basket, grunts, and answers, "'Bout 15 pounds."

"How much you want for 'em?"

"I'll sell all of 'em for... five dollar."

"Give 'em to me," says Edna Marie.

Sorting through the basket of wet flounder, trout and butter fish, Edna Marie talks about living on the Island, where electricity was only recently hooked up, where plumbing is scheduled to be put in as part of the state health department's Brown's Bay cleanup project and where she was raised as one of 16 children, "all married and off the Island now."

"It's nice in the summer," says Edna Marie. "Real pretty. But it's hell in the winter, to tell you the God's truth."

According to Edna Marie, it's her husband who loves the Island enough to stay. When he's not working on the water, Harry Truman puts in hours at one of the seafood houses, packing fish and shellfish. But he's happiest away from the mainland.

"I love it on the Island," murmurs Smith, a stocky 35-year-old who is rarely found without a Carolina blue baseball cap perched on his head. "There's no people bothering you there."

Before hopping in the truck to drive his catch to Hampton, Smith agrees to meet back at this spot in five days, to take a pair of visitors out to the Island.

Five days later, Smith doesn't show. James West, Roger Maris' father, strolls over from a nearby trailer and says Smith is working at a packing house this morning. He adds that Edna Marie and the children are at Newport News' Riverside Hospital, where Peggy Sue West is giving birth to a child.

A few hours later, Smith shows up and wordlessly approaches a boat with two other men. One of the men turns to the visitors and asks, "Who the hell are you?"

After they identify themselves, the man complains of the host of television and newspaper reporters who have invaded Guinea in past years, "exploiting these people." Then he brusquely tells Smith to shove off, and their boat disappears around a marshy bend.

As the wake smooths and silence returns, Roger Maris West and another man saunter over from a nearby house. The man introduces himself as a lawyer who keeps a getaway house here on Jenkins Neck.

"I reckon I'm the only person living around here who wasn't born here," he says, turning toward West for affirmation.

West nods.

Saying he'd rather not be identified, the lawyer picks up an oyster from a bushel sitting in the water, cracks it with a knife, flicks the meat into his mouth and nods in the direction of the boat that has just left.

"I'm kind of pulled both ways about this thing," says the lawyer. "These people are interesting and admirable. They're living a unique lifestyle, the same way they did hundreds of years ago. Their lives are tied to the tides, the wind, the rain, and it makes them more tolerant of things, of life's hardships.

"But I know how they feel," he adds, squinting toward the seclusion of Big Island, the last piece of Guinea to remain immune to the tides of change.

"They're entitled to their own lives and privacy, just like you and me."

And for a brief moment, before sliding out of sight behind a stack of crab pots, Roger Maris West smiles.

December 2, 1984

Bittersweet Dreams

Oh Lord, I sing just like I hurt inside.
—Patsy Cline

It has been almost 25 years since the wintry March day Patsy Cline came home to Winchester, home to be buried.

People in this Shenandoah Valley town still talk about that day, about the thousands of people who lined the four-mile funeral route from downtown to the hilltop cemetery beyond the city limits. They remember the cars jammed bumper to bumper from sun up to sundown, the hundreds of state troopers called in to control the crowd, the mountain of flowers banked high beside the grave and the throng surging forward to grab a blossom in remembrance.

"Patsy," wrote a local reporter the day after the 1963 event, "got a funeral worthy of royalty."

But that's about all Patsy Cline ever got from her hometown.

When she was alive, she never got a Patsy Cline Day. She never got a key to the city. The only thing the town ever gave her was a chance to ride in its Apple Blossom Parade. And when she did, they laughed.

Now, a quarter century after she died, little has changed. There are no signs at the city limits telling visitors this was where a music legend was born, raised and launched. In a town that prides itself on its history, there is no monument to the woman whose voice still stirs hearts wherever it is heard — everywhere, apparently, but here. You'll find Elvis on the jukeboxes around Winchester, but you won't find Patsy.

Patsy Cline's mother still lives here, but hers is a life of bitter seclusion. It's ironic that the last song Patsy recorded before she died in a light plane crash was "I Fall to Pieces." And it's ironic that few people in Winchester care to put the pieces back together.

"People are surprised we don't have more on her," says Cheryl Robinson, who mans the desk at the visitors center out by the interstate. "They ask us what there is to see of Patsy Cline's life, and we point them to the cemetery."

"You'd never know she was from Winchester," says Fran Ricketts, who works the counter of a movie museum in the center of town. "People around here would just as soon let her memory drop."

"It's sad, real sad," says Bobby Carter, a downtown barber who just resigned as chairman of the Patsy Cline Memorial Fund. "Look at Staunton. They do everything they can for the Statler Brothers. But Winchester does nothin' for Patsy."

"This is a very cliquish town, sir," says Harold Madigan, who owns the drugstore where Patsy Cline worked as a teenager. "It's like all small towns are. You're either all the way up on top or all the way down on the bottom. You're either on the holiday cocktail party list or you're on the beer joint list."

There's no question which list Patsy Cline was on.

"Patsy," says Madigan, "was not part of the in crowd."

A quarter century after her death, she continues to be shut out. A book and a movie have been made about her life, her fan club grows every year, a new generation of young people have discovered her music, other country legends sing tributes to her memory. But in the town Patsy Cline called home, she remains an outsider.

"It's funny," says Jim McCoy, a former disc jockey, leader of the first band Patsy ever sang with and a pallbearer at her funeral. "Funny that she's a bigger star outside her hometown than she is in it."

"I hear that from all over the country," says Charlie Dick, Patsy Cline's husband and the father of her two children. Dick — a Winchester native like Patsy — now lives in Nashville, as do the children. That city inducted Patsy Cline into its Country Music Hall of Fame in 1973, 14 years before Winchester finally consented to name a quarter-mile stretch of asphalt leading to a shopping mall "Patsy Cline Drive."

"I don't pay a hell of a lot of attention to anything up there anymore," says Dick. "But people I know stop through, see nothing, then call me and ask me, 'What's wrong with those people, are they nuts?'"

It's hard to say why Patsy Cline remains shunned by the people she grew up with. But just a walk through the town yields a few clues. Despite the interstate highway and suburban development that have swelled it into a city in the last two decades, Winchester remains a town small enough to walk through.

Walk past Handley High School and talk to the kids there. They've heard of Patsy Cline. They know she was a singer. Their parents, aunts and uncles went to school with her, back when her name was Virginia Hensley. But there are no pictures of Virginia on the school walls. No trophy case honoring a world famous graduate. After all, she dropped out of Handley High her sophomore year, 1947, the year her father deserted the family, forcing his oldest daughter to go to work to support her mother and sister and brother.

Drop in at Gaunt's Drug Store, where Patsy was hired when she quit school. Harold Madigan was only 8 years old then, but he remembers the girl who poured him Cokes at the soda fountain. Now that he owns the place, he's set up a minishrine of sorts: Half a dozen black-and-whites of Patsy wearing a cowgirl skirt, leaning into the microphone at the Lorton Fire House on New Year's Eve, 1957, backed up by Sonny Hawthorne and the Blue Rhythm Boys.

The snapshots are easy to miss, nailed to the rear wall, behind the rack of walking canes and convalescent aids. But Harold Madigan is proud of those photos, proud, in his own small way, to keep alive a memory few of his neighbors care about.

"She was real down to earth," he says, coming out from behind his pharmacist's counter to look at the photos. "Even after she made it big, she'd come in here with her hair all up in rollers and she'd give us an update, tell us about the people she was working with, the records she was cutting. It was real important for her to let us know how she was doing. The kid had to work so hard for every durn thing she got."

One of the first places she worked was the stage of the Palace Theater, where a fellow named Jack Fretwell ran Saturday morning talent contests for kids. Ask where the Palace is today, and you'll find it burned down, replaced by a real estate office. But back in the late 1940s, it was a place where a teenager with a strong voice or nimble feet could get noticed.

"They'd come on and sing, dance, play the violin, the accordion, what have you," says Fretwell, who is 72 now, a retired beer distributor and director of a drug rehabilitation clinic in town. "There were a lot of those kinds of places in those days. Just like the Ted Mack hour and the Arthur Godfrey show."

Fretwell remembers a 7-year-old tap dancer — "a black boy," he recalls — who was a Palace star and went on to tour nationally. But he says Patsy Cline was by far the biggest thing to hit his stage. The Grand Ole Opry's Wally Fowler caught her Palace act one Saturday morning in 1948 and urged her to come to Nashville.

That trip didn't work out, and it wasn't until she appeared on Arthur Godfrey's "Talent Scouts" television show nine years later that Patsy Cline moved beyond the local Moose clubs, drive-in theaters and car dealerships where she sang into any microphone she could find. She paid her dues, but the respect of some of the people in town apparently had a pricetag she would never be able to afford.

"Patsy wasn't exactly society," says Fretwell. "These small towns can be funny about that. People resent somebody from the wrong side of the tracks being successful."

The Palace, and most of the places like it, are gone. The heart of Winchester is now malled off, its old shops replaced by trendy cafes where young emigres from metropolitan Washington discuss stock prices while classical music drifts out of the sound systems. Patsy Cline is nobody these transplants knew in the old days, and she's no one they're interested in now.

Fran Ricketts, who takes tickets at Madigan's Movie Museum — owned by Harold's third cousin and located at the center of the mall — confirms the neglect. She says "four, maybe five" customers a day pay $2 for a tour of the bits and pieces of Hollywood bought at auction by her boss. Included among the exhibits is a display of a dress worn by Jessica Lange in "Sweet Dreams," the 1985 film of Patsy's life, named after one of the songs that made her a star.

"I don't think I've had one local person ever come through here just for what we've got on Patsy," says Ricketts. "As far as local people go, they couldn't care less."

Walk east from the well-kept historic heart of town, downhill in the direction of the railroad tracks, and the downtown scene suddenly shifts. Paint peels. Porches sag. It only takes two blocks to reach the bottom of the hill, where back yards butt the B&O tracks. Unlike the well-to-do west side of Winchester, not much has changed here since the 1930s, when the Depression drove farmers off their land and into town, where they sought work in the apple packing or textile factories or on the railroad.

This is Kent Street, where Patsy Cline's parents moved after she was born in the nearby village of Gore. And this is where her mother sill lives, in a plain whitewashed two-story house with a rusted metal glider on the porch, trash cans out front and a small set of chimes tinkling in the chilly breeze.

Patsy bought Hilda Hensley this house after she finally made some money in Nashville. That was in 1960, when she became a regular on the Grand Ole Opry. Patsy bought her mother a brand new gold Cadillac that same year. It's tired and worn now, but it still runs.

Sometimes the Cadillac is parked at the curb, sometimes it's gone. But whether Hilda's home or not, she never answers her door. Instead, she has friends do it. Or relatives. Folks around town say she's been like that for years, a hermit in her own home, driven into a cocoon by years of bitterness and disappointment.

"Her mother did everything for Patsy, and she did it alone," says Harold Madigan, who still fills Hilda Hensley's prescriptions. "Her attitude now is, 'You didn't help me when I needed help. So the hell with you.'"

On this December morning, the white-haired woman who answers the door says she's Hilda's sister. She says Hilda's out, visiting her brother. The woman says she's from "out in the county" herself. She says her own husband died young, and she raised seven kids by herself.

"It was rough," she says. "Hilda and her children had it rough, too. But we survived. All of us. We made it all right."

The woman says Hilda still "gets around pretty good." She says Hilda visits Nashville "pretty often" to see her grandchildren. Asked if she means Charlie Dick's two children, the woman bristles.

"Those aren't Charlie's kids," she says. "Those are *Patsy's* kids."

There are grandkids,too, says the woman. And plenty of other family to keep the loneliness away.

"The way she sees it," says the woman, "she's got lots of memories. Some bad ones, but mostly good."

It was the bad memories Hilda was thinking about back in 1984, when the Hollywood people came to film the movie about Patsy. Instead of choosing Winchester, they went 25 miles north, to Martinsburg, W.V. And Hilda Hensley told People magazine she was glad they chose that site. Said Hilda: "I don't think she's been treated fairly by the Winchester people."

That magazine clipping is in the downtown Handley public library, in a folder thick with yellowed newspaper and magazine articles dating back to the days Patsy was singing with local groups like the Kountry Krackers at places like Watermelon Park, over in Berryville. Leaf through the clippings and they show the itinerary of her short 30-year life.

One local newspaper column notes that both novelist Willa Cather (1873) and singer Virginia Patterson Hensley (1932) were born in Gore, a village 12 miles north of Winchester. "Like Willa Cather's novels never could," wrote the columnist, "Patsy Cline's aching voice shimmers across the airwaves to millions."

In another clipping, this one from the Washington Star, Hilda told a reporter, "I was 16 years old when Patsy was born. All my life I'd had hand-me-downs. But when she was born, she was mine. We grew up together. We were hungry together."

Other pieces of the early years:

Hilda was married to Sam Hensley, who had been a master blacksmith at the Norfolk Naval Shipyard. At 4, Virginia won a tap-dancing contest. At 14, she walked into local radio station WINC and knocked

"Joltin" Jim McCoy off his seat with her voice. At 15, her father deserted the family. At 16, she quit school and went to work at Hunter and Elsie Mae Gaunt's pharmacy, just up the street from her house.

The Rev. Nathan Williamson, who conducted Patsy's funeral service in 1963 and who addressed the fan club gathered at her grave this past September, once said of Patsy's Kent Street neighborhood: "The people there did not have much of this world's goods."

Even though she was a well-known regional star before she was 20, it took Patsy years to break away from that neighborhood. Years of singing in churches, armories, American Legion halls, race tracks, radio stations and $8-a-night barn dances. Years of wearing the rhinestone-studded cowgirl outfits her mother sewed for her by hand.

When she joined a local group called Bill Peer and the Melody Boys in 1952, Virginia Hensley changed her first name to Patsy. She changed her last name a year later, when she married a truck driver named Gerald Cline.

There were extramarital romances along the way, including a fling with a local linotype operator named Charlie Dick. Patsy divorced Cline and married Dick in 1957, the same year she stepped on the stage of Arthur Godfrey's "Talent Scouts" television show to sing "Walkin' After Midnight." She froze Godfrey's famous applause meter that night, had herself a national hit, was asked to appear at the Grand Ole Opry and rode a float in Winchester's Apple Blossom Parade.

"She still hadn't got in the big time," recalls Gene Bowers, a 62-year-old electrician who was in the jukebox business back when Patsy began putting out the hits. "I can remember her riding in that parade, people laughing at her. They didn't think much of her."

Not long after that parade, Patsy and Charlie moved to Nashville. But it still took three more years for her to finally become the star she'd always wanted to be. Meanwhile, she was a regular on regional TV shows with names like "Old Dominion Barn Dance," "Louisiana Hayride" and "Ozark Jubilee."

In 1960 the Grand Ole Opry made her a member of its cast, and she was on her way. In 1962, her career peaked with appearances at Carnegie Hall and at the Hollywood Bowl. That same year she was named Billboard magazine's female singer of the year.

Then, on the rainy night of March 5, 1963, returning from a benefit concert for a Kansas City deejay, a Piper Commanche piloted by her manager Randy Hughes slammed into a Tennessee hillside, killing Hughes, two singers named Cowboy Copas and Hackshaw Hawkins, and Patsy Cline.

According to a story that ran on the front page of the next morning's Winchester Star, all that could be found of the passengers was "a silver belt buckle engraved with the name Hackshaw Hawkins" and "a woman's red slip hanging from a tree."

Beyond her dedicated fans, Patsy Cline's memory lay dormant until 1980, when the film "Coal Miner's Daughter" let the world know how much Patsy had meant to Loretta Lynn, who still credits Patsy Cline as one of the greatest influences in her personal and professional life.

A biography of Patsy published in 1981 added to the surge of interest in her life. The book, by a New York writer named Ellis Nassour, detailed Patsy's sexual affairs as well as her professional career. Although even her biggest fans admit she was "a real party gal," as Harold Madigan puts it, they say the book was exaggerated. And besides, they say, her life beyond the stage had nothing to do with her achievements on it.

"There was a lot of trash in that book that I don't think was needed," says Bobby Carter, the barber. "She was a star. I don't think the personal stuff matters."

But it apparently matters to people in Winchester, even after a quarter century. The guys having lunch in the downtown Open Kitchen restaurant grunt when her name is mentioned.

"There's some around here who think she's a star," says Bob Herbaugh, a 41-year-old construction worker bending into his hamburger. "Others hold the opinion she was nothin' more than a bar fly."

The boys in the Red Star Inn feel the same way. Patsy used to sing in this bar at the south end of town, but that doesn't mean much to the men in flannel shirts, drinking their Budweisers and arguing about aid to Africa.

"Ask anybody in this town, and they'll tell you," says Butch Creswell, a 40-year-old welder. "Patsy Cline was nothin' but a whore."

Creswell takes a swig of his beer, then softens his words.

"You can't say nothin' bad about her music. But this here, this is a small town. And you know how small towns are."

Winchester Mayor Charles Zuckerman knows. In May 1986, when the Winchester City Council voted 11-1 against a proposal to rename a city street after Patsy Cline, Zuckerman cast the lone dissenting vote. That left it to the county to give the two-lane road leading to the cemetery her name. Last September when her fan club dedicated a bell tower at the cemetery in Patsy's honor, Zuckerman admitted he was "a little embarrassed that the city of Winchester hasn't done anything to commemorate Patsy's name."

He still feels the same way.

"I guess maybe the people in Winchester don't think she was the star people everywhere else think she was," says Zuckerman. "I really don't blame anybody in particular. It's just unfortunately one of those things that happen.

"Sometimes the local people are the last to recognize one of their own."

On a weekday morning in December, the grounds of the Shenandoah Memorial Park are empty. Leaves are off the trees, and gray clouds swirl in from the east. A lone sedan with West Virginia plates crawls through the cemetery, past the pond and the bell tower. At the top of a small rise, the car stops, idles for several minutes, then moves on.

"Yeah," says Sonny Chapman, the cemetery manager, "we get about six to eight of them a day. Weekends even more. We see the out-of-state tags, we know what they're looking for."

It's not much to look at, Patsy Cline's grave. Just a flat bronze memorial with no more flowers on it than any other. The name DICK is stamped on the heart of the marker. In the corner, engraved in smaller letters, are the words "Virginia H. (Patsy Cline) 1932-1963." The grave would be easy to miss, even for people who know what they're after.

"We wanted to put the bell tower right next to it," says Chapman. "Or at least a sign, something to let people know where it is. But Mrs. Hensley doesn't want it. She doesn't want *any* of it."

Hilda Hensley skipped that bell tower dedication in September. It was too little too late, say her friends.

Bobby Carter feels the same way.

"The bell tower and that little stretch of road," he says, shaking his head. "That's all there is."

Maybe that's all there ever will be. Carter quit that fund-raising committee last month, after one of it own members slurred Patsy's name. Jim McCoy no longer deejays in Winchester, spinning Patsy Cline songs "so people won't forget." He runs a bar now in West Virginia. The Patsy Cline Fan Club, headquartered in Massachusetts, keeps pushing for some signs at the city limits, but none has been built.

And people like Jack Fretwell just sigh and shrug. As far as Fretwell is concerned, everything would have worked out all right if Patsy Cline's life had just lasted a little bit longer.

"You can't really blame this town," says Fretwell. "If she'd had another two or three years, people around here would have been convinced she deserved their respect.

"That's what it is," he says. "She just died too soon."

January 3, 1988

Skin Game

This is a story about a porno vampire and video star named Spider Webb, about a motorcycle model named Ronnie LaRoux and about an 87-year-old pinup girl named Elizabeth Weinzirl.

But mostly, this is a story about tattoos.

More specifically, it's about the Tattoo Expo '89, a display of some of the most stenciled skin in the world, a gathering of truly illustrated men and women held recently in Richmond.

The press release promised "an intense weekend of optical and audio assault on the senses." It vowed to have us understand "one of modern man's most primal urges, the urge to be forever different." There would be "numerous personal collections of tattoo history and memorabilia," including exhibits from the San Francisco Tattoo Art Museum and from the Tattoo Archives in Berkeley, Calif. There would be "50 of North America's most talented Tattoo artists," as well as some of "Europe's tattooing elite." There would be live music from a dozen bands with names like GWAR, the Formaldehyde Blues Train and the Electric Crutch Band.

Which all sounded interesting enough. But what really caught my eye was the woman with the violin.

Actually, she was standing on her *head*, a bow in one hand, her instrument in the other — standing on her head wearing almost nothing, while a demented figure waving a crutch danced above her. This was all in a set of photographs advertising the Spider Webb Studios in Derby, Conn.

What exactly this had to do with tattooing I did not know.

But the man with the crutch was Spider Webb, and that was enough for me.

I hopped in my car and headed toward Richmond.

The Holiday Inn Koger Center South looked like a fairly respectable place. Fancy, in fact, with an atrium lobby, ferns and fig trees, bow-tied desk clerks and a babbling indoor fountain. But the bodies sprawled across the lobby furniture and bellied up to the hotel bar were not your standard conventioneers.

To the extent they were clothed, most wore leather and chains. They clanked when they walked. Bandannas around the head were *de rigueur*. So were ponytails — on the men. And earrings on everyone — as well as rings on other parts of the body. A thin blonde, her head shaved except for a tuft in front, wore three gold rings in her left nostril, one in her eyebrow and one in her upper lip. She was chatting with a woman in a green gown, whose arms, from shoulder to wrist, were writhing with tattooed serpents and orchids.

They were standing next to a life-size poster of porn-film star Seka. The poster was signed, "To Spider, Lustfully Yours, Seka."

Beside the poster, between the bar and the fountain, was a display of wall-sized panels plastered with X-rated photographs of every part of the human anatomy — most, but not all of them tattooed. A sign to the side of the display read WEBB'S WALL OF WEIRDNESS.

This was definitely the place.

Dante saw it first, but his Inferno was nothing compared to the scene inside the Peabody Room of the Holiday Inn.

Stepping into that ballroom was to wade into a sea of undulant, phantasmagorical, festooned flesh. Screaming flesh. Howling flesh. Flesh come alive with dreams — and nightmares.

Booths lined the walls, displaying the wares of the tattoo trade, collected from nearly every state in the union. But the show was the crowd itself, the bodies, erupting in cataclysmic, kaleidoscopic bursts of color and chaos, images of death and danger, of sex and sinister strangeness. It was as if the darkest demons prowling in the subconscious depths had been summoned to rise up and seep through the skin.

A frightening sight. But for people like Crowe, it's a business, pure and simple. Crowe — "Just call me Crowe," he said when asked his name — was tending a booth by the door, selling T-shirts he'd made at his York County tattoo studio. A fellow artist stopped and asked him about the "$200 Reward" sign posted above his booth.

"That's for the bootleggers, the scratchers," said Crowe. "I'm just gettin' sick of the bastards. They're killin' me. I mean, I'm havin' $180 weeks. *Weeks!* So I'm after them."

Crowe, it turned out, was a co-organizer of this event, along with a couple of Richmond tattoo artists named Lady and Ace. Crowe said there are more than 100 tattoo "parties" around the country every year, but that this Expo is one of the two largest.

"We get the word out through mailing lists, magazines, but mostly word of mouth," he said. "This is a close-knit culture, the tattoo network. I probably know 99 percent of the people here."

Crowe said he and Ace were expecting 2,000 people in the course of the three-day event. "That's about four times the crowds they get at the European shows," he said. "We're really the pace-setters over here."

Crowe himself was up at Coney Island earlier this year. And he's headed to Amsterdam in the spring for an international tattoo exposition.

"It's no different from a hardware convention, where hardware people get together and BS about hardware," said Crowe. "Or a dentist convention where dentists get together and talk teeth."

This crowd was talking nothing but tattoos. They were stopping one another in the hall, pressing flesh in a way no politician could understand, posing for Polaroids and, basically, generally, unabashedly reveling in one another's skin. New tattoos were greeted like babies, with cuddles and coos all around. And above the shouts, hoots and hugs, above the rock 'n' roll booming from background speakers, above the drone of tattoo videos playing on screens all around the room, was the incessant buzz and hum of electric tattoo machines.

These people weren't just sitting and chatting. They were tattooing — each other. This, as Crowe explained, was a rare opportunity for the best tattoo artists in America to treat themselves to themselves.

"That's not something we normally get to do," said Crowe.

There was Dr. Strange, from Watertown, N.Y., ("Let Doc Be a Kin to Your Skin," read his card). There was Dixieland Dermagraphics of Panama City Beach, Fla. ("18 and Sober Required"). There was "Fip" Buchanan from San Diego, and Kevin "Wear Your Dreams" Cronin from Houma, La. And there was a fellow named Slamm, who didn't have a booth but had driven 20 hours from Maine just to be here.

"It's *great*," said Slamm, a 52-year-old carpenter and tattoo artist who said he's been sketching on skin since he was 12.

"I'm seeing a lot of people I haven't seen in a long, long time," he said. "Right now I'm looking for someone I ain't seen in years."

I asked him who that was.

"A man named Spider Webb."

I finally found Webb's booth, two tables down from Skin Deep Tattooing out of Waikiki Beach, Hawaii. This was one of the only spots in the room where someone was not in the process of being tattooed. The man himself was nowhere to be seen, but his cronies were working the counter, selling the Spider Webb line of comics ("Tattoo Vampire"), books ("Pushing Ink — The Fine Art of Tattooing"), record albums ("Sonick Plague," by the Electric Crutch Band, featuring the Webbettes) and assorted odds and ends (a pair of swastika-embossed BVDs tacked to the wall were labeled "Adolf's Undies" and priced at $3,750 — "Serious Inquiries Only").

I asked where I could find Spider.

"He'll be around," said a huge man with a tattooed snake coiled around his massive forearm. "The band's playing tonight."

That would be the Electric Crutch Band. I asked if the girl with the violin had made the trip.

"Girl?" he asked. Then he stopped and smiled.

"Oh, yeah," he chuckled. "The girl."

I wandered through the swirl, past tables covered with bottles of brightly colored ink, boxes of tissue paper and bags of rubber gloves. The people pressing past were in various states of undress. For men, the standard garb was a muscle T-shirt (muscles optional) or simply no shirt at all. Women wore tops cut as low as possible and bottoms sliced high, all the better to reveal tattoos crawling into points unknown. A woman in white heels and a white miniskirt strolled past, her thighs crawling with a zoo of wild animals. As I counted the animals on her skin, a voice drifted up from a nearby crowd.

"... and then I had Spider Webb."

I pushed my way through the throng and came upon an old woman sitting in a chair. A puff of white hair, a pastel-print dress, a white sweater to keep off the chill, she looked like anyone's grandmother. Most of the year, which she spends in a retirement home in Portland, Ore., she is no more than that. But when she gathers the strength and the dollars to make it to one of these conventions, she becomes Elizabeth Weinzirl, "The World's Greatest Tattoo Fan."

That's the title of the video showing on the wall behind her ("$29.95, A *Must* For the Serious Tattoo Collector"), and of the 8-by-10 color photographs showing her reclining 87-year-old body, nude and tattooed from neck to knees ($10), and of the 1990 Elizabeth Weinzirl Calendars stacked on the table in front of her.

Elizabeth had plenty of stories to tell, of her first tattoo back in 1947, of her appearance on the television show "Real People," and of the time she showed up in Esquire magazine. But all I wanted to know was how she knew Spider Webb.

"Who?" she asked, putting even more creases in her wrinkled brow. Then she waved her hand and reached for a photo album.

"No, no, no," she said, turning to a shot of her tattooed stomach.
"I've got a spider *web*," she said, "right here, right on my tummy."

By late afternoon, a rumor was going around that Spider Webb had been seen talking to a tall redhead, offering to trade a T- shirt for a trip to her room. Word was they'd last been seen heading upstairs.

So I bided my time, ushering the willing to a hallway outside, where our photographer was taking pictures. Everyone was polite, eager to be photographed. There is not much shyness at a tattoo convention.

But Ronnie LaRoux was different. When I asked her if she'd like to sit for a photo, she launched into a dizzying rap about release forms and her portfolio and permission from her tattoo artist, whom she said is "really big."

Finally, after she got the OK from her artist, LaRoux was ready.

"OK," she said, all business, no nonsense, "This is the one everybody recognizes."

The photographer focused on her tattooed shoulder, but Ronnie knew better.

"If you want a photograph of me," she said, ripping off her skirt, "*this* is the one you get."

And there she was, standing in the crowded lobby of the Holiday Inn, in her pink alligator high heels and cherry red panties. The tattoos creeping up her calves were incidental, at least to the dozens of on-lookers jostling for a peek.

It was only right to stay on the subject of tattoos. So I asked Ronnie LaRoux if she planned on having her body embossed any further, or if she was done.

"Done?" she asked, not taking her eyes off the clicking camera. "Nobody's *ever* done."

I was.

I could have stayed till midnight, when things were supposed to really get rolling. Maybe I would have been able to see what Spider Webb actually does with that crutch.

I could have stayed all *weekend*, and maybe seen a lot more.

But as I pointed my car back toward Norfolk, I had no doubt...
I'd seen enough.

October 7, 1989

Mike D'Orso was born in Portsmouth, Virginia, in 1953, the first of four children of a Naval officer. By the time he finished high school near Washington, D.C., his father's submarine career had taken the family to 13 cities, ranging from San Diego to Key West to Frankfurt, Germany.

After graduating from the College of William and Mary with a degree in philosophy, D'Orso traveled around the country, working odd jobs including driving a dump truck, tending a small grocery store at a Rocky Mountain ski resort, working as a golf course greenskeeper and sorting mail for the postal service.

He taught high school for one year before earning his master's degree in English from the College of William and Mary, where he wrote his thesis on Beat writer Jack Kerouac. An excerpt from that thesis was published in the academic journal "Studies in American Literature."

While in graduate school, D'Orso was a writer and photographer for the college's office of university communications. He also wrote a weekly sports column for the Virginia Gazette newspaper and co-wrote a song recorded by country music singer Mel Tillis on his 1981 album "Rain."

After finishing graduate school, D'Orso spent three years as senior writer for *Commonwealth Magazine*, a regional magazine, before joining the staff of *The Virginian-Pilot and The Ledger-Star* newspapers in Norfolk, where he has been a feature writer for the past six years.

Among D'Orso's national and regional awards for writing in fields ranging from sports to medicine to minority affairs were his selection as 1987 Writer of the Year by the Virginia Press Association, and a 1988 National Headliner Award for feature writing.

He has been included three times in *Best Sports Stories*, an annual sportswriting anthology published by *The Sporting News*. His first book, *Somerset Homecoming*, written with the subject of one of his newspaper stories, was published by Doubleday in 1988 and was nominated for the Pulitzer Prize in history.

D'Orso is among a collection of journalists invited to contribute to an anthology to be published in 1991 by Random House's Vintage Books. Proceeds from the book will go to an anti-poverty organization called Share Our Strength. He has also written a chapter on research methods for *Feature Writing Secrets*, a book to be published in 1991 by Writer's Digest Books.